Management in Health Care

Management in Health Care

Neil Wheeler
School of Health Care
Oxford Brookes University

Diana Grice
Berkshire Health Authority
Reading

Stanley Thornes (Publishers) Ltd

First published in 2000 by:
Stanley Thornes (Publishers) Ltd
Delta Place
27 Bath Road
Cheltenham
Glos.
GL53 7TH
United Kingdom

03   04   05   06   /   10   9   8   7   6   5   4   3   2

A catalogue record for this book is available from the British Library

ISBN 0-7487-4038-4

Typeset by Northern Phototypesetting Co. Ltd, Bolton, Lancs.
Printed and bound in Spain by GraphyCems

This book is dedicated to Austin, Fiona, Kirstie, Alexander, Benjamin, Calum and Daniel. This band of people have unrelentingly striven to teach me what I now know about management and I will appreciate them for ever. Rather than using didactic teaching, these mentors have presented me with a constant stream of learning challenges and opportunities and have taken the trouble to give me instant feedback on every task. There can be no doubt that this experiential learning supplemented by academic enquiry has been very effective in enabling me to learn existing theory and generate new ideas. I strongly recommend it to the reader.

Neil Wheeler

CONTENTS

INTRODUCTION

PURPOSE

This text sets out to enable the reader to understand management in the specific arena of health care, and to come rapidly to the point where he or she can practise management with proficiency. It is written for the benefit of those studying to become professionals or managers in the health and social care arena. It seeks, also, to assist those practitioners moving into management in those settings. The text sets out all of the foundation material necessary for sound understanding and practice in health care management. The book acts as a foundation point of reference for those studying health care management at a higher level, anticipating additional study in those areas selected for special expertise.

The text covers three general topic areas:

- how to manage oneself;
- how to manage organisations; and
- how health and social care organisations are managed.

The text sets out to meet three specific and related needs:

1 to provide sufficient management knowledge and understanding to enable the student to meet the requirements of an honours degree;
2 to provide management skills, knowledge and understanding sufficient to enable the clinician or manager to enter practice with a very high level of proficiency;
3 to act as a source reference for professional practitioners and managers in practice and to support them as they progress in management.

The theoretical insights and the pragmatic guidance given, as well as theoretically sound, have all been tested and proven in the workplace and, furthermore, could be achieved by all readers, albeit they are the ideal. It is recognised that not every reader will achieve all of the recommendations because of local circumstances and personal priorities. None the less, the text unapologetically sets out the ideal as the recommended course of action which should always be a goal.

The text is based upon extensive experience and research regarding the requirements of the health care professions for management knowledge and the content reflects that. It is understood that health and social care can never be considered simply as a business, but there are business principles able to improve efficiency and effectiveness which may be productively applied in these settings. These disciplines are described in their original language and adapted where necessary to fit the setting. Terms such as 'value for money' and 'efficiency' are used throughout the text because they are essential, although it is understood that they may be interpreted in different ways in some health and social care settings.

In postmodern management, progressively more emphasis is placed upon individual autonomy, with employees of a high calibre and high educational attainment having significant ability to make their own decisions about their strategic aims and immediate objectives. If these aims are dynamically aligned with those of the organisation, achievement for the organisation is also achievement for the individual. The individual is expected to supply much of his or her own direction and motivation and contribute to achievement of the corporate aims without the direct and detailed instruction that was required by management over recent decades. This is particularly evident in the health and social care industries. Achievement in this setting therefore requires high levels of organisational understanding. There are certain specific skills and knowledge required in health and care enterprises and a raft of generic skills. Together, these form the content of the text.

It is hoped that the student will make significant use of the text during undergraduate training and thereafter make reference to the text as issues – e.g. time management or the distinction between full and marginal costing – arise in the early years of practice.

STRUCTURE

The text is organised for the convenience of the reader, and recognises that health care students and practitioners are under constant time pressure. Consequently, it has been written to enable the greatest return for the reader for the time invested, thus enabling you to be efficient in your research or studies. The book may be read for any degree of theoretical understanding or for clear instruction on how to perform management in health care, or for a rich combination of theory and practice.

Each chapter stands alone. Where it is necessary to build upon notions illuminated in earlier chapters these are clearly identified with a section reference.

Each chapter consists of three parts:

- Part 1, 'Introduction', sets the scene for the topic area.
- Part 2, 'The theoretical framework, supplies essential management knowledge for professional and managerial practice,
- Part 3, 'The practice', which might equally be called 'And now, how to do it', supplies pragmatic guidance about the practice of management in health care.

Sections 2 and 3 may be equated to: methodology – the science of what is done – and method – what is done. The text thereby meets the dual need for knowledge and practical ability.

Where appropriate, part 3 of each chapter will apply principles primarily developed for management of organisations to management of oneself. This will enable the reader to benefit personally both in the work setting and in other aspects of a well-rounded life. For example, the discipline of marketing described for application to a large corporation, such as an NHS Trust, may equally be applied to marketing yourself, and maximising your career achievements, or even marketing a good diet to your children.

CASE EXAMPLES

Where it is considered helpful, the points made are illustrated with brief case examples. These are manufactured specifically to fit each point to be made, from extensive experience of functional and general management. The examples are not, however, direct histories and any similarity to individual events is purely coincidental.

GUIDANCE

Although considerable benefit would be gained from reading a chapter in its entirety, the text is set out to make it also easy to read any one of the above sections individually. Therefore, for example, the section 'The practice' sets out to carry the necessary information to ensure good performance. The section 'The theoretical framework' carries the theoretical notions that underpin these ideas. You may chose to skip between sections in order to gain a robust understanding.

In reading this text, as with any textbook, you might usefully consider the following advice:

- Decide in advance what you want to gain by reading the piece. That makes it easier to know when you have succeeded,
- Note from each piece a short quotation that encapsulates the point made.
- File the reference in two or three key areas in a comprehensive lifelong filing system (see Chapter 2). This should include all information necessary to enable the piece to be used as a reference in a future paper.

1 Managing Time

Introduction

This chapter addresses, in 'The theoretical framework', the notion of actively managing time and the importance of that notion to: (1) the individual, (2) the patient/client and (3) the employer. In part 2, it gives pragmatic instruction on how to manage time to the best advantage of all concerned.

Efficiency

Time is a finite resource, and the effectiveness of the individual is largely a matter of the efficiency with which his or her time is exploited. All full-time employees have the same amount of time to commit, but their value to the employer depends upon the amount and quality of productivity that they can achieve with that resource.

$$Efficiency = output/input = value/costs$$

The employee needs to reduce his or her costs and maximise his or her productivity in order to maximise efficiency. It is possible to be very busy, working hard and continuously – even to the detriment of one's health – and yet to produce output of low value, because the work produced, although high volume, is of low value. Alternatively, the employee can achieve a constant, manageable and healthy work rate applied to high value activities and have a very high value output when measured in terms of benefit to patients/clients. An important distinction, therefore, is that between volume of work done and value of work done. This achievement requires examination of the work that presents and selection of the essential and productive tasks in order to ensure that time be used to the greatest benefit. This principle is equally important if the value to be maximised is profit earned or patients/clients treated or even leisure time enjoyed. Regardless of the currency considered, to maximise the value of the work achieved is essential.

The purpose of time management is to achieve the most with the available time. However, although it is possible to define high reward in relation to simple productivity, it might equally be used to mean the work that the individual will find most rewarding. Therefore the benefit to be maximised is not just that to the employer and client/patient, but also to the individual. It is foolish to waste leisure time on a task that delivers low personal reward when a more rewarding task is waiting, just as it is foolish to produce low value productivity when highly productive tasks go undone. The discipline of good time management may be applied to all aspects of life. This self-evident fact is not always translated into action. The following chapter discusses areas where the individual can reconceptualise practice to be more effective and then progresses to section 2 to show mechanisms that might be useful in making the most of the time available.

This subject is chosen for Chapter 1 of the text to reflect the importance of the material and to recognise that time management practice underpins all management behaviour, including study.

THE THEORETICAL FRAMEWORK

Deadlines

Good time management enables workloads to be made even, eliminating peaks and troughs and ensuring that deadlines are achieved in good time without last minute anxiety. It may be that immediate time pressure is a convenient motivator and it is easier to work reactively to impending deadlines. However, this routinely results in unnecessary failure to achieve because, perhaps, illness interferes with work during the final week before a deadline. One week of illness may, in reality, be seen as a poor excuse when a task has been ongoing for six months. Additionally, it may be argued that high workloads result in work being achieved only at the last possible moment. In reality, again, this is a false thesis. It takes no longer to perform a task ahead of a deadline than it does at the last minute. On the contrary, work may be lighter when addressed in advance of a deadline because more can be delegated and advantage can be taken of pre-existing work rather than always beginning from first principles.

Waiting lists / waiting times

It takes no more time to perform a task when it is requested than to perform it six months later. Therefore, waiting lists do not ease a workload. If a waiting list is roughly static, then the volume of work coming in is the same as the volume of work being performed. If more work was coming in than the service could perform, then the waiting list would be expanding, and vice versa. The static waiting list, which is damaging the reputation of the department, is unnecessary, being simply a reflection of an accumulation of work at some time in the past. In the NHS, waiting list initiatives are made periodically to remove these lists and allow departments to respond to work more appropriately to demand. This type of initiative is also appropriate for the individual. This is explained below.

Anecdotally, managers may comment that they come up with a waiting list when they want one, although generally they consider that good management results in very little waiting. In fact, waiting can be used deliberately for a number of reasons:

Queuing theory

Queues are necessary to smooth the activity level of employees. If enough staff were employed to eliminate all waiting, then there would be periods of idleness at times of low demand. Therefore even in the most customer-friendly situation, some waiting will be involved at peak times and resolved during quiet times. The queue becomes dysfunctional when it is not cleared even during the quiet periods.

The individual, in the same way, might at a busier time accumulate a pile of work waiting for attention which will be cleared when the workload is in a lighter phase. However, if the clearance does not happen, then the queue has become dysfunctional and the overall relationship between workload and resource needs to be re-examined. Note that this is not simply a matter of demanding more resources. Rather, it is commonly an exercise of reshaping and reprioritising expectations, i.e. workload and resources should both be considered in order to repair the balance between them

Queuing theory suggests that to some extent queues are self-limiting. When a queue is at a certain length then those desiring a service or product will not be willing to wait and will therefore choose not to consume, or will choose a substitute service such as private care. This may be used as a discrete method of rationing and it may be said that, in the NHS, waiting lists cannot be eliminated because removing the rationing influence of waiting lists would result in a dramatic increase in demand.

Occasionally, an individual may use the rationing effect of a waiting time for services to control his or her workload, i.e. claim to be unable to respond quickly to manager demands as a strategy to reduce the demands made. He or she might stop delivering in order to stem demand. This strategy carries a risk in terms of gaining a reputation for failure to perform. However, if time will not allow success, then it is better to refuse a task than to accept it and be seen to fail to deliver.

A manager who wishes to appear to be extremely busy and productive when bidding for additional resources occasionally engineers a waiting time for services. This strategy might be adopted by the individual, but at some risk.

Reactive or Proactive?

At any particular moment, individuals may be operating reactively or proactive. When reactive, they are solving problems and performing tasks as they present themselves; when proactive they are considering in advance those tasks that could be done and choosing those that will deliver the highest value results and choosing the most efficient time to perform them. Proactive time managers, therefore, select high value activities and allocate them to particular time slots where they can be best achieved. Reactive managers, however, perform tasks as they present regardless of whether they represent the best use of time.

Management, at all levels, involves a significant amount of problem solving. It is possible to find solutions to emergent problems and maintain fluent running of the organisation with a reactive approach. However, if a sense of strategic direction is in place through a proactive management style, then the solutions found, in addition to solving problems, also help move the organisation towards its longer-term goals.

Reactive use of time leads the individual to feel frenetically busy and even out of control, and yet results in him or her reaching the end of each week without achieving those tasks that he or she considers to be the top priority. This is a stressful and frustrating experience and the high level of activity does not deliver commensurately high productivity. Proactive management of a schedule will result in the individual being in control of his or her time and achieving that which he or she considers to be of the highest potential benefit (Fig. 1.1).

Reactive	Proactive

• Frenetically busy
• Stressful and unrewarding
• External control of priorities
• High/medium/low value tasks achieved
• Work done as it arises
• Short-term solutions to immediate
  problems which ignore long-term plans
	• Controlled workload
	• Reduced stress and increased satisfaction
	• Personal control of priorities
	• High value tasks achieved
	• Work done at the most effective and efficient time
	• Solutions to immediate problems also advance
	  long-term plans

Figure 1.1   Reactive/proactive management

Parkinson's law

Parkinson's law was coined with a degree of humour but proves to be startlingly accurate. It states that the task will expand to fill the time available. Thus, however much time you allow for a task, that time will be consumed. Meetings allowed a full morning will consume all of that time, albeit that most of the agenda is covered in the final half hour. The same meeting given a shorter time window will also complete its agenda – particularly if scheduling puts lunch at the end of the meeting. Pressure will be felt to finish on time and eat, with the consequence that business is achieved in the time available. Thus, the 'law' is reversible. Many tasks will shrink to fit into the time available

Most attention goes to the early agenda items when there is a feeling of freedom and as the deadline for the close of the meeting moves nearer, items receive progressively less attention. Experienced meeting practitioners exploit this phenomenon to the full. When they want to receive detailed attention for their item, they ensure that it appears early in a meeting agenda, and if they want their question to be passed on the nod they will arrange for it to appear at the end of a tiring agenda.

The knowledge of the amount to be done and the time available operates at a semi-conscious level in most people to enable them to budget time and achieve their goals. Thus if a workload increases or decreases it will still, generally, be completed in the time available. Thus is Parkinson's law sustained. This practice breaks down when the workload is too great or when a novice practitioner fails to accurately estimate the time demands of the tasks before him or her. This is seen more and more frequently in current health care settings, and may result in reduced reputation and self-esteem, leading to 'burn out'. At this point active management of time becomes crucial.

Routine and exceptional strategies

If it is implicitly accepted that the working time extends until late in the evening or into the weekend, then Parkinson's law states that the workload will expand to fill that time. If, alternatively, an explicit limit is set to the time available for work, then the workload will tend to fit within that time. Accepting that a good clinician or manager is one who lives a well-balanced life requires that adequate time be protected for non-work activities.

Occasionally there is an exceptional reason for working beyond the working week, and this is expected of the health care professional or manager. In such circumstances, an employee will work evenings and/or weekends to complete a special task. To be available for such effort might be seen as essential in many jobs. However, when this exceptional strategy is happening routinely, leading to extended periods of evening and/or weekend working, then workload and time management needs to be reviewed using the strategies explained below, in 'The practice'. This means that to occasionally take work home is normal, but to routinely do so is an indicator of poor management. For many people, drift will occur, leading to a gradual expansion in the working week and the exercise of workload and time management review will be needed on a regular basis.

Managing a diary

Well-managed appointment diaries will contribute to making a sound plan for getting the most from the available time. A diary will show meeting start times and the maximum probable duration (Fig. 1.2). The diary should also show the time needed for travelling between meetings and recovery, natural breaks, collection of papers/briefing for the next meeting, etc. If these transition times are not protected, then contributions at each meeting will be significantly impaired. It is generally better to be occasionally unavailable for a meeting than to earn a reputation for high attendance but poor time keeping and badly briefed contributions.

Meetings serve the purpose of communication and decision making, but rarely produce anything. If a high number of meetings are to be attended, it will be necessary to protect time to act on the decisions made and the information gained. If this is not the case then it is difficult to see the justification for attendance. The diary must show a sufficient amount of time protected for action based upon meeting decisions. In some cases, it will be necessary to mark out slots for work, thus making these times unavailable for meetings. Failure to do so can result in a diary being filled with meetings, leaving no time for resultant work. This gives a false impression of the work that can be carried out. The result is that the individual uses all work time for meetings and then either fails to deliver on consequential tasks or carries out these tasks outside of working hours. If this occurs then poor diary management has resulted in acceptance of a workload that is not achievable within the paid week. This is acceptable in emergencies, as has been said, but will lead to failure if it continues indefinitely. Corrective action is taken by altering diary management practice to show enough time free from meetings to allow action to be taken on meeting decisions. Whenever a meeting booking is accepted, the diary is immediately marked out with sufficient time to prepare, travel to and from the meeting and act on the conclusions, in addition to the full duration of the meeting itself.

Clinicians not involved in such a high meeting load will find that the same difficulty arises when the diary is filled with direct client contact. This leads to associated work being performed outside of working hours. If this is the case then, again, the solution is to adjust diary management practice to allow non-contact tasks to be performed.

	Mon	Tues	Wed	Thurs	Fri
8.00am	Preparation	Keep free to act on	Preparation	Keep free to act on	Preparation
9.00am	Meeting A	Meetings A & B	Meeting D	Meetings	Meeting E
10.00am	⇓ ⇓	⇓ ⇓	⇓ ⇓	⇓ ⇓	⇓ ⇓
11.00am	⇓ ⇓	⇓ ⇓	⇓ ⇓	⇓ ⇓	⇓ ⇓
12.00	Return to base	Preparation	⇓ ⇓	⇓ ⇓	⇓ ⇓
1.00pm	⇓ ⇓	Meeting C	⇓ ⇓	⇓ ⇓	Return to base
2.00pm	Preparation	⇓ ⇓	⇓ ⇓	⇓ ⇓	⇓ ⇓
3.00pm	Meeting B	⇓ ⇓	⇓ ⇓	⇓ ⇓	Keep free to act on
4.00pm	⇓ ⇓	⇓ ⇓	⇓ ⇓	⇓ ⇓	Meeting E
5.00pm	⇓ ⇓	Return to base	Return to base	⇓ ⇓	⇓ ⇓
6.00pm	⇓ ⇓	⇓ ⇓	⇓ ⇓	⇓ ⇓	⇓ ⇓

Figure 1.2 Diary example

Realistic goal setting

In the final instance, Parkinson's law notwithstanding, time is constrained and there is a finite amount of work which is going to be achieved. The individual who accepts only achievable work on to his or her workload will have the experience of success and earn a reputation for achievement. The individual who, through good nature, allows more on to the task list than is ultimately achievable will know failure and earn a reputation for non-delivery, in spite of the fact that both individuals have performed to the same level. Therefore in good time management, the ability to say 'no' is essential and, paradoxically, will earn a reputation for achievement which always saying 'yes' cannot earn.

In summary

It is critical to control time rather than be controlled by time, to make time deliver that which is the greatest priority to the individual rather than to someone else and to maintain equilibrium in a very turbulent environment.

THE PRACTICE

Examining and revising the management of available time will bring you a sudden improvement in productivity, reputation and job satisfaction. The exercise requires a forceful period of standing back, which is difficult because when it is needed is when it is most difficult to achieve. The cartoon might say, 'When I have time, I am going to get organised.' However, the exercise has a payback time measurable in days, and within weeks the 'time profit' is significant.

The time management revision exercise is one that you should repeat throughout your career. Time management cannot be got right. Objective analysis sets you up for a period, but drift immediately sets in and the exercise requires repeating on a regular basis. In time you will learn to notice when the exercise needs to be repeated. However, as a guide it is appropriate to see a time management review as a twice yearly event.

Conscious insight into time usage is an essential precursor to improved time management. There follow suggestions for a practical approach, firstly to give you insight into current time usage, and secondly to improve your use of time.

Time use analysis

Gaining an explicit picture of how you are using your time is the first step to improving that use. It may be a baseline against which you will make improvements, or it may be a diagnostic tool to see where time is wasted, but it essential that any concern about time efficiency be based upon an assessment of the present situation. There are a number of approaches to assessing your time usage.

Descriptive diary

A diary of your day's activities, completed at least hourly, describing what you have done over that last hour will capture all of your activity. This can then be analysed after a period of perhaps a week and you will gain a detailed picture of where the time goes.

This is a very rich form of data and allows all activity to be accurately recognised. This device has the advantage of spotting time usage that you could not predict. However, it will be a very costly exercise in terms of time. Although there is certain to be a swift payback, after which you will have gained at least as much as you lost, you may still feel that the exercise cannot be afforded in the short run.

Time log

After a predetermined interval throughout your working day you stop work and tick the box that best corresponds to the activity that you have been doing during that period. This requires you to categorise all the possible activities in advance. Since the ticking boxes exercise is very quick, the intervals can be very short. It is common practice to carry some kind of alarm that will alert you to the passage of another time interval. Intervals may be as short as a quarter hour or as long as an hour. The defining factor is how quickly you change activities. What is the longest interval you can choose and be confident that it will have been spent on just one main activity? The log can then be quickly analysed and data collated about the aggregate hours spent on each type of activity. You must ask whether the items you spend most time performing are your highest priority. If they are not, then why are you giving them so much time? The limitation of this device is that all of your real life activities have to be squeezed into categories and often categorisation is unsatisfactory. Sometimes several definitions are possible. Should you call getting an unnecessary telephone call an interruption, or a telephone call, or client-related work?

Time sampling

As a still cheaper option, it is possible to take a sample, either at random – which requires an assistant to say 'Now!' to you periodically during the day – or regularly, which requires an alarm to go off at preset intervals. When the call comes, note down what you were doing during the previous quarter hour. This involves less data collection and analysis, but delivers less complete information. Time sampling might be done as an intermittent diary entry log or by placing the relevant activity into one of a range of preset categories in a time log. You might make this sampling exercise more representative by considering a diagonal slice. Week 1 Monday, week 2 Tuesday, etc. will give you a picture of each weekday but over a period of five weeks so that monthly patterns are also reflected.

Whatever your method of collecting activity information, you will wind up with a statement of where you are deploying your time and you can compare that with your list of priorities. Are you spending the greatest amount of time on top priority tasks, or are you being drawn into spending time on tasks that you do not consider to be of optimum importance? If the latter, then you must better control your choice of activity.

Prioritising

Having measured your actual use of time, it is necessary to decide your ideal use of time. All potential tasks need to be captured on to some sort of list and you need to decide, seeing them together, what is the most important.

First, make a list

It is necessary for you to record emergent work as it arises, in order to remove it from your active memory. Just as a computer slows down when its random access memory (RAM) is overextended, so you will observe that your own mental processes are impaired by having to hold a long list of duties in your head. Talking to colleagues who have 'a lot on their mind', you will note that their speech and responses are slowed. Record your emergent tasks and then let them go. You will address them later along with tasks that have arisen from other sources and then you will decide on their importance and urgency, thereby deciding which to do and when. In order to do this you will need to carry around a suitable 'to-do' list. This will have a section for the tasks you are carrying out today and another for the tasks that you are collecting for later consideration. This list must be in one place only. Avoid having a plethora of scraps of paper and sticky yellow notes. One clinician made this list on the inside of her uniform hem. It worked acceptably until she sent her 'notes' to the cleaner and lost everything. The method recommended is to designate one section of your personal organiser 'Today's to-do' and another section 'New tasks'. You can then keep to your planned priorities and consider new tasks alongside tasks arising through other channels in order to set new priorities.

Second, establish priorities

Potential tasks present themselves by an array of routes, and you must learn to rapidly sift and categorise them. Generally, it is possible to designate any task's importance as 'A' 'essential', 'C' 'non-essential' or 'B' 'maybe'.

'A' tasks need storing, and attending to as soon as is possible. These are the tasks that you will put onto your 'Today's to-do' list. Choose a time for them to be done that will allow you to meet deadlines and to do the task when it can be done to the best effect for the least effort, i.e. essential case notes or meeting records are most easily made if they are done immediately after the event, not put off until your memory is challenged. However, telephone calls may be best performed in batches, when you have desk time and interruptions can be controlled.

'C' tasks do not need doing. This does not mean that they can be put aside for doing later. If they do not merit doing now, then they will not merit doing later unless their priority changes and they become 'A' tasks. These 'C' tasks are stored for a period because they may become important later as a result of developments. A client situation may change, or your manager may follow up the task. Either of these developments could redesignate a task from 'C' to 'A'. At this time, the papers are retrieved and the task joins the 'A' list for attention as soon as desirable. If you feel that a task must be done, but can be left until later, then the task is no less important, only less urgent. Any task that is essential, regardless of time frame is an 'A' task.

Tasks are in the 'B' category because of indecision. You must carefully reconsider and recategorise these tasks. Thus, everything either goes into an 'A' pile, for attention or a 'C' category for storing in case they later develop into something important. As you get better at prioritisation, the B pile will disappear. Only in the very rare event that all work in the 'A' pile has been completed, without exception, should a task from the 'C' pile be addressed. If a task has been put into the 'C' category but your feeling is that it must be done eventually, it has been wrongly categorised. Perhaps it was important but not urgent – see 'Urgency/importance' below. This can be seen as a way of validating the categorisation process. If the lists feel right, then the process is working. If the feeling is that the 'C' pile cannot be comfortably ignored, then the categorising needs further work. Periodically the contents of your 'C' pile can be transferred to a waste bin for disposal, or if you are very unconfident, they can be filed away – the further away the better.

Beware the medium through which the task has emerged

It is important to ensure that you categorise tasks according to content rather than medium. Many people feel disposed to attend to requests received verbally, by telephone and by email, and allow tasks received by paper mail to fall behind, which often means to be left undone by default. It is not unusual to find 'C' tasks being completed in preference to 'A' tasks simply because they came by telephone rather than by letter. This is a waste of the time resource because a low reward task has been performed in preference to a high reward task that came by another route. Note, however, that you can exploit this phenomenon in trying to get colleagues to give priority to your 'A' tasks. If your task is not their priority, they should not do it, but you can exploit this common mistake and get their help. Do they respond best to written, spoken or electronic messages? If you want a colleague to give high priority to your work be thoughtful about the channel through which you transmit it.

Ensure that it is your priority

If another person passes a task to you, then they will have assessed it as important but only to them and their priority list may not match yours. It is essential to assess potential tasks according to priority against your own objectives. It is important not to allow your priorities to be distorted by those of others. Inevitably the priorities of your manager will influence yours, and in a perfectly managed organisation the priorities of the whole guide those of the individual with the consequence that priority conflict cannot happen. Where priorities do not match, however, it is necessary to negotiate compromise rather that letting your personal priorities be deflected by those of an assertive colleague. If you simply decide not to perform tasks passed to you by a colleague, because they are not your priority, then it is essential to be explicit about this reality, saying 'no' because the alternative is to appear to fail to deliver.

It is a manager's task to ensure that individuals' goals are well aligned with each other and those of the organisation. See Chapter 7.

Urgency/importance
All tasks can be placed on two continua:

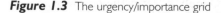

Figure 1.3 The urgency/importance grid

Seeing these together allows a grid to be composed – see Figure 1.3. In this grid, tasks v, w and x are important and should be categorised 'A' and be performed. Broadly, they would be performed in order of urgency, i.e. v, x and then w. Task y is a trap. Urgency, which simply means that the task must be done very soon if it is to be done at all, can lead to immediate action where no action was the better response. This means that an unimportant task has taken priority over an important task simply because it is time bound. Tasks y and z should be categorised 'C' (unimportant) and the swiftness with which they would have been done is therefore irrelevant because they are not to be done at all. This urgency trick is often used to pressure others into performing a task that they would otherwise call unimportant. A questionnaire with a deadline, for example, is more likely to be returned than one without. The sense of urgency is mistaken for importance. The thought is 'I had better do this now because it is urgent', rather than 'Should I be doing this at all?' Consider only whether a task will deliver you sufficient benefit to warrant your time. If the answer is 'yes', then do it. If the answer is 'no', then do not do it. Do the 'yes' or 'A' tasks in the order of urgency, making adjustments for the time at which they may be most efficiently done, but not risking failure to meet the deadline.

Jobs for today
Because it is not sensible to make prioritising decisions whenever a time slot arises, you will need to make a list. You can devise your daily to-do list either early in the morning or last thing the previous day as you like. The important thing is that it is done. Look at the list of 'A' tasks and select those that can realistically be achieved in the time available. Always select the highest priority. There is a temptation to select the tasks that neatly fit the time, even if that means performing the odd 'C'

task because it fits and there are no 'A' tasks that can be completed in that time. You must steel yourself to address 'A' tasks first, and probably only. This requires that major tasks are broken down into manageable components and one of these components is handled in the available small time slot, rather than addressing a 'C' task that happens to be conveniently sized.

Prioritising: conclusion

So, whenever a potential task comes to your attention, it goes on to a list. Daily, the list is examined and the first question is 'Am I going to do this at all?' This is essential, whether the task came by letter, over coffee or by any other means, and whether the task is tightly time bound or not. If the answer is 'no', then a record of the task joins the 'C' pile in a remote part of the office just in case it becomes important later. If the answer is 'yes', then the task joins the 'A' pile and is performed with the priority deriving from its deadline and at a time when it can be performed most efficiently and well. Time pressures on a task or the direct approach from the supplicant must not distort this decision process.

Junk mail, of course, is thrown away immediately it leaves the envelope.

Perform in the present

Once you have prioritised your jobs and are working through a plan, focus on fulfilling the plan. Do not concern yourself about what you are not doing. When the prioritisation is done, then the plan is made and you should focus single-mindedly on achieving the best results. This attention to the present will allow you to perform each task to the best of your ability and achieve the best outcome. If you perform tasks with a part of your attention elsewhere, considering the things you are not doing right now, then your performance will be impaired. The benefit of the planning and decision process is that the decisions are made and your responsibility, now, is to carry out those tasks to your very best ability and not to worry any more about the prioritisation process. Other important tasks will be elsewhere and they should be considered in their turn with equal dedication, but not allowed to impair your immediate performance.

Focus on performing the current task as well as possible without also reliving guilt about an earlier failure or rehearsing anxiety about a future challenge. There are lessons to be learned from failure, and that should happen, but once the lesson is learned through sensible reflection, it is important to release it and focus on the current task. This attention to the present can be a very liberating experience and will result in better enjoyment of life and improved performance.

This principle should be applied to all facets of your life. If you have decided to spend an hour out of a busy day with your mother, children, friends, lover, etc., then do so whole-heartedly, enjoy it and ensure that they do too. Do not allow it to be impaired by having your attention distracted by other tasks. Recreation is necessary for health and consequent work productivity. However, many of us feel uncomfortable about leisure or holidays and approach them with diminished energy, thereby deriving impaired (inefficient) benefit. Once you have made the decision that this is the most important way to spend that piece of time, then that decision is made and you should not revisit it or fret about the things that you are not doing. Opportunity cost tells us that there are always other things that could have been done. One activity is always at the expense of another. However, once the top priority has been chosen, then that is the best use of your time and the other possibilities must be released. When you have made a decision in favour of an activity, pursue it with single-minded attention, maximise the benefit gained and enjoy the liberating effect of focussing on the present.

Strategy and goals

In order to decide your priories it is essential to have an explicit understanding of your desired achievements. This will require you to have carefully considered and well-expressed strategic and operational goals.

Strategic goals

Strategic goals are your long-term intentions. This short list is a clear statement of what is to be achieved by performing your job over a defined period, and what you want to make of your position. Additionally, the strategic goals will include your individual development intentions and aspirations for your career as a result of achievements in the past. These goals must be discussed in detail with your family, manager and colleagues, so that they are agreed and understood.

Operational goals

These are your short-term targets, and eventually they will add up to achievement of your long-term goals. They may be in relation to problems that present themselves, or routine work opportunities. For each area of involvement, it is important to be conscious of the planned outcome and to ensure that all activity undertaken will advance your goals. Indeed it must not just advance your goals, but must advance them and more than would any alternative activity. Without this focus on goals, it is difficult to assess the importance of a possible task. It becomes easy to perform tasks that are generally a good idea but which will not deliver the greatest possible benefit for you. This results in always being very busy and constructive, but without having the best possible quantity and quality output.

In achieving short-term goals, there may be a wide range of possible routes. Strategic objectives are achieved by careful choice of the routes by which we achieve operational objectives. If there are a number of ways to achieve a short-term goal, pick one that also constitutes a step towards achievement of a long-term objective.

Prioritising, within an explicit framework of goals, focuses effort and results in greater achievement without greater effort. This is what was meant by the popular expression of the 1980s,

Work smarter, not harder. (Lakein, 1984)

The slogan may appear trite, but the notion is correct. Another useful slogan might take the form of a question on a poster on your wall:

Which of my objectives were advanced by that last task?

If the answer is 'None' then ask yourself why you did it. If it was a necessary task, then the objective list is incomplete. If it was an unnecessary task, then don't do it again!

CASE STUDY 1.1   BASIC GRADE OCCUPATIONAL THERAPIST (OT) IN A DISTRICT GENERAL HOSPITAL (DGH)

Strategic goals

1   to reduce the average length of stay of patients following hospitalisation;
2   to reduce the average readmission rates of patients;
3   to gain the experience and reputation necessary to enable promotion into a senior community-based position.

Operational goals

1. to assess and facilitate personal independence in daily living skills in each referred patient;
2. to facilitate safe return home for each referred patient.

The patient presents with a request for a device to assist with dressing, a daily activity that has become difficult.

A device could simply be issued, thus satisfying the immediate demand. However, consideration of the operational goals would lead to exploration of the problem to identify the cause. This would enable the OT to spot and resolve related difficulties that might otherwise impede independence and discharge.

A number of solutions might offer themselves to the dressing problem, but the OT will accept only the one that delivers the best step towards achieving strategic goals 1, 2 and 3, i.e. the intervention must ensure swiftest possible discharge combined with the lowest possible likelihood of readmission and constitute good experience for a potential community occupational therapist.

In this case the OT made an assessment of the home setting to know exactly what the patient would require on discharge and what would be required to ensure safe continuance at home. All of the strategic goals were thus addressed.

Delegation

If a task is to be done, by the above criteria, then the next thought is 'By whom?' Delegation to another is not to be seen as shifting the load. Making one person busier in order to make another less busy will not benefit the organisation. However, if another person can do a task better, quicker or cheaper than you, then delegation is appropriate. Frequently, delegation is to a subordinate. If that person can perform a task as well as you, then he or she will do so at a lower hourly cost, therefore increasing the efficiency of the organisation. In the case of administrative staff, it is usually the case that a good secretary can type a large document in less time than a clinician, to a superior standard and on a lower salary. In this case, delegation is a three-fold winner. Additionally delegation may be practised to protect the time of hard-to-recruit specialists such as clinicians by passing generic work to easy-to-recruit generalist employees.

If no staff time is available at the grade to which you would like to delegate, then this is a sign that the 'skill mix' is not correct (see Chapter 3). The NHS favours expensive, qualified staff over unqualified assistants and secretaries and this impedes delegation. It can often improve patient care to increase the available time of less expensive staff such as secretarial support even at the expense of a reduction in more expensive qualified clinicians.

If a task is not important enough to be done, then it cannot be delegated.

There is a temptation to delegate a task that is difficult to categorise between 'A' and 'C'. We do not think that a task is important enough to do personally but, not liking to refuse, we pass it to someone else. If it does not need doing, then it cannot be delegated. If the decision is that a task does not warrant doing by all objective criteria, but none the less it feels wrong to leave it undone, then this is a cue to reconsider the criteria. If, however, genuine 'C' tasks are delegated because the manager does not like to say 'no' then the organisation rapidly degenerates into a 'C' task organisation, and the reduced cost of the labour employed is counteracted by the low value of the output.

In delegating there is a sequence to be followed:

1 Ensure that the task is really necessary – 'A' not 'C'.
2 Identify any essential skills needed to perform the task.
3 Select the lowest point in the organisation at which the task could be satisfactorily performed. Identify an individual who is suitable and has time. Identify the protocols for passing work to that individual.
4 Set the objectives for the task.
5 Communicate the task, with context, parameters, standards for success, monitoring arrangements, time frame.
6 Brief colleagues in the organisation that the task is delegated, and confer any necessary authority.
7 Monitor, directly if necessary, but by exception reporting if possible (i.e. require a report back only if the task is not proceeding according to plan). This allows complete freeing of your time.
8 Evaluate and recognise the achievement. The small cog in any machine may be

just as important as the large cog. Similarly, the subordinate can be just as important as the manager in achieving results.

9 Consider whether this delegation points to the need for permanent change in processes and responsibilities.

Note: temporary or permanent delegation might alter job descriptions and/or grades.

Delegation: conclusion

- Only delegate tasks that are justified within the organisation's resources and priorities.
- Delegate to an officer who can perform more effectively or efficiently than yourself.
- Tell everyone who needs to know.
- Delegate authority.
- Monitor as much as is necessary.
- Feedback, recognise and reward.
- Consider whether the delegation can become a permanent change in routine and practice.

Use every moment

There are periods in the day that are traditionally wasted. When tasks are identified and prioritised, some can be allocated to non-traditional work times. Reading reports should be possible on train journeys, when outside an office waiting for an appointment, etc., provided that the need for confidentiality is remembered. This is only possible, however, if you keep a few such reports with you for such eventualities. Always ensure that you have pen, paper, highlighter, etc. at hand, so that these opportunities can be fully exploited even when they arise unexpectedly. Therefore, if there is a risk that you will be kept waiting by someone, take some work to do, and always have some work on hand for the time when you are kept waiting unexpectedly.

Handle paper only once

Time is wasted by repeatedly reading a message that contains a job and setting it aside to do at some future time. Once tasks are categorised, then try to pick up the document again only when you are going to deal with it. Decide immediately who it goes on to, what the reply is, what the job will be, etc. Then the message can be filed or thrown away. It is often quicker and clearer to write a reply on to a letter and send it straight back. You may like to photocopy the message, with reply, for your records. Encourage colleagues to write an immediate reply to you about your queries by putting a reply section on the bottom of memos and letters.

Break up tasks into manageable slices

Question: 'How do you eat an elephant?' Answer: 'One slice at a time.' How do you address a huge task when your desk time is never more than half an hour? The answer is to break the major task into manageable small half-hour tasks. Perhaps a major task cannot be scheduled, but a string of small ones always can. This is also a good approach to a task that is too daunting to begin. See the task as a sequence of small steps and set out on the first step. Thus address the daunting 'A' not the unthreatening 'C'.

Major task: Go though the files and remove records for all those clients who have not been active in the last two years.
Smaller task: Deal with surnames: A and B.

Without this active disaggregation, the task will be left until a full day can be committed, and this may not be soon. The minor (but 'A') task can be scheduled into any normal day.

Major task: Revise the skills mix for the ward you manage.
Smaller task: Ask staff to complete a time audit for a day/week.

Spring cleaning is, for most people, a daunting task, but to clean and organise the kitchen cupboards can be motivating and rewarding. The rest of the kitchen and the lounge can then be scheduled for other days, and the kitchen success will help you motivate yourself for the next room.
   Therefore:

Major task: Spring-clean your home
Smaller task: Clean and organise the kitchen cupboards.

Many 'A' tasks can be overwhelming, and you might never reach the situation in which you can address them. This leads to inaction and demoralisation, because you know that a really important task is not being addressed. You then attempt to feel better by working relentlessly on 'C' tasks. The result is that you are exhausted, unproductive and still anxious about failure to address the real task. This is a good way to achieve burnout. Breaking up a task allows you to feel good about each step of achievement, and this periodic reward is essential to help maintain your moral and motivation. Breaking up huge 'A' tasks into manageable small 'A' tasks is therapeutic and ensures that you are highly productive by spending all of your time on 'A' tasks.

Interruptions

Being interrupted in your work is very inefficient. If you are working on a task and a colleague enters your office for a five-minute query then you are likely to lose up to half an hour's productivity in giving that five-minute's attention. You may spend ten minutes in moving your attention to the new subject and coming to grips with the matter, five minutes of productivity, five minutes receiving gratitude/pleasantries, and ten minutes recovering your position on the task upon which you were working. Thus, you have lost half an hour to achieve five minutes' productivity.
   Avoid interruptions however you can. Often, work can be performed at home

or away from the workstation, thus making you unavailable for interruption. The telephone can be transferred to a colleague or answer service. If you do not want to be interrupted at your workstation then you might have a 'Do not disturb' sign. However, you may feel that this is very negative. To turn the position to a positive one, publish 'office hours' when you are available to deal with colleagues and receive telephone calls, and encourage enquiries at this time. This will make you appear very welcoming and save a lot of time in the abortive calls and visits that arise when your colleagues do not know when would be a good time to call you.

Make maximum use of breaks

Breaks in the working day are very constructive and result in a net increase in productivity. Being in a position to break for lunch and even tea/coffee on most days can be seen as an indicator of good organisation and time management. Productivity is better when you are refreshed, but the value of breaks is far greater than that. It is during your breaks that you will have freewheeling thoughts about your work and will recognise alternative, more efficient ways in which tasks may be achieved. Additionally, during informal conversation over lunch much fortuitous communication can occur that can save many hours of unnecessary work.

When you are having a break, focus whole-heartedly on that break. Do not do it with guilt or anxiety about what you are not doing. If you feel guilty abut work not done, then you will still not be doing it, and you will also diminish the benefit you could gain from the break.

Meetings

Meetings consume a great deal of time. This time may be time well spent. However, some meeting time may be committed to material from which you will not benefit. Challenge the need to attend all meetings. If attendance is indicated, check whether you need to attend for the full meeting or whether you can attend only for selected items. Do not feel slighted by being allowed to attend a meeting for one item only; it simply means that you are too busy to sit through a full meeting of unproven importance. When you are running a meeting, there are a number of requirements on you as chair (see Chapter 3). Concerning time management, as chair of a meeting you have a duty to constrain discussion to the point that time committed is justified by the achievement. A two-hour meeting with 20 attendees costs the organisation the equivalent of one week's salary. One weekly meeting with 20 members, therefore, consumes the equivalent of a full-time employee. Are you sure that each meeting is worth that?

Making effort count twice

With many activities, there is the opportunity to benefit from synergy. A task, once completed, may be utilised for various other benefits. The case report written for the referring general practitioner might, with only a little additional work, become a teaching resource for your student, or the focus of a journal article. It will be far less time consuming to write the teaching resource or journal paper immediately after completing the case report than it would be to recall the information later.

Time and motion analysis

Time and motion analysis became fashionable and then unfashionable in the 1950s, 1960s and 1970s. Although a sophisticated analysis is rarely thought appropriate now, the principle of performing routine tasks efficiently remains valid. Consider those tasks that you perform repeatedly, which consume a significant part of your working week. Review how you go about those tasks and consider whether they could be performed in less time if the circumstances were altered. Alterations might involve changing the location of the task, the time of day of the task, the order in which tasks are performed, the location of equipment stores, etc. in order to enable the task to be performed in less time. This principle is evident in the location of ward-based stores. If storage of dressings and other consumable materials is as close as possible to the areas in which they are to be used, then time and energy in collection will be minimised. If your dishwasher is close to your crockery cupboard, then the task of emptying it is far more quickly performed. If it cannot be close, then use a trolley and make a single journey. Do not carry a few plates over and over. These examples are small, but clearly correct. Look at where your time is spent, and ask whether improved time and motion practices could reduce the time they take. If one task takes on average ten hours a week, e.g. filing, and you could reduce this by 20% by moving the filing cabinets, then this one-off reorganisation will net two hours' benefit per week with the benefit recurring indefinitely.

Systematising routine tasks

Time is expended on the process of deciding how to respond to situations. It is wasteful to respond in less than the most efficient manner. Therefore, take time to set up systematic ways of performing routine tasks. This will save future thinking time, ensure time efficiency and, additionally, reduce time-consuming errors.

Form letters

Create letters that with minimal tailoring can be used in bulk situations. This considerably reduces time use and, also, ensures that all letters cover all necessary aspects of the matter in hand and are easily read because they are always in the same format.

When replying to a memo or letter, it is frequently possible to write a response on the received memo and return it. This saves a preamble reminding the recipient of his or her letter and saves typing. If a permanent record of both pieces of correspondence is required, then photocopy the document with your reply written on. You can save further time by encouraging colleagues to write on and return your letters and memos, by having a 'reply' section at the foot. This saves you time in reading letters and makes it more likely that you will receive your reply by return of post.

Setting standards

Tasks must be performed to the standard necessary for success. To perform to a lower standard is unacceptable, but to perform to a higher standard is to use resources wastefully. To produce ten results to the required standard is often better than to produce eight results at far more than the required standard. Therefore decide what standard is necessary and ensure achievement of that standard. Do not strive for excellence unless that excellence will make a substantial difference. Excellence will consume time and thereby reduce your volume of output. You can perform more tasks if you perform them to the required standard than if you perform each to a level more than the required standard. However, poor quality is not at all efficient, so you will need to allow a safe margin for error in quality to ensure that you always meet the required standard. Additionally, you must continually improve quality in order to remain acceptable. However, to reduce responsiveness and reliability in order to achieve excellence is not good quality.

Biorhythms

Recognise your most and least productive times of the day/week/year. Most people know that they are capable of greater achievement in the morning or in the afternoon. If you work best in the morning, then apply this period to your most demanding tasks, and during the afternoon, if this is a poor time for you, perform the routine tasks that require less of your focused attention. If you spend the morning getting the routine work out of the way so that you can have a good run at the difficult tasks after lunch, then you have used your most creative time on routine tasks and are left with the difficult work when you are least equipped to manage it. If you can barely stay awake after lunch, do not schedule desk tasks for that time. Rather make that a time for individual meetings, where the other person will offer enough interest to keep you alert. However, do not fall asleep in company! Power napping may be preferable to public poor performance, and is best done alone.

Do not present for work if you are not fit

As a final thought, although you are urged to make the very best of every minute, there are times when you are sufficiently unwell or distracted to be unable to perform to an acceptable standard. On such occasions, your efforts might do more harm than good. It is better not to attend for work than to attend and perform so badly as to damage your reputation and create a huge workload in correcting your mistakes. Therefore, if you are going to perform work of negative net value to you, then do not present for work.

Conclusion

How much value you achieve in exchange for your time, is the only measure of the efficiency of your work.

Efficiency = output/input = value/cost

Make every moment of your time deliver as much of the most valuable output as you can. Perform only the most valuable tasks, perform them as efficiently as possible and use all of the above tactics to maximise your efficiency. Consider your life holistically, so that you achieve the most for your employer, your family and yourself. It is easy to be angry with others about your diverted priorities, but in the final analysis how you use your time is your direct responsibility and that of nobody else. Your failures are your fault and if these suggestions are followed then your successes will be entirely to your credit.

REFERENCE

Lakein, A. (1984) *How to Get Control of Your Time and Your Life*. Gower, Aldershot.

FURTHER READING

Mackenzie, R.A. (1981) *About Time! A Woman's Guide to Time Management*. McGraw-Hill, New York and London.
Oncken, W. (1984) *Managing Management Time: Who's Got the Monkey?* Prentice-Hall, Englewood Cliffs, NJ, and London.

2 THE MANAGEMENT OF INFORMATION

INTRODUCTION

The 21st century may be described as the Information Age. Up until the 18th century, the majority of human endeavour was expended on agriculture. In the 19th century the industrial revolution saw most human effort moving to manufacturing industries, with mechanisation enabling the agricultural industry to maintain and increase output with only a very small segment of the human workforce. The 20th century saw manufacturing industry able to increase output and dramatically reduce the need for a human workforce through the information revolution. The segment of the total population employed in manufacturing has shrunk and will continue to do so. This has been made possible by the process of intelligent automation. Human labour is shifting to the management of information as the major means of generating wealth. Information and knowledge have become the dominant product underlying a large proportion of industrial activity, and the sole product of a long list of professions from law to stockbroking. Thus, it has become essential for all employees active in any industry to be skilled at handling information. As agricultural skill moved from being essential for survival to being unnecessary for most of the population, so the ability to manufacture is also becoming unnecessary for most people. Whether manufacturing develops into a hobby activity, as agriculture was modified into gardening, remains to be seen. What is clear is that 'knowing things' is replacing 'making things' as a way of earning a living. Alongside the shift in production from food through goods to information, is the steadily growing service sector made possible by increasing wealth and leisure. This chapter examines the management of information in health care, the largest of the service industries.

Managing information includes the development of computing skills, but equally important is the management of information in other formats. It is essential in health care that information is held, is accessible and is recognisable where and when it is required. This chapter considers how this is made possible, by considering the principles that apply to all storage media.

THE THEORETICAL FRAMEWORK

Storing and retrieving information – a personal database for life

The amount of information that will be necessarily collected by a new health or social care professional throughout his or her career is massive. Having the information is of no value, however, unless it can be retrieved when it is needed. Therefore, information must be locatable. Further, information must be easily locatable because anything less will be an inefficient use of time. It is essential for every new professional to devise a system for storage of information of all types which is robust enough to see him or her through a lengthy career. What is not practical is to wait until enough material has been accumulated for the individual to realise the need, because by then the exercise will be almost impossible.

It is necessary that storage systems are logical and transparent because, although in early years a quixotic system may be made workable by a good memory, once the system has grown large it will be progressively more difficult to track items at need. When it begins to be a time-consuming exercise to find a particular item, that is the time to revise and update a system. However, if no system exists at all, it will be nearly impossible to impose one on a mountain of accumulated information. Material will be lost.

It is essential, therefore, to be scientific in information storage as early as possible and to build a database that manages information from every source. The professional always notes the source of any useful reading. A report into internal communication carries more weight if the author can say, 'According to Swansburg (1990), 75% of a manager's time is spent talking and listening.' This is more persuasive than if it said, 'Most of a manager's time is spent on talking and listening.' Equally, the author will be believed more easily if he or she can say 'A study reported by Swansburg ...' instead of 'I read somewhere ...' or the non-attributed and never believed 'Research has shown ...'. Therefore, it is essential that the professional clinician or manager record sources for information held and make note of content and source from books they have read. Additionally, this referencing system will allow additional research when necessary. In early years of practice, good memory may allow the individual to go to the book in question with little effort, but as the material accumulates (and memory deteriorates!) this becomes less possible. Notes from reading should be integrated into a unified information system, not a vast array of card indexes, each compiled for a different purpose. The notes from an inspiring book should be filed alongside the instructions for patients following, say, total hip replacement, if they relate to the same subject area.

The system devised will hold all of the information collected in a lifetime's study. However, that is of no value unless the recorder knows broadly what is there in order to initiate retrieval. Again, a sound and logical ordering will allow a comprehensive grasp of content.

A good information system, therefore, has a number of qualities:

1 It is unified, carrying all of the collected information from a lifetime of endeavour. It is even difficult to achieve demarcation between work and domestic life, and therefore it may be advantageous for the system to cover all areas of life. Information will be in paper and electronic format, but this need not result in two systems. Rather there should be a single system evident across both media. Thus if the nurse wishes to collate all that he or she has on a chosen subject he or she will interrogate the same headings in both media as different branches of a unified information system.
2 The system must be transparent. Where any piece of information is to be found must be self-evident and unambiguous. This will prevent information loss and reduce the time involved in accessing it.

3 It must be flexible and infinitely expandable to accommodate new information and new categories of information.
4 Sources must be clearly identified so that they can be attributed and so that when further research is indicated this can be done with maximum efficiency.
5 The professional clinician or manager must know, in broad terms, what the system holds in order that when an opportunity to benefit from what is held it can be quickly exploited.

It should be noted that information of many types might be needed at a future time as legal evidence. Therefore, in some situations, the manner of storage is critical because it may, one day, be read aloud, by a hostile advocate, to a coroner or judge. See Chapter 3.

Different media

Information may be recorded in a variety of media, and there is currently no system that meets all needs. Each has benefits, and can play a part in a unified information system. Paper records remain important legal documents and this has not been superseded by IT systems. Card index systems have the benefit of portability, accessibility and ease of sorting for small records. IT-based systems are almost infinitely expandable, flexible and are potentially very easy to interrogate. IT systems are being devised to mimic the benefits of other systems, e.g. single-write CD-ROM systems allow a record to be dated and to have unchangeable permanence, thus replacing the evidence value of a written record. However, they cannot match the portability and instant access of some paper systems.

Recording patient/client information

Separate, or unified case notes

There is a debate in all health care settings about the unification of case records. Traditionally each professional group has kept records about each patient or client treated. These records serve a number of purposes. They are primarily to enable the clinician to plan, monitor and communicate treatment interventions. They also allow a colleague to take over a case if necessary. Secondarily, records allow quality audit and serve as evidence in judicial enquiry.

Where the clinician considers that the treatment and progress need to be known by colleagues he or she will write a summary in the medical case notes and/or nursing records. However, this practice has many shortcomings:

1 There is significant duplication of effort.
2 It allows the risk that the clinician omits information that a colleague would wish to know.
3 Biographical patient data are collected repeatedly, which duplication of effort places unnecessary strain on the clinician and patient/client.

Minimal biographical data may be more easily managed by making centrally printed labels available to all clinicians. This eases the burden on patients/clients but, in the interest of confidentiality, it covers only the minimum data.

Many hospitals and services have developed a unified case record that carries the detailed notes of all of the clinicians involved with a patient/client. This avoids duplication of effort and ensures that all clinicians have access to all information. However, there are various ways of devising unified records, each having its pros and cons.

Continuous, or sectional

Unified case records may carry continuous entries in chronological order regardless of author, or there may be a section for each profession involved with the patient/client. The chronological order system allows the reader to follow the experience and progress of the patient holistically, but requires careful skip reading if the reader is to track a specific event such as wound care. The profession-specific approach, more widely found, allows each profession to monitor their own area, but requires constant flicking between sections to put together the nursing, physiotherapy and occupational therapy interventions that might constitute the intervention package after a surgical intervention. This demarcation process might encourage clinicians to be parochial in what they read when faced with a heavy caseload and can result in important information being missed.

The physical location of unified records may also present difficulties. Generally, records are kept on wards so that they can be accessed in the presence of the patient. However, that may be inconvenient when accessing records to record information and later for departmental audit. If the unified record is part of a ward round, case conference, etc., then it is not available to the clinician for an extended period. Additionally, there can be a need to access records in department to audit quality or enact supervision. This has resulted in a variety of devices to achieve a unified record and a department record simultaneously. This partially defeats the object of a unified record, and demonstrates an inadequacy of the unified record notion. Attempts to overcome this inadequacy include photocopying records in order for them to be in two locations. In settings where the IT services allow, records are held on a central computer server and accessed at terminals at all clinical settings. This requires extensive security measures to protect confidentiality and may involve stepped access so that levels of authority only allow access to restricted levels of data. Thus, for instance, managerial and administrative authority might allow access to information about category, length of stay and location, but not diagnosis and social situation. Additionally, the system has to allow a distinction between read-only access and the right to change or add information. The central server based system, once security has been ensured, has considerable potential benefits. Access terminals need not be in the same building or organisation as the server. Following the publication of *A New NHS* (1998), trials have been conducted into allowing Health Centres and GP Practice Surgeries to access central NHS Trust records and receive instant and reliable information about investigations and treatments concerning their patients. The amount of information made available in this way is limited, but the opportunity for growth is clear.

System in recording ensures that records will be read

Once information becomes freely available across organisational boundaries, the volume, already great, is likely to increase rapidly and the time taken in reading will become the limiting factor. A clinician who wants his or her records to be read by colleagues should set them out in the most accessible and transparent way possible. Records in chronological script, while logical, can be insufficiently rewarding to justify the time needed to read them. The reader may either attempt to skip read the paper and risk missing important material or decide not to look at the work at all, because time does not allow. If there is a consistent system in the way records are made, with headings and subheadings then the reader can rapidly find the areas that concern him or her and gain essential information at minimal cost. A good system is logical, transparent, consistent, comprehensive and universally employed.

In a logical recording system, information is given in causal sequence and such as Presentation, Examinations, Interventions, Outcomes and Aftercare. This will mean that the reader is able to anticipate each step in the information chain and will more easily absorb the material offered. Additionally, if the reader is to skip read the paper, it is more likely that he or she will find the pertinent material.

To achieve transparency, the system requires its logic to be easily identifiable and well signposted. This may be best achieved by the clear use of headings and subheadings.

To achieve consistency the reporter must always adopt the same order and presentation in report writing. He or she must resist variations wherever possible. This is more difficult than may appear. It requires considerable forethought, because the system that seems logical in the first instance may not be sufficient when an unusual case arises. To change order to meet emerging conditions will set back the reader who has become accustomed to an established style. Therefore the system adopted should be tested in the abstract in order to ensure that it is truly robust. The general rule 'Adopt and adapt a proven method' applies to recording systems, however simple the job may appear to be at first sight. It is advisable to adopt an existing recording and reporting methodology, with adaptations if necessary, because it will have been developed over time to meet all eventualities. Two popular systems are the Subjective, Objective, Assessment and Planing (SOAP) approach and Problem Orientated Medical Recording (POMR) systems.

To be comprehensive, a recording/communicating system must have one methodology that meets the whole need. There must not be a string of other communiqués needed alongside the central record in order for the picture to be complete. Rather, a recording/communicating system must be devised that comprehensively meets the need. It should seek to sweep up the functions of the plethora of forms and notes that arise in unplanned practice.

Uniformity in a recording/communicating system requires that the same system be employed by all members of a profession who are involved with the same client group, and if possible on a much wider basis.

Legal Documents

Medical records are legal documents, and NHS Trusts are required to keep them, in their original paper form, throughout an episode of care and thereafter for many years according to a complex schedule. A Trust can be required to produce these records by a coroner, or a judge in criminal or civil proceedings. Recognising that all clinical records might become designated 'legal documents', the clinician should systematically employ content and language in the recognition that it may be read aloud in a court by an adversarial advocate. This caution encourages the clinician to be thorough and accurate in record keeping, but it should not place a burden greater than that required by good clinical practice. The best defence against embarrassment in a court is not the so-called 'defensive medicine' but consistent good practice.

The definition of a 'medical record' is imprecise but can encompass a wide range of clinical documents. However, the NHS Trust has the power to designate some records as 'transient' and destroy them after an episode of care has ended. Transient records are those notes made to facilitate treatment and communication, but not necessary to establish the rationale or progress of the treatment involved

Many NHS Trusts are copying old medical records on to microfiche or read-only CD-ROM devices. This results in a very significant saving in space, and leads to records that are more durable and easier to access or search. However, although these records are often accepted in court, it is unclear whether they completely discharge the responsibility on the Trust to keep the original documents. Consequently, most NHS Trusts make the transposition on to microfiche or read-only CD-ROM devices, but arrange for the original papers to be stored at a low cost location.

Right of access

Data protection legislation initially gave individuals access to any information identifiably referring to them held on a computer. This rarely included medical records, since they were primarily paper-based documents. Medical records legislation was adjusted to close this loophole. Any patient in a hospital has the right to obtain, on demand, a photocopy of his or her hospital and other medical records. Each NHS Trust has a procedure by which application may be made and the information must be made available within a reasonable timescale. The Trust is entitled to charge for this service at a rate necessary to defer costs incurred. The rate of charges may be the marginal costs, i.e. photocopying etc, or full costs, which include staff time, and overhead costs. Thus, the charges can vary considerably. Trusts are also expected to arrange to restrict some information where it is deemed clinically damaging to the patient, or to support the patient when he or she receives unpleasant information through this right.

Revisions made to data protection legislation in 1999 extend rights of access to personal information on paper as well as computer databases. This gave patients access to all of their records upon demand and effectively superseded access to medical records legislation.

Duty of confidentiality

All employees of a NHS Trust and others contracted to carry out work for the NHS or Social Services are bound by a duty of confidentiality. They may not divulge that a named person is receiving or has received treatment or care without the consent from the individual. Failure in this duty is a gross misconduct resulting in dismissal. This duty is reinforced by the codes of conduct of all health and social care professions, in which failure can result in removal from a state register. This requirement is self-explanatory and it is very rare that a clinician will knowingly breach it. However, clinicians are at risk when they discuss a case in a place where a member of the public may overhear them. There is also an expectation that patients are not named in management meetings where this information is not necessary for a decision to be made. It is the case that all managers and administrators are bound by confidentiality rules, but personal information should not be communicated to, or sought by, any individual who does not need to know that information.

Government information collection

The NHS is centrally controlled and locally managed through progressively independent provider units (NHS Trusts). This has made it extremely difficult to know how much activity is taking place, whether that activity addresses the highest priority need locally and whether it represents the best value for the public money consumed. Prior to the 1983 general management reforms ('The Griffiths Report'), responsibility for ensuring priority provision and value for money was entrusted to local managers and clinicians. They were considered the best judges of local need and priority. However, professional loyalty, known as 'tribalism', and self-interest, presented as 'empire building', were possible distractions from balanced judgement. During the 1980s, the Department of Health developed machinery to collect data about the productivity of service providers. Activity data are collected in three categories: individual patients/clients, service productivity and individual use of time. Health Authorities are required to submit information about morbidity and mortality within the catchment and the plans to improve the health of the local population.

Individual patient data are collected in the form of minimum data sets including; referral route, biographical data, residence, diagnosis, treatment, length of stay and outcomes. These data were formerly used to track patients for payment, and more recently for quality assurance purposes.

Service productivity data involve identifying and counting events. Events identified are contacts (initial or follow-up) and episodes of care. This collection may take one of a variety of forms.

Individual use of time is recorded through an annual time-sampling exercise. This requires clinicians to record, retrospectively, how each unit of time was spent, by placing it into a predefined category. These time segments are aggregated to allow an understanding to emerge of the detailed practice of each profession. Time sampling was described in detail in Chapter 1.

These data are collected and passed to the Department of Health. The results are collated and each provider is shown where they appear in comparison with the national and regional norms. This feedback loop helps managers to know when changes are required. It is intended that this collection of data should be of primary benefit to local managers as near as possible to the workforce and the supply of data to the Department of Health should be achieved as a by-product of this local good management practice. Therefore, the data should be easily available to managers at department and ward level for their immediate action and the NHS Trust or Department of Health should be incidental beneficiaries of information collected to meet the needs of immediate managers.

The data collected, however, have not proven to be robust and if applied inflexibly provide a perverse incentive to good practice. Clinicians pressured to increase episodes of care and/or reduce length of stay in hospital may find it disadvantageous to accept complex cases. This would result in cases that show a good prognosis being accepted for treatment in preference to those who are in circumstances that are more difficult. For example, a patient needing a prosthetic hip, but otherwise fit and living with supportive family can be treated and discharged in little more than a week. However, another patient for a similar procedure living alone in poor housing and with other joint pathology will need far longer rehabilitation. The latter patient is a higher priority for treatment, but to treat that patient may result in apparently inefficient practice if the returns are treated insensitively.

Where a department, such as physiotherapy, is crudely assessed according to number of patient contacts, its staff could feel pressured into improving their figures by offering more treatments in groups, delivered by non-professional helpers or simply offering treatments of a shorter duration. This practice may result in reduced care but give the impression of higher productivity if raw data are examined insensitively.

Importing notions of productivity into health care, therefore, presents difficulty because of the unique nature of every episode of care. However, it is necessary to maximise the amount of care that is achieved with the finite resource available and, for this reason, statistics about treatment are necessarily collected. The duty upon managers is to look dynamically at this data and use it intelligently, not mechanistically, to maximise the care achieved with the resource available.

In patient data collection a number of other statistics are important. These may be defined as below:

Midnight bed state = the number of heads on pillows

Midnight bed state is a physical count of the number of patients sleeping in NHS beds at midnight, conducted by nurses.

Bed occupancy = number of patients / number of beds × 100

Bed occupancy is the percentage of beds occupied on any given day. Ideally, this should stand at around 90–95%, meaning that 90 to 95 out of every 100 beds are occupied. This figure indicates that beds are not lying idle and therefore being wasted, but there are some beds available for emergency admissions. Higher than 95% occupancy is rare because of the time between discharge and admission (turnover time).

In some mental health settings, patients are discharged on trial. In this case, a bed will be reserved to ensure that they can be rapidly readmitted at need. This bed will show as occupied. Where a number of patients are on leave pending discharge it may be unnecessary to retain a bed for each of them. Five patients on leave might require only two beds reserved. This can result in more patients being technically in hospital than there are beds. This situation gives a bed occupancy of more than 100%.

'Hot Bedding', in which beds are filled on the same day as the previous patient was discharged, may also result in the appearance of double occupancy.

Length of stay = number of days or part days between admission and discharge

Length of stay (LoS) figures are known for every hospital or NHS Trust. However, this statistic can be misleading. To compare LoS between hospitals can tell little unless the case mixes are matched, the use of day surgical units is similar and the socioeconomic and demographic profiles of the populations are well matched.

Turnover interval = number of days/part-days from admission of one patient to admission of the next

The turnover interval is greater than the length of stay because of the turnover time the time from discharge of one patient to admission of the next.

Communicating information

Information frequently becomes important only when it is communicated.

Communication is a process involving a transmitter and receiver. The transmitter encodes information and transmits it, and the receiver receives and decodes it. Error can be introduced at any of these four stages.

Encode: transmit: receive: decipher

It cannot be assumed that material transmitted is received as intended. However, it can be assumed that what is received is based upon what was transmitted. Walton (1997) describes this as the 'arc of distortion' (Figure 2.1).

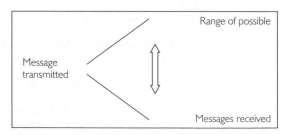

Figure 2.1 The arc of disortion

The task of the parties to the communication is to minimise the depth of the arc. However, it should be understood that distortion cannot be entirely eliminated and therefore the system must allow for a degree of misinterpretation. The communicators cannot know that the exact message has been received, but can be confident that understanding is somewhere within this arc.

One-way and two-way communication

Communication can be seen as a one-way or two-way process. One-way communication, such as radio or newspaper communication, lacks an opportunity for checking accuracy of understanding, whereas two-way communication allows checking by both parties. However, one-way communication is under the control of the transmitter, whereas two-way communication allows the message to be diverted by the questioning process so that the planned message is not adequately covered during a conversation.

Selecting the best media

All communication media have strengths and weaknesses. Qualities to consider include immediacy, permanence, reciprocity, control, accessibility and plausibility. Each quality will be important in different settings.

Immediacy

Immediacy is achieved by telephone, or verbal communication with people in the near vicinity. This may be paramount where timeliness is the dominant requirement. However, it has the disadvantage that little planning can be applied to precisely what is communicated. For this reason, much legal advice is given in the written form. Verbal communication also has the disadvantage of impermanence. This information will suffer from distortion of memory as well as communication distortion.

Permanence

Permanence is achieved by paper communication. This is necessary when either the sender or the receiver is expecting to refer back to information later. Verbal communication is frequently followed up with a written record, thus achieving both immediacy and permanence. This need for enduring information might also be considered when giving public presentations. Where visual aids to communication are by photographic slide, acetate overhead projection, or electronic data projection then once the slide has been changed it is no longer available. The speaker and the audience are denied the opportunity to refer back to that information as the presentation proceeds. Posters or flip charts, however, provide a useful reference throughout a presentation.

Reciprocity

Reciprocity allows communication to be two-way, thus ensuring accurate reception. This means that better understanding is achieved by conversation. The principle is employed in public presentations by encouraging discussion from an audience. Reciprocal information giving is generally verbal, but consideration should be given to written reciprocal communication by letter, with email offering a swifter substitute.

Control

Control is achieved by planning and is easiest to achieve in the written form. This results in sensitive matters being resolved by letter in preference to telephone communication. Where a sensitive issue arises in conversation, it is advisable to seek time to check the correctness of any response. It is for this reason that adjournment is so common in industrial negotiation. Where sensitive material is to be transmitted in a public forum, it is normal to use visual aids and personal briefing notes not just to better convey the message, but also to maximise control over information conveyed.

Accessible

Making communicated information accessible requires careful consideration of the receiver. Communication must be under conditions to suit the recipient, not the communicator. Material must be available at a time and place where sufficient receiver attention can be given. This means that conveying essential information to patients/clients who are distressed by any aspect of care may be unsuccessful. It may be impossible to convey details of treatment in the same interview in which the diagnosis has been revealed, or to give health promotion advice in a session including uncomfortable treatment.

Information must also be in language accessible to the recipient. Technical language (jargon) presents a known bar to understanding that clinicians strive to avoid. However, many clinicians overlook difficulties caused by language that is culturally specific. A receiver from another culture, social class or locality may apply different meanings to the words used. Language must be planned from the perspective of the recipient rather than the communicator.

Plausibility

Plausibility is essential in communicating information. Research has shown that audiences are persuaded by three factors in a communication (Mehrabian, 1971). Least persuasive are the words spoken. More persuasive is the intonation and voice quality when presenting. Of greatest importance are the body communications given when speaking. Mehrabian observed the relative importance of these three factors in persuading an audience to believe a message and, more critically, he pointed out that maximum effect is achieved when all three devices are in harmony. Therefore, it is important to ensure that the spoken message is correct, then voice qualities support the message and finally demeanour, eye contact, etc. are compatible with the message that is being delivered. This convergence best ensures understanding and cooperation.

THE PRACTICE

Storing and retrieving

The difficulty in exploiting information is finding it when you need it. The common complaint of new post holders in any profession and at any grade is the difficulty they find in coming to grips with their predecessor's filing system. The worst filing system is one without logic. This occurs more commonly than might be expected, because information storage starts small with the owner knowing what is where. The stored information incrementally grows until it is unmanageable and the system collapses. Once collapse has occurred, retrieval is a very difficult task and procrastination ensures that it is not achieved. The lesson is that you must establish your information storage systems early in your professional life, with a natural home for all types of information created ahead of need. This requires you to have a measure of discipline, because it involves you proactively planning to create efficiency that will only pay off at some indeterminate future time.

Information is commonly stored by one of three logics. Each may be appropriate according to the data stored. They are: alphabetical order, chronological order and a category–subcategory decision tree.

Alphabetical storage

Alphabetical storage is very common but rarely very satisfactory. This involves attaching a title to every item and storing every new piece of according to that title. Difficulty arises because it requires absolute consistency of designation. 'Personnel' information may also appear as 'Human resource', 'Welfare' , 'Pay & conditions', etc. With such a system, you are faced with a wide range of different files that may hold information relevant to your enquiry. Secondly, information correctly categorised and filed is separated by the vagaries of the alphabet. Information on 'Dressing materials' could be in an entirely different place from information on 'Post-amputation stump bandaging'.

Alphabetical categorising is appropriate for information that is essentially homogeneous, such as patient/client records. Therefore, where there is no categorical logic to follow, titles are unambiguous and no interaction between data is needed, then an alphabetical system will enable your individual records to be easily found.

Chronological storage

Some records are best categorised by when and in what order they occurred. Thus, we record diaries sequentially, rather than having a section for work, another for domestic and a third for amorous encounters. The chronological logic makes retrieval possible and is very helpful for identifying cause and effect relationships. Case records contain information in time order, but it would be illogical to store accumulated knowledge according to the date on which it was acquired. None the less, much information is so stored. Undergraduate study is in one place, sporadic continuing professional development follows and MSc or PhD learning is in another quite separate place, categorised according to when it was gained, not according to what it is. However, when you want information it will be subject specific, not specific to what course you learned it on. Therefore, it follows that you need a storage system that follows content, not the time the material was gained.

Category–subcategory storage

Much of the information collected at work and domestically would benefit from being stored, not simply according to its defining title, but according to the category in which it sits. Categories at the initial stage can be very large and clearly defined. By a series of subcategorising, it is easy to reach some very specific definitions by which to store data. The right category is easily located by answering a small number of clear questions, with the result that items are reliably categorised and related items are close together. 'Mobilisation after stroke' lies beside 'Unilateral transfers', although they are distant on an alphabetical scale.

This is the basis of the very successful Reed Classification System for disease and treatment which enabled dramatic improvement in the classification of disease and NHS interventions.

Figure 2.2 shows an embryonic system for storing information. By answering three unambiguous questions the searcher has reliably navigated to stroke treatment and can access all information on patient transfers. There is no ambiguity about the description and location of the material required. Had the searcher said 'Stroke' in preference to 'CVA' or 'Care' in preference to 'Treatment', the result would have been the same. It is the idea that navigates the searcher, not the actual word chosen. This minimises the possibility of mistake or duplication. The exercise required no memory about what was where or knowledge of other than the elementary fact that the system works upon a decision tree notion.

The above system lends itself to management of a filing cabinet or the files on a computer. In both cases, it is essential to decide the logic of the categories as soon as the system is started. In paper, or electronically, this system allows for near infinite expansion, devising new categories and subcategories as the need arises. What is essential is that nothing is stored that has not been categorised according to the system. In paper systems, the practice is to keep items in a 'To be filed' tray until time allows its correct categorisation. Many people fail to use the same discipline with computer storage of files and file carelessly because of lack of time. The consequence is that much material is known to have been filed yet is irretrievable. The solution to this problem is to have the electronic equivalent of a 'To be filed' tray. You could keep a directory on the computer called 'Temporary' or 'To be filed' into which new files are placed if time does not allow for their immediate careful allocation. These can sit until time allows you to correctly store them.

It is important to have only one filing system through all aspects and phases of your life. The same decision tree that defines your filing cabinet sections should govern choice of computer directories, and one directory set should carry files

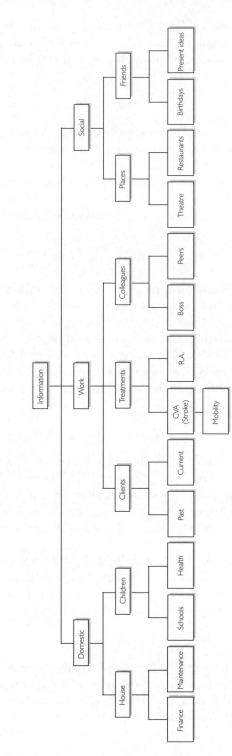

Q:
Information needed. Is it: domestic, work or social?
Is it clients, treatments or colleagues?
Is it CVA, RA, etc.?

A:
Work.
Treatments.
CVA.

Figure 2.2 A decision tree

from all of the software you use. There will be a 'CVA treatment' section in your personal filing cabinet, and on your computer. A search for 'CVA Rx' information will involve looking in both of these places, but in each case you will be looking under the same chain of headings.

Personal organisers

Personal organisers also come in paper and electronic forms, and both can revolutionise your effectiveness by ensuring that you always have fundamental information to hand. Alternatively, they can be reduced to the level of very expensive and clumsy diaries. In addition to diary pages, the personal organiser has a number of useful components to dramatically increase your effectiveness. These include the items below. Use them as a start point, but you should be continually adding to the list.

Contacts directory

This should far exceed a telephone number list, by including simple information gleaned about each of your more regular contacts. If they mention the progress of their children in one conversation, then there is great advantage to be gained by enquiring about the same at future meetings. All contacts should be in this book, domestic, social and work and the book should never be out of your reach. Do not make the mistake of having one address book at home, another at work, etc. This will inevitably lead to your needing a critical number and offering the weak excuse, 'It's in my other book.'

To-do lists

Whenever a task emerges it can be captured instantly, ready for review according to whatever prioritisation schedule you favour. See Chapter 1. This list will always be complete and up to date, and will prevent you from collecting a plethora of small lists and yellow notes that are lost or time consuming to collate. Since the personal organiser is always with you, nothing can be missed and there is always a record of current workload to hand.

Your to-do list might have two sections. The first is the sheet showing the tasks that have been through your prioritisation process and that you are working on at present. The second list is for collection of emergent tasks, which you will consider alongside tasks from all other sources in your next prioritisation exercise.

Meeting planners

Where you are chair or a member of a meeting, it is good to give the meeting a page in your personal organiser. Whenever an item occurs that is relevant to the meeting it can be immediately noted and by the time the call for agenda items comes out, you have a ready-made list. Additionally, it will make a useful reference during the meeting.

One-to-one interview planners

It is good to give a full section to each of the most critical contacts in your life. As items emerge, it is easy to note them and when you next meet, either by chance or for a planned meeting, you will have a ready-made agenda for discussion. If you do not do this, then you will be unable to control the relationship with your boss/subordinate/peer. Additionally, brief notes about previous conversations will allow you to create continuity in your discussions and remember any personal information that they might have chosen to disclose.

Project planners

If you are responsible for part or all of a project, then contacts will pass you helpful information and suggestions about it at opportunistic moments. If each project has a page in your personal organiser, then you can capture them as they occur. Additionally, you will always be in a position to report the current position of any project when challenged.

Back it up

Data is always vulnerable. Personal organisers are notoriously easily lost and may even be stolen. There have been cases of personal organisers held for ransom. This system, like all data systems, needs to be subjected to a back-up system. In the case of an electronic organiser, computer copying is possible, and this should happen frequently. Paper systems are difficult to back up, but many people keep two systems with a desk organiser held by a secretary to mirror the personal portable one. Contact list and allied information might be periodically photocopied.

One comprehensive organiser

You will only carry one organiser with you. Therefore have just one, and use it for all functions. If necessary, have one with a lock so that you are happy to store personal information alongside work information. You will know that the system is working when you cease to find the need for other systems and, above all, when you stop leaving yourself messages on sticky yellow notes.

Databases

You will collect data on many things, particularly patients/clients and subordinate staff. You will find that you want to use these data for a wide range of purposes and, for some, the data collected will be in the wrong form. Much analysis and research is performed using secondary data, i.e. data that already exist because they were collected for another purpose. If a database is created with the broadest consideration of its potential uses, then the data collected can be ordered and stored in such a way that its retrieval will be simple and unambiguous. Attempting to discover whether air quality affects patients' sleep, a researcher may want to correlate recorded pollen counts with nurses' records about patients' sleep. However, although records cover this information most reliably, it is frequently not in a form that makes it good for this purpose. The difficulty arises in two areas:

1 Sleep information is not always recorded in the same place on the sheet/computer, and is therefore prohibitively time consuming to collect.
2 The expressions used to describe sleep can vary and are therefore difficult to find. Additionally, it is an assumption that two expressions such as 'Slept well' and 'Had a good night' mean the same, which may not be correct.

If, however, the data had been collected with research analyses in mind as a possible use, then the terminology could have been standardised and the structure of reports made accessible by strict ordering and headings. When information is so clearly a valuable commodity, it is sensible to collect it in such a way as to maximise its value. This need cost no more, but requires creative thinking at the outset of any data collection exercise. Indeed careful consideration about order and terminology at the outset of a data collection exercise will reduce the long-term cost of collection and recording as well as increasing the eventual value.

Where it is likely that a type of data will be wanted in the future for any purpose it is helpful to place a signal that can be found by a researcher or computer search. This might involve consistent use of subheadings etc.

Ideally, you will have one database for any subject. All information about clients will be on one system, rather than one for their medical needs, another for their care arrangements and a third for their schooling. If these three types of data are stored separately, then the opportunity to interact with the data is lost, and the danger of data being lost between two homes is considerable.

Collecting information

It is necessary to build up a body of information and there are a number of disciplines for doing that. All of the following are well used in health care settings:

Observation
Observational data usually refer to the scientific data collected by professionals such as nurses. It is according to recognised protocol and follows a standard checklist format. The procedure is well proven and reliable. It offers a useful model that can be transferred to a range of other situations.

Questionnaires
Questionnaires are used throughout the health care industry, but are not always conducted to a very high standard. A basic protocol, as follows, might be helpful.

1 Identify the purpose or overarching question to be answered by the questionnaire, i.e. devise a form of research statement for your enquiry. Questionnaires appear rambling and intrusive when wide-ranging data are requested because the enquirer asks everything 'just in case'. The purpose of your enquiry should be placed on a real or virtual poster in front of the questionnaire designer and used to ensure that questions are focused and justified at all times.
2 Search the archives to find an existing questionnaire that could be used or adapted. This gives the benefit of using a proven tool and the opportunity to

correct errors reported by the previous researcher. Creating your own questionnaire is time consuming and there will be errors that would not be present in a previously tested device.

3   Modify the questionnaire or devise from scratch if necessary, and challenge the right to ask every question against your research statement. To ask a question that is not necessary to meet your purpose is unnecessarily intrusive and may result in a reduced response rate.

4   Order questions logically. Cluster questions on one subject together, and tell the respondent when you are about to change the subject.

5   Intersperse closed questions with open text invitation, allowing an opportunity for explanation. This reduces frustration on the part of the respondent and increases the response rate. Put an optional, free text question after each series of closed questions to allow the respondent to elaborate if he or she wishes. However, do not open with a free text question, because that may give the impression that the questionnaire is challenging to complete and will reduce the response rate.

6   Start with easy questions and build up to more searching or intrusive ones if necessary.

7   Consider the analyses that are to be conducted and ensure that the data collected will be suitable. For example, most regression and some correlation tests require continuous or interval data whereas other tests can manage with categorical data.

8   Check for leading or pejorative language that might guide the respondent to a particular answer.

9   Check for double questions, such as 'Was your ward clean and tidy?' If it were clean, but untidy, how would you answer? If you needed to ask for this information, then two questions would be required.

10   Format the questionnaire to look as professional as possible. This improves the response rate.

11   Write detailed instructions to the respondent or the staff member who is to administer the questionnaire.

12   Pilot the questionnaire, make changes in response, re-pilot, make further changes and only then administer the questionnaire.

13   Overpersonalised questionnaires, e.g. to individuals by name, are not proven to gain a good response rate, but small incentives such as competitions or free pens do help.

14   It is important to report and publish questionnaire work in order to become a resource to others collecting similar data.

Interviews

You may wish to interview informants to gain information. Interview data are capable of delivering very rich information, but the process is time consuming and subject to interpretation by the interviewer. There is much that can be learned by interview, but it is important to recognise limits regarding the extent to which opinions expressed may be generalised to a wider group. It is also important to ensure that since the interviewer must selectively report what was said, what is reported does derive from the interviewee and is not projected by the interviewer.

Again, a sequence of events should be followed:

1 Identify the purpose or overarching question to be answered by the interview(s); write a research statement. Interviews may appear rambling and intrusive when wide-ranging data are requested because the enquirer wants to ask everything 'just in case'. The purpose statement might be placed on a real or virtual poster in front of the interviewer and used to ensure that questions are focused and justified at all times.
2 Search the archives to find an existing interview protocol that could be used or adapted. This gives the benefit of using a proven tool and the opportunity to correct errors reported by the previous researcher. Creating your own schedule is time consuming and, again, there will be errors that would not be present in a previously tested device.
3 Challenge the right to ask every question against your purpose statement. To ask a question that is not necessary to meet your purpose is unnecessarily intrusive and may unnecessarily distress an interviewee.
4 Order questions logically. Cluster questions on one subject together, and tell the respondent when you are about to change the subject.
5 If the interview is a highly structured one, involving closed questions, intersperse the closed questions with opportunity for open discussion.
6 Start with easy questions and build up to more searching or intrusive ones.
7 Guard against leading or pejorative statements and language that might guide the respondent to a particular answer.
8 Write detailed instructions for the interviewer, even if you are to conduct the interviews yourself; this is essential as a discipline for your thinking and as a permanent record.
9 Pilot the interview process and make changes as a result.
10 It is important to report and publish interview exercises in order for them to become a resource to others collecting similar data.
11 With due consent, record and transcribe the interviews and analyse by looking for themes in respondent comments, e.g. 'Three out of the four interviewees observed that financial constraints were playing a part; R1 said, "I think that …"', etc.

Group interviews

A small group of respondents may be more revealing in their comments because they can respond to and build upon each other's contributions. This cannot happen in individual interviews. It may be helpful to interview between two and six respondents together. The protocols for this are as for individual interviews.

Focus groups

In order to learn something about the views of interested parties a group of stakeholders might be brought together and asked to have a free-ranging discussion in the general area of your interest and seek to achieve some consensus about their wishes. This provides information about what people might think, given information and the chance to discuss the matter in depth. It is better than interviews and questionnaires in that it allows respondents to give a very considered view after discussion and subject to negotiation with other interested parties. However, it is important not to make false assumptions about the honesty of members or the generalisability of the conclusions.

The part played in a focus group by the researcher is to collect a representative sample of participants and facilitate the event. Facilitation involves assuring confidentiality, thereby encouraging honesty, leading brainstorming and negotiation discussions and supplying relevant information, where requested. By this means, health authorities have sought to collect informed public opinion about priorities for committing limited resources.

Sociological observation

A different kind of observation is conducted in sociological and anthropological enquiry which involves being present when interactions occur and making interpretations about the meaning of them. This is a valuable but highly skilled activity. Managers seeking to employ this means of data collection need expert tutelage and assistance.

Participant observation

It is recognised that it is not always possible to observe social interaction without affecting that interaction with your presence. Participant observation therefore allows that the observer is a part of the group and data are collected on that premise.

Ethical considerations

If your data collection may be considered research, then it might be necessary to ask your local ethical committee to examine your plans. If in doubt, it is always advisable to consult the committee chairperson.

Conclusion

Information is not just a tool of industry, but a major product. In health and social care, an important part of the service that you provide will be what you know or what information you can access at short notice, rather than what you do. The sheer volume of information that you will acquire in your career will be massively more than in previous generations, and you need to be highly efficient in how you handle it. How well you can acquire, manage and communicate your information will be a major determinant of how valuable you are to your clients or patients.

REFERENCES

DoH (1979) *Patients First*, The Griffiths Report. HMSO, London.
DoH (1988) *A New NHS Modern and Dependable*. HMSO, London.
Mehrabian (1971) *Tactics of Social Influence*. London, Prentice-Hall.
Walton, M. (1997) *Management and Managing: Leadership in the NHS*. Stanley Thornes, London.

FURTHER READING

Oppenheim, A.N. (1982) *Questionnaire Design, Interviewing and Attitude Measurement*. Pinter, London.
Swansburg, R.C. (1990) *Management and Leadership for Nurses*. Lippincott, Philadelphia.
Taylor, M.C. (1999) *Evidence-Based Practice for Occupational Therapists*. Blackwell, Oxford.

3 THE MANAGEMENT OF PEOPLE

INTRODUCTION

Health care providers in the public or independent sector are human resource focused institutions with a collective workforce exceeding one million people. The efficiency and effectiveness with which these resources are deployed is the critical factor in determining organisational success.

This chapter addresses the selection, development, management and accountability of staff and identifies the players. It addresses how the individual manages others and how individuals manage themselves to their best advantage and to that of the organisation.

'The theoretical framework' provides the necessary information and 'The practice' provides pragmatic guidance for successful practice.

THE THEORETICAL FRAMEWORK

The rise and fall of line management

Traditionally, the NHS has been managed along military lines, with a continuous chain of command all of the way from the government Department of Health (DoH) to the clinician with the patient. This involved very deep pyramid-shaped organisation charts, with strict accountability. Managers held a span of control in which, generally, less than ten people reported directly to any individual. This ensured close supervision and firm control. Arguably, however, this control was unnecessary for self-motivating people such as health care professionals, and it has become ever less necessary as the academic level of attainment has drifted upwards. Simultaneously, the autonomy of clinicians and managers has been greatly increased.

Since the NHS reforms of 1990, 'The NHS and Community Care Act', there has been a trend towards flatter structures in which many people can report to one manager. This is achieved by making the individual more responsible for his or her own actions and less reliant on direct supervision. Managers and clinicians have a set of objectives to achieve for the organisation; these objectives encapsulate the job, and the individual is given licence regarding how to address them. The task of the manager becomes strategic planning and negotiating objectives with development opportunities to facilitate individual achievement. Additionally, individuals may break away from line relationships by becoming members of client or task focused teams. These teams may be semi-permanent or transient, depending on the nature of the tasks to be undertaken.

Outsourcing and tendering

In many situations, the need to manage subordinate staff has been eliminated entirely by buying services in from a specialised service provider. Early examples of this were cleaning and grounds maintenance services. These services were bought in, subject to tender, from professional cleaning and gardening organisations. There were benefits and disbenefits in this practice, but the eventual cost savings were sufficient for the practice to be continued and extended to other services. Now, a wide range of support services is outsourced in this manner. The process is even applied to some of the more peripheral clinical services such as the Nurse Bank.

Where an existing direct labour team wanted to continue to deliver services but on a contract basis, they had the right to compete as an 'in-house' tendering organisation bidding for the work on an equal basis with external tenderers. These in-house teams also tendered for business with other health and social care providers and a complex picture of provision emerged. Alternatively, some departments chose to buy the hardware from the organisation, take over contracts of employment for the staff and become independent traders. This was known as a 'management buy-out'.

As management of the service was devolved to NHS Trusts, which are a group of hospitals at most, it has become uneconomic for them to employ technical experts such as engineers and lawyers. Consequently, these services, also, are commonly acquired by retainer contract with private sector engineering and law firms. The same model has been used to employ management consultants to help NHS Trusts to achieve a wide range of short-term projects.

Thus, as predicted by Handy (1990) in his discussions of shamrock organisations (see Figure 3.1), an NHS Trust has come to employ three categories of employee. These are:

1 A core of directly employed clinical and managerial staff who are of high calibre and have a high level of commitment to the organisation.

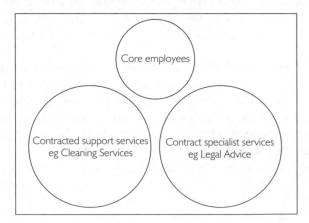

Figure 3.1 A shamrock organisation

2 A large number of non-professional staff who are employed indirectly through contracts with other organisations at market-controlled costs.

3 A small number of highly technical individuals contracted to supply specialised services.

Managing supply and demand

Many of the NHS professions have experienced long-term staff shortages standing at 10% and more. This periodically becomes worse during demographic downturn periods. There will be periods when the output of young adults from schools and universities cannot satisfy industry's needs. The result is a mismatch between supply and demand. Traditionally, this shortage has been met by recruitment that is more aggressive, leading to leapfrogging among salaries and inflation, but not resolving the difficulty. Seeing the problem as a two-sided mismatch where demand exceeds supply and then addressing both sides of the equation leads to some more creative solutions.

Demand > supply

The mismatch is corrected by increasing supply and/or decreasing demand. Each of these may be addressed passively (short-term measures) or actively (long-term measures).

Short-term measures for reducing demand for permanent staff include: relying on bank/agency staff, increasing overtime working, reducing quality and reducing output.

Short-term measures for increasing supply of staff include: intensifying recruitment, increasing salaries, relaxing recruitment standards.

Long-term measures for reducing demand for staff include: redeploying staff, addressing skill mix issues, increasing mechanisation, improving training, improving staff efficiency, improving retention.

Long-term measures for increasing supply of staff include: removing inappropriate discrimination and stereotyping, improving local status as an employer, building relationships with universities, schools and other educators, optimising employment packages.

It can be seen that the long-term measures will improve the performance of the organisation while the short-term measures detract from performance. Short-termism may be necessary to overcome acute difficulties, but for the overall health of the organisation it is the long-term strategies that are required. A dependence on short-term responses, sustained over an extended period, will result in deterioration to the point where continuing viability may not be possible. Ideally, as in all planning, short-term responses to difficulties will be chosen that are compatible with the long-term strategic intentions.

The human resource (personnel) department

Most NHS Trusts employ a department of human resource (HR) staff, who perform three distinct functions:

1 The largest part of an HR service is working with managers to ensure that recruitment, supervision, training and employment termination are conducted by line managers to the organisation's greatest advantage.
2 Many HR departments also act as organisation development (OD) facilitators. In this, they are supporting the management of change and seeking to achieve an efficient, well-motivated workforce and a healthy organisation.
3 The final and often smallest part of an HR service is attention to the welfare of the employees. This is important to an employer as a route to gaining maximum performance and minimising casual absenteeism. Additionally, a reputation for care and attention to employee welfare will make a significant, and cost-effective, contribution to recruitment and retention of staff.

The employment lifecycle

Employment requires workforce planning, recruitment and selection, choosing and applying a form of contract, initial and continuous staff development, continuing management and appraisal and termination.

Recruitment and selection

Attracting and employing the right combination of staff is one of the most important functions of a manager and the area where the most expensive mistakes are to be made. In appointing an individual, a junior manager may be committing an NHS Trust to spend between £10,000 and £1 million. Few other expenditures of this magnitude are devolved to junior managers without complex caveats and fail-safe mechanisms. It is essential to perform this task well. It is necessary to be explicit about the responsibilities of the post, the consequent candidate qualities required and the means by which these qualities will be evaluated. A clear statement is required of the standard to be accepted, in order to be assured that the best candidate is also a satisfactory candidate. 'The best of a bad bunch' will make an unsatisfactory appointment. The requirements must be assessed objectively and an appointment only made when successful performance can be assured. Once a number of candidates have been demonstrated to be satisfactory, then the best of this group should be appointed without consideration of race, gender, age or other irrelevant qualities. In an environment of uneven skill supply, objectivity is particularly important in order to counter pressure to make an appointment at all costs.

It is not, however, expected that a newly appointed post holder will commence a position able to perform all aspects of the job to the level ultimately required. In the case of promotion, or transfer to a new field, a period of induction and development is anticipated. In this case, the task of the selection panel is to choose the candidate who has the aptitude for the task and the learning skills necessary to come up to speed in the time available. A choice often exists between a candidate who already has the desired skills, but demonstrates limited inclination to develop, and a candidate who would need to learn new skills in order to perform, but shows aptitude for the position and enthusiasm to learn. The decision in this case may depend on the time available to the service before full performance is required. If time can be allowed for extensive induction, then the candidate with aptitude is preferable. However, if immediate performance were essential, then a different decision would be made. This highlights the benefit of succession planning in order to avoid the need for hasty appointments or choice of a capable employee over an employee with potential. It is generally considered that a newly appointed executive will spend up to two years growing to peak performance in the position, three years performing at peak, and up to two more years satisfactorily coasting before he or she should seek new challenges. This period may be extended if dramatic in-post changes cause an employee to be addressing entirely new challenges within an existing position.

The pressure to appoint in health care is great, since during periods of staff vacancy patients and clients will go untreated. Cover of a vacant post by colleagues is possible only for short periods. If long-term colleague cover is practical, then what was that person doing during periods of full staffing? However, to be rushed into a doubtful appointment because of a patient waiting list is to risk a mistake that could take many months to correct. Leaving work undone because of difficulty in recruiting is not good management either, and may jeopardise a contract or the quality of services. If a position proves difficult to fill, then it is good practice to appoint a support worker or member of another, more plentiful, profession on a fixed-term contract who can give best-next treatment for a limited period during which time a more careful recruitment exercise can be conducted.

Types of HR contract

Where direct employment remains the favoured option, e.g. with clinicians and service managers, a number of options are available.

1 Many staff have substantive contracts (permanent) that confer the possibility of employment for life, subject to acceptable performance.
2 Alternatively, as with the General Management scheme, staff may be awarded rolling three-year contracts, with the option of renewal at the end of each year. Thus, managers always have two or three years of a contract to run. However, this distinction has proven to have limited impact. Where performance is satisfactory, contracts can be expected to be renewed indefinitely, and not to do so would constitute dismissal, which is potentially subject to the same protection as substantive contracts. Where performance is unsatisfactory, individuals are required to leave at very short notice, with due compensation, and the two or three years remaining in their contract becomes irrelevant. This type of contract has been explored for the employment of some clinician staff, but the belief that it gives the employee no tenure is not proven.
3 A truly fixed-term contract may be used when a task will discontinue at the end of the contract period. This device is commonly used for finite development projects, and a cadre of worker has emerged who chain these fixed-term positions in order to build a varied career. However, it is common practice for staff to achieve career security by seeking the next job before the current contract ends. This often results in staff leaving before the task is satisfactorily com-

pleted. Some attempts have been made to employ clinicians on short-term contracts in order to retain staffing flexibility. However, these schemes remain rare because they are difficult to recruit to and, unless the job can be demonstrated to have ended, then failure to extend the contract constitutes dismissal and the employee may yet be protected under employment law and nothing has been gained.

Equal opportunities
In all industries, you must recruit a workforce that reflects the population. This imperative is reinforced by the following legislation:

Disabled Persons (Employment) Acts (1944 and 1958)
This Act require large employers (more than 20 employees) to employ a minimum of 3% of their workforce from people registered as disabled. They are also required to designated some posts as exclusively for people with disabilities and record their efforts in this direction. The legislation is difficult to enforce, but gives a guide to good practice that is appropriate to follow.

Rehabilitation of Offenders Act (1974)
This legislation allows offenders to deem their offence 'spent' and therefore not declare it when seeking employment. However, this legislation has no impact on the health and social care industries, as they are, generally, exempt and may require full disclosure from all candidates. For details see *The Home Office Guide to the Rehabilitation of Offenders Act* (HMSO, 1974). For some positions, such as those involving access to children, employers are required to obtain police records for candidates before appointment. As there is no authority for these to be obtained in other situations, much relies on the candidate's honesty. As police records become more available to the people to whom they apply, employers are beginning to require that a transcript be obtained and presented by the candidate as a part of the application process.

Sex Discrimination Act (1975)
This law makes it illegal for employers to discriminate between candidates on the grounds of gender, sexual orientation or marital status. Direct discrimination has become very rare and is quickly challenged. However, indirect discrimination remains common in that rules are written which unintentionally disadvantage one group. Employers have a duty to recognise the implications of their actions in this regard and make correction in order to give the organisation greatest recruitmen advantage as well as to meet statutory requirements.

Positive discrimination, favouring one underrepresented gender or group, is illegal under the Act, but positive action to remove barriers is legal and desirable. The law occasionally allows some posts to be for one gender only where there is clear evidence that the other gender would be unable to perform the duties involved.

Race Relations Act (1976)

The law makes it illegal for employers to discriminate between candidates on the grounds of race, colour, nationality or ethnic background. As with sex discrimination, direct discrimination has become very rare and is quickly challenged. However, also as with sex discrimination, indirect discrimination remains common in that rules are written which unintentionally disadvantage individual groups. Employers have a duty to recognise the implications of their actions in this regard and make correction in order to give the organisation greatest recruitment advantage and to meet statutory requirements.

Positive discrimination, favouring members of an ethnic minority group, is illegal under the Act, but positive action to remove barriers is legal and desirable. The law allows some posts to be for one group where there is evidence that another group would be unable to perform the duties involved. Religion is not protected by this legislation, except where a religion such as Judaism may also be deemed a race.

Workforce planning (manpower planning)

In a rapidly changing health service, there is rarely an occasion when a vacant post can be filled without consideration of alternative possibilities. This exercise of deciding the ideal team constitution should not simply be performed when a vacancy arises. The service manager should at all times know the ideal make-up of his or her department, and be looking for opportunities to move towards this position. In this way, the manager is proactively planning the service, rather than simply reacting to vacancies as they arise.

'Workforce planning' is a term given to the projection of staffing needs over a number of years in order to identify the extent to which training of new professional staff must be commissioned. Managers are asked to project their employee needs up to an identified point in the future. This information, when aggregated, tells how many of each profession will be needed at that future time. Taking into account the known rates for wastage from each profession, it would be possible to know how many new members of each profession should be trained each year. The NHS is unusual in that it carries out this exercise internally and pays for the training of its own workforce. Most other professions, lawyers, accountants, teachers, etc., have their workforce trained at the expense of Local Education Authorities (LEAs), and the market forces of supply and demand ensure that broadly the right number of people elect to be trained. However, market forces lead to short-term periods of famine and of plenty, and it is only when seen over a period of years that a balance is achieved by these mechanisms. Recognising the great investment made in health care professional training and the importance of steady availability, the NHS seeks to control workforce supply. However, this exercise is imperfect for two reasons:

Lead time

Allowing that the shortest training time for health professionals is three years and that universities need at least a year to change recruitment numbers, the minimum lead time needed to make changes to supply is four years and projecting workforce needs forward for at least four years is inherently difficult. The changing NHS environment periodically calls for an increase in the performance of a particular staff group. However, considering the lead times involved, it may take four or five years before a response can be achieved.

Wastage rates

Workforce planning requires predictable rates of wastage from a profession. The service must train, for example, enough new nurses to replace all of those who are expected to cease to practise and also to satisfy the need for a growing service. The number of nurses leaving the profession will, however, vary according to external and internal conditions, many of which are out of the control of the service. In conditions of economic growth, nurses will leave the NHS to take work in other industries, or take career breaks supported by successful partners. In times of recession, however, these opportunities are fewer, and wastage is less.

If the actual wastage coefficient is different from that assumed in calculating the future need for new staff, then the output from the universities will be either too few to meet need or too many so that some people will have been trained at great expense and not employed. The DoH managed this exercise for some professions, and District Health Authorities (DHAs) for others, until the NHS and Community Care Act (1990) passed responsibility for making workforce plans and commissioning training to consortia of the NHS Trusts and DHAs who were to become the main employers.

This workforce planning exercise may be measured by its results. For the larger professions, such as nursing, the supply has been close to demand, although generally slightly low, but for smaller groups such as physiotherapy and occupational therapy, there has been a consistent shortfall of supply amounting to 15–20% for many years.

Skill mix analysis

To ensure that the most efficient and effective service is provided with the resource available, a service should routinely assess the tasks that are to be performed, the type of operative needed to perform these tasks and, by aggregating this material, the number and type of individuals needed. Clearly, not all of the tasks that could be done should be done. An exercise of prioritisation is required. This is the same as the exercise described in Chapter 1. The task of the manager is to make prioritisation decisions for all of the resources available to the department. This will include the uncomfortable duty of deciding to leave some tasks undone, because they do not deliver adequate value to the organisation and the patient to justify the cost. This method of identifying ideal staffing by task analysis can appear reductionist, missing some of the more complex behaviours of individuals. The work of a department may be more than the aggregate of the tasks identifiable. It is necessary, therefore, to check the validity of a task-based department plan, by asking whether the derived 'necessary team' feels right to the members of the current team. If the answer is 'no', then it is necessary to ask whether the concern arises from tribalism, a protectionist approach to one's own profession, or whether something needs to be added in order for the model to be comprehensive in its consideration of the responsibilities of the service. The ability of experienced performers to intuitively know when an answer is correct is a valuable tool. However, this should only be used as a way of checking validity of some findings, and not as a reason to abandon the scientific approach to workforce planning.

Skill mix analysis will result in changes, not just of skill mix within professions, but also between professions. Progress from uni-professional to multi-professional management resulting from the Griffiths Report (1980) and the NHS and Community Care Act (1990) has made it progressively easier to effect inter-professional skill mix changes. This skill mix analysis will replace a member of staff from one profession with one from another or with one of a different grade. However, although most managers routinely review the intra-professional skill mix, far fewer routinely review the inter-professional skill mix. The emergence of generic employees at assistant grades in clinical settings has been a clear result of this change, but this occurs only in small numbers reflecting the reluctance to move resources between professions.

Staff development

Employees, once in post, need to be enabled to perform at their most effective level. This entails a sequence of management actions.

Induction

On starting in a new position, an individual needs to be orientated to the organisation and made aware of policies and practices. This is achieved through an induction programme. The induction should be phased in order to give information and insights at the time they are required and at a rate that they can be usefully internalised. Knowledge of safety procedures cannot be left until the second month, while being told the names of 40 colleagues on day 1 is unhelpful. A comprehensive programme should exist at each supervisory level. This may be adapted to suit the situation at each appointment. If a new programme is devised for each appointee then a number of failings are likely to occur:

1 The programme is at risk of missing a key item, because it did not occur to the manager.
2 Inconsistency renders the employer open to a charge of negligence towards an employee if he or she was not given information that was given to another employee. This would be particularly important in the incidence of industrial injury. It is difficult to define what must be told when, and such cases are difficult to prosecute. However, it is easy to demonstrate that an employer has not performed to its own standards as defined by behaviour towards another employee. To tell one employee and not another would be very difficult to defend.
3 It is time consuming and inefficient to repeatedly reinvent the induction wheel.

4 The unnecessary time demand may result in procrastination over this important task.

Objective setting and the personal development plan

As performance begins, a process of individual performance review (IPR) should be initiated. This will set out the objectives to be achieved by the appointee in doing his or her job during the period selected. It will also look at the skills needed to achieve these objectives. Any shortfall in skills will become the basis of a personal development plan (PDP). Agreed employee aspirations regarding future objectives or promotional opportunities will also be reflected in the PDP.

The PDP will show the agreed learning for the individual and identify the means by which this learning will be achieved. Routes to learning will include attendance at courses, but of equal importance will be mentoring and coaching, job swaps, project work, visits to other workplaces, shadowing, etc. If qualification is felt to be essential, a University Accreditation Procedure for Experiential Learning (APEL) scheme might register this learning exercise. This would give academic credit for learning that has both free-standing value and currency towards undergraduate/postgraduate qualification. Most universities have an APEL mechanism, often accessible through an independent study module at undergraduate or postgraduate level, although in many cases there will be a charge for the service. PDPs may be based upon a profile that describes the balance of abilities in an individual and a portfolio that contains the evidence to substantiate that profile.

Individual performance reviews

In the first IPR meeting, objectives will be set for performance and learning. When the employee returns for a second IPR interview, typically after six or twelve months, it is possible to appraise the extent to which they have achieved the objectives that were set. This enables the interviewee to gauge the value of his or her work and to explore routes to enhance his or her contribution. Following this appraisal, there will be another round of objective setting and a review of the PDP. If the employee is subject to a performance-related pay (PRP) agreement, then this interview will set the value of the bonus to be awarded.

Goal alignment

The objectives set constitute an agreement between the individual and the manager about the contribution that he or she is to make to the organisation. It is the responsibility of the manager to ensure that the objectives of all of the individual employees aggregate to the objectives of the department. If the objectives of the individual are well aligned with those of the organisation, these collectively will meet the organisation's needs and there will be no conflict between the individual's personal aspirations and those of the organisation. Therefore, there is an important task for the IPR interviewer, generally the manager, to ensure that the organisation's objectives for the individual are compatible with his or her objectives for job satisfaction and advancement. If this is achieved, then the individual is intrinsically motivated to perform the duties required of him or her. This will minimise conflict and maximise productivity.

Industrial relations

For an organisation to negotiate individually with many hundreds of employees is impractical. Therefore, employers frequently encourage the involvement of trade unions (TU). A responsible TU seeks to maximise the benefits of employment for members but, although distribution of benefit may be contentious, TUs recognise that a healthy organisation is better placed to benefit employees. There is much common interest between employers and employee representative organisations. The TU is likely to come into conflict with managers over the treatment of individual employees, but again it is in the interest of an organisation that procedures are rigorously applied and TU attention helps to supervise this process. For these reasons trade unions are well recognised throughout the NHS and Social Services Departments. TU representation has traditionally been through Whitley Council groupings in which the membership of each committee is understood and remains constant across the country. This makes management of industrial relations simpler and has ensured consistency of pay and conditions, thereby preventing salary leapfrogging and consequent cost escalation.

Salaries and broad conditions are agreed nationally by Whitley Council groups and the Department of Health, informed by independent pay review bodies. Local Whitley Council committees agree local conditions with local managers. With the amalgamation of many specialised TUs, the constitution of Whitley Councils locally and nationally has become less complex.

To obtain statutory rights, a registered TU must be demonstrably independent of the employer, and formally recognised by the employer. Responsible employers such as NHS Trusts and Local Authorities (LA) are generally open to recognising TUs for the reasons described above. However, where an organisation refuses to recognise an independent TU, legislation allows for a ballot to be held and if 50% of the workforce vote in favour of recognition, then recognition is mandatory. A recognised TU has the right of consultation, representation, with reasonable time off, protection for stewards and the appointment of Health and Safety Officers in each workplace.

Absenteeism and staff availability

Department plans need to reflect the finite time that employees will commit to their work. Many departments appear to operate on the assumption that employees work 52 five-day weeks in every year. Managers can appear not to know that employees take holidays, become ill, undergo training and bear children. Notices advising patients that services have been curtailed due to routine and predictable staff absence might well be taken to indicate incompetent management. Taking emergency action in response to predictable events, such as maternal confinement, is unsatisfactory. Therefore a department plan, showing the work to be performed and the team that will perform it, must be based upon the person-days realistically available to the manager, and this should reflect the certainty of many types of staff absence.

Reflection of absenteeism will take two forms. The aggregate volume of work to be achieved must be based on a maximum of a 45 week year, not 52. Plans must exist to ensure that priority work is performed during periods of staff absence, rather than reactive action being taken with ad hoc cover arrangements made.

Casual absenteeism in the form of uncertificated sickness leave and absence without leave are seen as an indicator to the quality of management and general morale of a service. This is an important area for monitoring and high levels of absenteeism point to departments in need of improved management attention.

Terminating contracts

Employees may leave an organisation by one of a number of routes. How the manager handles this separation is extremely important to the individual, those remaining and to potential recruits.

Progressing to another position

The NHS and Social Services Departments operate a general principle that for employees to develop their abilities and increase their contribution to the service overall is desirable. Thus, individual employers will, normally, assist employees to develop new skills in order to move to another NHS Trust or a Social Services employer in a more senior position. The NHS Trust to which an employee moves will, normally, assist with the cost of relocation such as house sale and purchase expenses. However, this assistance is generally only available where there is evidence that the move is to the benefit of the service as a whole. The usual test of benefit is that the individual is moving for a promotion, i.e. he or she is to contribute in the new position at a higher level than in the former position. Where an individual is moving from one employer to a very similar function in another then there is no net benefit to the NHS as a whole, and relocation expenses are not normally paid.

Career breaks

Many employees in the health and social care industries will consider one or more career breaks. Most commonly, these relate to caring for children and other dependants. However, they may also be for further study, travel, sabbaticals, etc. Career breaks, including those for child rearing, should be considered for male as well as female employees.

It is not uncommon for individuals to plan a short career break, but never return to the employer or even the service. This loss rate can be reduced if the organisation offers a managed career break scheme. A scheme might involve continuous communication and social meetings, technical updating, training opportunities, periodic episodes of employment and guaranteed re-employment. The cost of this scheme looks very good value when compared with training a replacement from scratch.

Dismissal

Employees who fail to perform the duties allotted to them, or who behave in an unacceptable manner, may be dismissed. The duty upon the employer is to manage this process by careful adherence to the recognised disciplinary procedure. Where an individual is unable to perform as required, it is usual for the employer to support retraining, explore alternative positions or to assist the employee to contact services capable of finding future opportunities.

Where unacceptable behaviour is concerned, there are clear procedures for warning the individual and, where appropriate, helping them to correct their behaviour. These are described below, and must be observed scrupulously if the disciplinary action is to succeed.

Redundancy and redeployment

A post may become redundant where the work involved is no longer required. Individuals cannot become redundant, although they are affected if their post becomes redundant. Only where an individual's skill is in a redundant area will employment become impossible without retraining. Redundancy in health or social care is unusual. Members of professions and experienced managers are normally redeployed within the organisation if their post becomes redundant. Standard procedures exist whereby post holders in redundant positions as a part of a reorganisation are considered for all emerging vacancies before formal recruitment may be commenced. This process normally accounts for redundant personnel. A duty to offer retraining is also attached to the redeployment imperative. If redeployment involves increased journey distances or rehousing, then it is normal for the employer to meet the costs involved.

There is a general rule in health care that there will be no voluntary redundancy. That is, the NHS will not pay redundancy expenses to an individual, who could be useful elsewhere, even if they elect to go. Only where there is no employment possibility is redundancy payment allowed. This, then, becomes compulsory redundancy. In the rare event that an individual cannot be deployed anywhere else in the organisation he or she will be compensated according to prenegotiated rates. He or she should also be assisted with finding other employment if appropriate.

Retirement

When employees are approaching retirement from the NHS or Social Services, it is usual for the employer to offer assistance with planning for retired life. Planning will be in a number of areas:

1 The service will offer financial guidance to enable employees to maximise the value of their retirement funds.
2 Assistance may be offered with time management, encouraging plans for use of increased leisure time. Experience shows that many people overextend themselves in an attempt to keep busy. Health and social service personnel are frequently prized in their community. They may become targets for local committees and other valuable work, and often report that they are busier after

retirement than before, and have difficulty in reducing their workload. This reflects a number of factors, and retirement preparation aims to help staff plan a balanced workload that will result in their fulfilling their aspirations.

3 Staff will be advised about the rules and prospects regarding casual or sessional re-employment. Such employees are a valuable resource, because of their experience and the flexibility with which they may be deployed.

Early retirement is unusual in health care, unless it is on the grounds of ill health. However, some professional groups, such as nurses designated Mental Health Officers, are enabled to retire at a fixed earlier age, and the NHS superannuation scheme alters its calculations of pension entitlement in order to allow this without disadvantage to the individual.

Accountability

Clinicians are accountable to: the patient/client, the employer, the profession, and to society (see Figure 3.2).

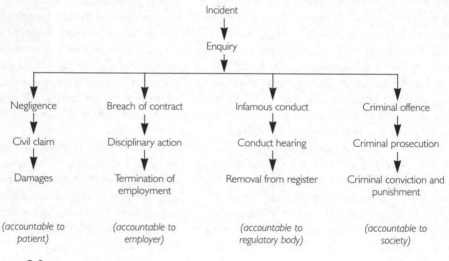

Figure 3.2 Lines of accountability

The patient/client

Patients/clients may resort to civil law. They may look for compensation for damages caused by a clinician who fails to take reasonable care over treatment. If a clinician has not acted as a reasonable clinician would have, then he or she is negligent. If this negligence can be shown to have caused damage then the case is likely to succeed. The award of damages seeks not to punish the clinician, but to make the wrongdoer restore the injured party to the financial position he or she would have enjoyed if he or she had not been wronged. A successful suit requires:

1 negligence by act or omission, as seen by comparison to a reasonable clinician;
2 loss, by the injured party, in terms of financial loss or loss of well-being in the form of pain or distress; and
3 causality, i.e. the loss can be shown to have been caused by the negligence.

The client may sue the clinician directly, or the employer by invoking 'vicarious liability' in which the organisation is said to be liable for the acts or omissions of those working on its behalf. It should always be remembered that although the employer pays for acts of negligence, the employee suffers the blight on his or her record, with consequent career limitation. It is also the case that the employer is not responsible for actions of employees while they are not working on the employer's behalf. Thus, if the error occurred because of a speech and language therapist exceeding his or her employment brief, then the suit may fall back on the employee. If a nurse gives careless advice to a friend in an informal setting, he or she is not working on behalf of any employer, and could be personally sued by the friend. It is sometimes mistakenly believed that issues of what is 'covered' are governed by a NHS Trust's insurance cover. In fact, NHS Trusts are not permitted by the NHS and Community Care Act (1990) to insure against negligence. Rather, they are required to guard against negligence through good quality management. Any successful negligence claim will be paid out at the expense of future health service provision.

The employer

An employer dissatisfied with employee actions has recourse to its disciplinary procedure. This will be on the basis that the clinician is in breach of the employment contract. Various levels of penalty exist including alteration of grading, alteration to location and supervision and ultimately dismissal.

Defence in these cases, in addition to understanding and observing the contractual obligations, as will be discussed later, is possible on the grounds of failure of the employer to comply with the requirements of that disciplinary procedure. Therefore it is of paramount importance for managers to know and follow the procedure carefully, keeping detailed records of each stage.

If a patient/client is not seeking compensation but wishes action to be taken against a clinician, they may ask the employer to take action under the clinician's accountability to the employer, utilising the complaints procedure.

The profession

The professional supervisory organisation, The United Kingdom Central Council for Nursing (UKCC) or the Council for Professions Supplementary to Medicine (CPSM) for Professions Allied to Medicine (PAMs), etc. may call the clinician to account. The examination is of possible 'infamous conduct'. Generally the questions put amount to 'In view of what has happened, is the person a safe and suitable practitioner?' and 'Has he or she maintained professional standards?' There are a range of sanctions, but the ultimate penalty is removal of the individual's name from The State Register of Clinicians, and therefore prevention of the right to practise as a state-registered clinician. Employment in the NHS, for example, would be effectively precluded to a clinician barred from state registration. This removal may be permanent or for a limited period. If a matter causing concern to the client or the employer is of professional misconduct, then they may refer the case to the CPSM for examination.

Society

The clinician as a citizen is accountable to society at large for actions and omissions. This is tested through criminal prosecution. It is rare, but not unheard of, for a clinician to be prosecuted under criminal law for clinical actions and a number of high profile cases have been in the press over recent years.

The prosecution must be in the public interest and will allege that the clinician has failed society. If it is found that the clinician has fallen short of what is required then criminal penalty will follow.

No personal insurance company, employer or professional body can indemnify the clinician against criminal prosecution or penalty. They may pay for legal representation, but cannot pay fines on conviction and, clearly, prison sentences will be served by the clinician in person and alone.

Repeated trials

An individual can be punished more than once for the same offence. In the case of the misbehaving health professional, this is often the case. This is reasonable when it is considered that each body is conducting its trial for a different offence, albeit arising from one incident. The employer dismisses the individual for breach of contract. Professional misconduct is considered separately and action taken. Neither of these events affects the patient's need for compensation, and if a crime has occurred then it must be addressed by a criminal court. Beverly Allitt was convicted of a crime, removed from the nursing register, and dismissed, all for different aspects of her misconduct and in different trials. None of these events addressed the right of victims and their families were able to seek compensation.

Dynamic tensions

Sometimes, as with Beverly Allitt, the views of all parties are in alignment and misconduct is agreed by all of the evaluating bodies. In other situations, the interests of the four parties do not so easily meet and there is a potential for conflict. Accountability can pull the clinician in several directions at once. It is the clinician's responsibility to resolve these contradictions. Conflict of demands does not excuse failure to meet a requirement and no one authority can indemnify the clinician against another. No 'orders' from a doctor or manager, can excuse a breach of duty to any of the four groups to whom clinicians are accountable.

Accountability, in conclusion

Lawyers cannot stop people from exercising their right to call clinicians to account. Clinicians have a position of trust and authority in the community and they must work without fear or favour, in the best interests of the client, acting on behalf of the employer, striving to uphold professional standards and maintaining the trust that society has placed in them. If the clinician has acted professionally and recorded those actions accordingly, then they are not at risk. However, it is their personal responsibility to meet the high demands of patient/client, employer, profession and society, and whoever promises to stand by them, they will be alone when complaint arises.

The professions

The NHS employs a bewildering number of different professions. Members of each profession express regret about the limited and stereotyped understanding of their group in the wider service. However, this does not always lead them to learn about and adopt a sympathetic understanding of their colleagues. Below, is a description of the core role of each of the professions involved in the health and care industry, as defined by senior members of each of the professions.

Art therapists

Art therapists use all of the arts as a medium for analysis and treatment of health disorders. Most, but not all, of art therapy takes place in mental health and learning disability settings, where art therapists have an analytical as well as therapeutic role.

Art therapists are generally trained to degree level, over three or four years, and are required to maintain their name on a state register in order to practise.

Mental Health NHS Trusts and other institutions may employ an artist in residence, who engages patients/clients in artistic endeavour for general therapeutic benefit. The artist in residence may not be a registered art therapist, and in consequence this function is separate from true art therapy.

Clinical psychologists

Clinical psychologists are involved in the formal assessment, diagnosis and treatment of patients in a mental health or learning disability setting. Clinical psychologists are becoming progressively more commonly involved in physical medicine contributing to pain control etc. Clinical psychologists are not supplementary to medicine and can, therefore, hold an independent caseload.

Clinical psychologists are psychology graduates who have undergone specialist education to MSc or PhD level in the clinical application of psychology.

Dieticians

Dieticians are employed in acute and community settings. They prescribe diets that will contribute to the recovery of patients with illness, or will prevent deterioration, etc. They also recommend easy but adequate diets for individuals for whom cooking and/or eating is difficult. Dieticians play a significant part in health promotion and disease prevention through public education as part of Health Promotion services or Public Health departments.

Dieticians are educated in university to honours degree level.

General managers

Since the Griffiths Report (1983) the NHS has employed general managers at all levels of the organisation. They have authority and accountability that cannot be diluted by notions of consensus management. General managers are employed on renewable fixed-term contracts, subject to annual IPR, and remunerated by a process of performance-related pay (PRP). There are no formal qualification requirements, although possession of a Master's Degree in Business Administration (MBA) is becoming the norm. General managers may be drawn from any of the professions or have progressed through a succession of NHS administrative positions. Occasionally, general managers are appointed to the NHS after a career in management in other industries or the armed forces.

General medical practitioners

General medical practitioners (GPs) are the primary contact for patients with any health need. The GP and his or her primary health care team provide about 80% of NHS treatments. If specialist treatment is required in the opinion of the GP, then he or she will refer to a consultant in a secondary care service. Ordinarily, patients have no direct route to secondary services, with the exception of emergency treatment, through an Accident and Emergency Department.

GPs play the pivotal role in Primary Care Groups (PCG) and Primary Care Trusts (PCT), which either advise Health Authorities in their commissioning role or take direct responsibility for commissioning or providing secondary services for the patients in their catchment.

GPs undergo normal medical education in universities and as House Officer, followed by a vocational training scheme involving NHS Trust positions as Senior House Officer, and in designated GP Training Practices.

Medical Laboratory Scientific Officers

MLSOs are responsible for provision and technical management of scientific equipment in hospitals. They are also involved in the wealth of technically sensitive screening procedures that are conducted by hospitals. Qualification for MLSO is through professional examination. Particular functions may call for graduate, master's or doctoral level education.

Midwives

Midwives work in hospitals and the community, preparing parents for the delivery of a baby, managing the delivery and caring for the new family for the first six weeks of the baby's life.

Midwife training is generally over three years resulting in an honours degree and state registration.

Nurses

Nursing is a profession focusing on caring for people, individually or in groups, covering the whole lifespan. They work with individuals to identify needs and plan together to address them. The viewpoint of individuals is fundamental to nursing in meeting needs. Nurses behave holistically, addressing physiological, psychological, spiritual, cultural and social needs, using scientific fact and empirical data.

Nurses are described as having two main functions:

1 They perform for people those tasks that illness or disability makes it impossible or dangerous for them to perform for themselves.
2 They administer a very wide of treatments prescribed by medical and other practitioners. Nurses are adopting a rapidly growing range of pharmaceutical and other treatments that they can prescribe and administer themselves.

Nurses are, usually, trained at university to degree level, or through Project 2000 Diploma and Advanced Diploma courses over three or four years. Both routes allow state registration with the United Kingdom Central Council for Nursing, Midwifery and Health Visiting and offer equal career prospects. All nurses are required to maintain their name on a state register in order to practise and maintain a portfolio of evidence which demonstrates continuing professional development (CPD).

Occupational therapists

Occupational therapy (OT) is concerned with the occupation of people. This is addressed in two ways:

1 The OT facilitates the individual performing all of the occupations to which he or she realistically aspires. This facilitation involves: teaching the individual new ways of performing where the old way is no longer possible, and altering the environment so that occupational performance is made possible. Environmental alteration may be as simple as supplying a handrail or as complex as building a new bathroom on to the home or workplace.
2 The OT uses activity as a therapeutic medium, i.e. he or she prescribes activities that will contribute to the patient/client recovering from illness or to holding back the progress of incurable disease. In addition to prescribing activity for in-patient or out-patient application, the OT will prescribe ways of carrying out normal life activities that are intrinsically therapeutic and developmental.

OTs are trained to honours degree level, over three or four years, and are required to maintain their name on a state register in order to practice.

Pharmacists

Pharmacists are licensed to purchase, store and retail controlled and uncontrolled pharmaceutical materials. They therefore meet the need for supply of these materials. Pharmacists also act as a source of expertise about the effects, side effects and interaction of drugs and other agents. Clinicians and the public consult pharmacists about drug issues. Pharmacists may operate as small businesses or be employed by larger retail outlets. General medical practitioners employ pharmacists in rural settings to operate from surgeries or Health Centres. Pharmacists in hospital supply medicines for in-patient use and to cover the period immediately after discharge. Hospital pharmacists offer a sophisticated advice service to clinicians and may contribute to ward round and case conference discussions.

Pharmacists are trained to degree level, over three or four years, and are required to maintain their name on a state register in order to operate.

Physicians

Physicians are registered medical practitioners who have chosen a non-surgical speciality, working in secondary or tertiary health care. Physicians may remain generalists (general physician) or specialise in care groups such as the elderly, rheumatology, etc. Physicians in secondary health care usually accept a patient only when referred by a general practitioner.

Physicians study medicine at university followed by a year in an NHS Trust as House Officer. They then seek employment in an NHS Trust as Senior House Officer, before joining a specialist training scheme as Registrar / Senior Registrar in posts approved by the Royal College of Physicians. When this period of training is satisfactorily completed and the relevant two-stage examinations demonstrate attainment of specialist understanding they become eligible to apply for a substantive post as a Consultant Physician.

Public health physicians

Public health physicians have a number of functions:

1 to monitor health status and assess health needs and advise upon the appropriate health care to be provided; this includes the application of evidence-based medicine;
2 to monitor and control communicable diseases;
3 to provide public health advice to the Health Authority, PCGs, PCTs, LAs, etc.;
4 the Director of Public Health is required to publish an annual report of the health of the catchment population and the health care provided;
5 to play a leading part in clinical governance within the catchment.

Public health physicians study medicine at university followed by a year in an NHS Trust as House Officer. They then seek employment in an NHS Trust as Senior House Officer, before joining a specialist training scheme as Registrar / Senior Registrar in posts approved by the Faculty of Public Health. When this period of training is satisfactorily completed and the relevant two-stage examinations demonstrate attainment of specialist understanding they become eligible to apply for a substantive post as a Consultant Public Health Physician.

The Director of Public Health is an Executive Director of a District Health Authority.

Podiatrists (chiropodists)

Podiatrists, formerly chiropodists, offer advice and treatment regarding the health and function of lower limbs. The aim of the treatment is to maintain normal foot function and therefore mobility. The service is primarily to the elderly and people with disabilities, but there is an important health promotion role with children, focusing on the impact of lifestyle on foot health.

Assistants are taking a growing role in treatment of toenails etc., although this is closely supervised by a qualified podiatrist.

Podiatrists train for three years, leading to an honours degree and state registration (SRCh). Podiatrists may elect to undergo a further five-year training to gain the title Podiatric Surgeon and practise surgery on the foot.

Speech and language therapists

Speech and language therapists (SLT) assess and train/retrain communication skills. They are involved with children in schools and at home. SLTs work in Acute Learning Disability and Community NHS Trusts assisting with treatment of patients whose illness impairs their communication, speech or feeding and swallowing function.

SLTs are trained to honours degree level, over three or four years, and are required to maintain their name on a state register in order to practice.

Social workers

Social workers provide a problem-solving service for disadvantaged people in the community. This may include ensuring that benefit income is claimed, but also can involve any other area of problem solving, such as housing, care services, education and employment opportunities, etc. Social workers play a major part in the discharge of people from hospital and their aftercare and may act as care managers, assessing and facilitating total care packages for people with disabilities living in the community. In the mental health setting the discharge plan is a formal requirement under the Care Planning Approach regulations

Many social workers undergo additional training to act as counsellors for people with mental health disorders. Approved social workers are agents for arranging compulsory admission of people under the Mental Health Act.

Social workers are normally trained in university to honours degree level or hold a Certificate of Qualification in Social Work (CQSW). They are required to maintain their name on a state register in order to practice.

Surgeons

Surgeons are medical practitioners who employ surgery as their primary therapeutic medium. They may remain generalists (general surgeon) or specialise in an anatomical region.

Surgeons study medicine at university followed by a year in an NHS Trust as House Officer. They then seek employment in an NHS Trust as Senior House Officer, before joining a specialist training scheme as Registrar / Senior Registrar in posts approved by the Royal College of Surgeons (RCS). When this period of train-ing is satisfactorily completed and the relevant two-stage examinations demon-strate attainment of specialist understanding they become eligible to apply for a substantive post as a Consultant Surgeon. When a surgeon completes his or her RCS membership requirements, he or she may cease to use the title 'Dr' and be addressed as 'Mr' or 'Miss'.

Tribalism

It has been argued in a number of DoH documents that members of a profession could, in theory, place the interests of their profession ahead of that of the service as a whole. This might present as an attempt to increase the resources allotted to the profession without being willing to consider that the same resources deployed elsewhere could have a greater patient benefit.

Successive attempts have been made to persuade members of professions to see the profession as their background, and the patient-focused team in which they work as the area to which they give their loyalty and for which they campaign.

This places individuals in a position of dynamic tension. It is important for them to seek the progress of their profession, improving standards and taking part in continuing professional development, etc., but they are encouraged not to hide behind professional protectionist barriers. For most employees, this means exist-ing in a matrix that shows them to be part of a professional and a patient-focused group simultaneously, and allowing neither to operate to the detriment of the other (see Figure 3.3).

	Surgery	Paediatrics	Elderly Care	Neurology	Etc.
Nursing					
Medical					
Physiotherapy					
Occupational therapy					
Speech and language therapy					
Diatetics					
Etc.					

Figure 3.3 Matrix management

Role blurring

There has been a long-running debate about the extent to which professions should allow overlapping and role blurring. This has been taken to the extreme where a single generic therapist is proposed whose members can provide all of the services currently associated with a wide range of professions. The emerging consensus is that a significant level of role blurring should be allowed in order to avoid clients being unnecessarily involved with a wide range of professionals, and to allow a clinician to deliver the care needed by an individual without unhelpful demarcation practice. However, there is very little support for the creation of one generic profession. Small rationalisations have occurred over the years.

THE PRACTICE

Recruitment and selection

There are a number of clear stages to follow in recruiting new staff. Carefully following these will prevent any resource and personnel wastage.

Confirming the post

Rarely can a vacant post be filled without revisiting the functions to be performed and therefore the person to be sought. This is explained in 'Workforce planning', above. Therefore when you have a position vacated by a colleague or subordinate you should initiate a discussion about the best use for the released resource in line with existing strategy. This will involve discussing what profession and what grade of employee must be recruited. A decision will be made by the immediate manager and ratified by a more senior manager authorised to appoint staff.

The job description

When you have confirmed the position, you must devise a job description. The job description, once published, becomes a part of the contract of employment. When an employee is in post, the job description may be altered only by agreement between manager and post holder. If an alteration is necessitated by a reorganisation and the post holder does not agree, then he or she is notionally redundant and the agreed redeployment procedures are employed.

The job description covers the following areas:

Title of post
A succinct, but accurate representation of the core function(s) to be performed.

Job purpose
A single paragraph that explains comprehensively, but in broad brush terms, the purpose of the post.

Term
Substantive / temporary / fixed term / fixed term, rolling. See 'Types of HR contract', above.

Location
Specifies the permanent base for the appointee.

Accountable to
The name of the post (not the post holder) to whom the appointee will report. In the case of health and social care professionals, this may be divided into:

• professional accountability – to a senior member of the profession – and
• managerial accountability – to a general manager in charge of the clinical area in which the appointee will practice.

Relationships
This section will explain the other posts to which the appointee will relate.

Duties
This will be a detailed, numbered list of the duties to be performed, covering the whole job and aggregating to the job purpose, discussed above. The duty list should be restricted to about ten items.

A catch-all clause is generally included of the type, 'Any other duties that the manager may require'. It is an error, however, to believe that this clause allows managers to add responsibilities at will. In fact, the clause is generally limited to duties that fit within the job purpose and are broadly in line with the list of specific duties.

The person specification
When the job description is agreed, then you can define the person that you require to perform the duties involved. This is usually described in terms of essential qualities and desirable qualities. It is not possible to appoint candidates who do not meet the essential qualities. The desirable qualities may be used to differentiate between satisfactory candidates.

Qualities are usually described under five headings as in Figure 3.4. Examples are given for illustration.

Post Title	Moving and Handling Trainer	
	Essential Qualities	**Desirable Qualities**
Physical	• Able to move & handle patients	• Highly presentable
Attainment	• SRN, SROT or SRPT • Knowledge of H&SAW legislation • Knowledge of ergonomics	• Experience of teaching
Intelligence	• Registered health professional	• Master's level qualification • Able to adapt to new culture
Aptitude	• Attention to detail	• Interpretation of legislation
Interests	• None essential	• Quality assurance
Disposition	• Able to relate well to all weekend shifts	• Able to attend international conferences

Figure 3.4 The person specification

Advertising

You must advertise the post in order to attract a wide range of candidates, thereby assuring the best available calibre of appointee. It may be possible to attract a satisfactory response through internal notification and word of mouth, but this is rarely considered acceptable, because it may not ensure equal opportunities to all parts of the community.

Regulations to be considered are routinely published by the Equal Opportunity Commission (EOC) and the Commission for Racial Equality (CRE).

The Institute of Personnel Management (IPM) published a code (IPM, 1990) which requires:

1 the person specification must be the basis for the advertisement;
2 a realistic description of the organisation must be included;
3 job location and salary or salary scale must be shown;
4 clear instructions should be given for application;
5 there must be no discrimination on the grounds of gender or race, unless within the exemptions in the prevailing legislation.

Your advertisement must attract and also inform. This maximises the recruitment trawl and yet ensures that the candidate list is appropriate by allowing individuals to screen themselves out if they do not meet the essential requirements of the post.

Advertisements must be appropriate to the medium. Therefore in a scientific journal the language will be different from in a daily newspaper. People do not read journals or newspapers as they do a novel. Rather, they skip read and browse. Most readers read the headlines. If they are interested by the headline, they read the first paragraph. This may satisfy them, or they may decide to read to the end. This also applies to advertisements and is demonstrated in the analysis below, culminating in the advertisement shown in Figure 3.5.

Your headline must tell the reader if this is for them, or allow informed screening:

Manual Handling Instructor – Manchester

This tells the potential candidate whether he or she needs to read the advertisement further.

A State-Registered Nurse, Physiotherapist or Occupational Therapist is sought to teach staff of all grades and professions in this busy NHS Trust.

This further information allows the candidate to continue assessing his or her suitability for the position. For those still in the running the next section describes the essential and desirable qualities in some detail:

Applicants should have good knowledge of H&SAW legislation and ergonomics assessment procedures. They should have a keen eye for detail and be available to teach night and weekend staff. A Master's degree and ability to interpret policy and legislation would be an advantage.

A penultimate section should describe (honestly) the attractions of the employer and locality:

> *Manchester is a thriving and vibrant city convenient for a variety of attractions, and the Manchester State General NHS Trust is ...*

The final section should advise the readership, which has now been reduced to serious candidates only, how to apply:

> *Application forms are available from the HR Department, tel: ... For an informal visit tel: ...*

Manual Handling Instructor – Manchester

A State registered Nurse, Physiotherapist or Occupational Therapist is sought to teach staff of all grades and professions in a busy NHS Trust.

Applicants should have good knowledge of H&SAW Legislation and ergonomics assessment procedures. They should have a keen eye for detail and be available to teach night and weekend staff. A Master's degree and ability to interpret policy and legislation would be an advantage.

Manchester is a thriving and vibrant city convenient for a variety of attractions, and The Manchester State General NHS Trust is ...

Application forms are available from the HR Department
tel: (*****) *********.
For an informal visit tel: (*****) ******

LOGO

Figure 3.5 Job advertisement

Shortlisting
The applicant list is screened against the person specification. Candidates who can be shown to fall short of the essential qualities are rejected at this stage. If this leaves a large applicant list, then further rejection is possible based on the desirable qualities.

Psychometric testing
Some qualities may not be assessable by reference to paper submission. For these, you may find it helpful to employ psychometric testing. Psychometric tests assess abilities and aptitudes. They predict performance, because they have been standardised upon large populations about whom much information is known.

A standardised test result may be reported with reference to people who are known to be successful in their chosen career. The tests are able to comment on how well the profile of a candidate matches that of individuals known to be successful in posts similar to the one to be filled. They are, also, able to indicate where a person lies in relation to the general population in terms of reasoning and problem-solving skills, leadership, etc. This is valuable if the person specification indicates a need for a particular ability, such as verbal reasoning.

Specialists in occupational psychology or HR management usually administer psychometric tests. The interpretation of this data is sensitive, and it is generally held that scores provide objective information to be considered alongside other information obtained from CV and interview observation.

Equal opportunities

In all industries, you must recruit a workforce that reflects the population. This will ensure that you have the best possible pool to select from and thereby you will obtain the best possible workforce. Additionally, if your workforce reflects the local population, then you will have a resource able to explain to one another the special requirements of each segment of the catchment population. This imperative is reinforced by the following legislation:

Disabled Persons (Employment) Acts (1944 and 1958)

You must employ people with disabilities where this does not prevent good performance. The Act asks you to consider targets to assess your achievement.

Rehabilitation of Offenders Act (1974)

You should not discriminate against a candidate where he or she has a conviction that is not relevant to the duties concerned. However, there is no right to withhold information when a candidate is applying for a position in health or social services and may have patient or client contact.

Sex Discrimination Act (1975)

You should be careful to avoid describing a position in such a way that one gender is in any indirect way disadvantaged. This would unnecessarily reduce your pool of candidates and therefore limit the calibre of your appointee. Indirect discrimination might include precluding part-time or job-sharing opportunities, which are more common among women than men. The use of physical lifting instead of hoists may again indirectly discriminate against women.

Race Relations Act (1976)

You should seek to employ an ethnic mix similar to the catchment population. This will require that you take steps to attract applicants from all sections of the community. You should consider your recruitment media, your public profile, your qualification requirements, building facilities, etc. All of these could inadvertently discriminate against individual ethnic groups.

Interviewing

The purpose of your interview is to assess the candidates against the essential and desirable qualities that you have preselected and published in your person specification. The interview, particularly, looks at those qualities that cannot be assessed from a paper application.

Where an interviewer is unsure what he or she is looking for, because he or she is not working from a clear person specification, the interview will be unsuccessful in choosing the best candidate. Furthermore, any appointment made will be very difficult to defend if an unsuccessful candidate makes an appeal.

Your interviews may be individual, by panel, or sequential (candidate moves from one interviewer to another until all panel members have assessed him or her).

The interview environment

Attention to the room layout is important. One hundred and eighty degree face-to-face seating makes the experience very formal and emphasises interviewer control. This effect can be enhanced if the interviewer(s) place a table or desk between them and the candidate. Ninety degree seating, without a table and in informal seats will have the reverse effect. There is no one correct layout for a room. You must make the decision according to the extent to which you want control or affiliation with the candidates. However, you should ensure consistency of approach to all candidates. This may require you to make a special effort where the interviews are to run over a number of days.

The questions

Your interview questions need to be primarily open in nature, aiming to achieve a balance in which your interviewee speaks for about 80% of the time.

The first question is normally predictable and serves the purpose of establishing rapport between interviewee and interviewer. You might ask a question about the interviewee's journey or comfort for this purpose. This also enables the interviewee to speak on an unchallenging topic and thereby release tension.

Your subsequent questions are then asked. These may be very varied in presentation, but essentially there are only three possible motives for your questions. These are:

1 to ascertain the extent to which the interviewee matches the person specification;
2 to establish the interviewee's motivation towards the position;
3 to establish that the interviewee understands the post, the employer and the implications of the move well enough to be making an informed choice.

You will examine these areas through a series of questions. Answers are sought in order to assess the match of the individual with the person specification. Your interview might take the form shown in Figure 3.6.

Welcome and introduction

↓

Rapport question

↓

Biographical details

↓

Questions about the candidate's education

↓

Motivation for application for the post

↓

Career to date, focusing on achievements

↓

Candidate's opinion about his/her match with person specifications with reference to personal profile and portfolio evidence, aspirations for the future

↓

Outside interests

↓

It is normal to allow the interviewee to ask questions of the panel during an interview, and these are often seen as indicators of insight and interest on the part of the interviewee.

Figure 3.6 Ordering the questions

Alternatives to interviews

There have been many studies of interviews and their effectiveness in personnel selection and they are consistently found wanting. Alternatives exist which may be considered, including:

- work simulation: such as typing tests for administrative appointments;
- group problem-solving activities and role-plays: used to observe candidates' performance in tasks similar to those to be performed by the successful candidate when in post;
- assessment centres: where a profile of strengths, weaknesses and aptitudes is established over a period of days;
- presentations: often used in conjunction with interviews to involve a wider constituency;
- predictive psychometric assessment: described above.

References

References are traditionally sought as part of a selection process. You may consider references at the screening (shortlisting) stage, interview stage or only for candidates to be offered the position. References are unreliable because the referee may be ill informed about the candidate, or may be biased in his or her commenting. At the worst, a reference may be the reverse of the truth because the referee as an employer does not want to lose a good employee or does want to lose an incompetent worker.

The reference is, however, a means of checking the truthfulness of information about job history given by the candidate, and may be used to reinforce detailed impressions gained from the interview and application form. References are usually taken up after shortlisting, but may occasionally be taken up only for candidates to be appointed, in order to verify the accuracy of information given by the candidate.

Appointing

Each organisation has a list of official appointing officers. Appointments must bear the signature of one of these. Following an appointment a member of staff is statutorily entitled to a written contract that sets out all of the conditions of the employment. The contract is binding upon the employer, but has limited control over the behaviour of the employee. Should he or she, for example, leave without notice, then there is very little sanction that can be applied. The contract sent to an employee will normally have a copy to be signed and returned. This is good practice, because it encourages the employee to read and own his or her contract. However, the signature, given or not given, has no great legal status. The employee is deemed to have accepted the contract by attending for work, and therefore the normal employment conditions apply regardless of his or her written response. You must send the contract with full terms and conditions in order to be able to demonstrate that the employee had the opportunity to learn his or her conditions of employment and therefore be held to account for compliance.

Offers

Employment offers are made verbally and/or in writing. Both are legally binding upon the employer. If you make an employment offer at interview, or by telephone thereafter, your organisation is bound to honour it, whether or not you have followed it up in writing. For this reason, it is important that you make explicit any conditions to the offers you make, such as 'subject to health assessment'. You cannot add conditions at the letter stage. It is important to be aware that any undertaking you make or receive at interview, such as 'You will support the appointees' need for training', will also constitute a part of a contract. It is important to use terms such as 'normally' or 'We would explore the possibility' at interview if you are not certain about your ability to follow through for the candidate who is appointed.

Probation

It may be possible for you to continue the selection process in the early months of an appointment by making the offer of employment probationary. If your appointee proves unsatisfactory, then he or she may be dismissed at the end of the probationary period before the employment has continued long enough for him or her to have rights against dismissal. You must, however, make the probationary nature of the employment clear at all stages of the recruitment and selection process and in particular in the verbal and written offers. Where workable, this is a satisfactory arrangement. However, many candidates already in substantive posts will consider this an unacceptable risk to take, and the recruitment pool would therefore be smaller. Additionally, in the case of internal promotions there may be continuity of employment, resulting in employment protection rights, making dismissal at the end of a probationary period impossible.

Rejecting

The majority of your applicants will be rejected. Many will be local residents and some will already be employees. Therefore, how you handle applicant rejection is very important for the reputation and image of your organisation. Some organisations have a policy of no response to unsuccessful candidates, but this misses a valuable opportunity to promote the organisation, and under no circumstances should it apply to existing employees seeking promotion.

Your unsuccessful applicants ought to receive a respectful and regretful notification of failure, and you might offer counselling about how to improve their profile and make themselves more suitable in the case of future vacancies. This is to the benefit of applicant and employer, particularly in the case of health and social care professionals where the national pool is limited and informal grapevine communication is rapid. Reputations of organisations may be built or demolished very quickly, and the impact of careless rejection practice on the quality of future recruitment pools can be dramatic.

Staff development and performance management

Once employees have been recruited, you have a continuing responsibility to develop them so that they give the most to the organisation and obtain the most personal benefit from employment.

Induction

On starting in a new position, employees need information in order to perform safely, efficiently and effectively. Some of this information is required on the first day but much of it is better introduced in a phased manner as the employee becomes ready to receive it. Essential information is, as shown in Figure 3.7, categorised as first day, week, month and quarter year. In some cases, where it is necessary to be able to demonstrate that information was given, a signature may be obtained for each component of the programme.

	These to be verified by employee signature	These are for employee's benefit
Day 1	• H&S procedures • Fire procedures • Rules of conduct, such as gifts policy	• Tour of department • Introduction to key colleagues
Week 1	• Employee responsibility to the organisation • Organisation responsibility to the employee • Terms and conditions • Procedures regarding: grievance, complaints, disputes and disciplinary action • Responsibilities such as state registration	• Tour of hospital (or equivalent) • Work schedules with explanatory policies • Workload apportionment • Involvement in social bonding activities
Month 1	• Payroll information • Staff development and advancement practice • Appraisal IPR & PDP procedures	• Services provided by the organisation and context • Enlightenment towards organisation • Involvement in social bonding activities
Quarter 1	• First objective setting meeting • Continuous professional development: initial plans	• Detailed analysis of the organisation's training offer

Figure 3.7 Example induction schedule

Drawing up an induction programme is the responsibility of the immediate supervisor. However, if desired, it can be made the responsibility of the employee to ensure that all information has been sought out, requested and understood. Any failure would therefore be the responsibility of the employee as well as the employer. This will improve the likelihood of successful training being achieved.

IPR and PDPs
Throughout the period of employment, each employee needs an explicit statement of what he or she is expected to achieve within the chosen period. This takes the form of a set of objectives agreed between the individual the supervisor. Since an experienced individual will know more about his or her job than anybody else, it is usual for him or her to draft the objectives in the first instance and then have them adjusted and ratified by the supervisor. The duty of the supervisor is to ensure that the workload is reasonable and that the objectives represent good prioritisation. The objectives of all subordinates should aggregate to the total objectives for the area under the supervisor's management.

Objectives need to be couched in language that allows for no ambiguity in order that the later evaluation presents no difficulty. A useful test for the robustness of an objective is that it is SMART (specific, measurable, achievable, relevant and time bound) – see Figure 3.8. An objective sheet might look as set out in Figure 3.9.

Specific	It is very clear what is to be achieved.
Measurable	Something can be measured to give an unambiguous indication about whether the objective has been achieved.
Achievable	It is realistic to think that the objective can be achieved in the time available.
Relevant	The objective is clearly relevant to the job and the needs of the organisation.
Time bound	It is clear by when the objective will be achieved.

Figure 3.8 SMART

OBJECTIVE SHEET

Objective No. 1:

Broad statement of objective:
To manage devolved budget

Processes:
I will control spend on budget for Mental Health Nursing, in order to achieve a spend of between 98% and 100% of target, while delivering the service requirements as per contracts held.

Caveats: (Subject to)
1. Secondment to training day on 'Revenue implications of capital spend';
2. Receipt funding of pay award;
3. Realistic funding of pay award;
4. Availability of human resources.

Signed:..(appraisee)

Signed:..(appraiser)

Progress report 1

Modifications

Signed:..(appraisee)

Signed:..(appraiser)

Progress report 2

Modifications

Signed:..(appraisee)

Signed:..(appraiser)

Figure 3.9 Objective sheet

You should agree 10–15 objectives and they should encapsulate the whole of the job to be performed. Some objectives will be of a maintenance nature, as in the above example, and some will be of a developmental nature, showing how your appraisee will change his or her service in the light of a changing environment.

If the individual does not have the necessary skills to achieve an objective, as above with 'the revenue implications of capital spending', then this will indicate the need for learning and will form a part of a personal development plan (PDP). The appraisee should also use this interview to discuss aspirations for promotion or enhanced duties in the future and if these are in line with service needs, then they, also, will form part of the PDP. As part of an IPR or appraisal interview, therefore, the employee will agree a PDP that shows how he or she will develop during the planning period. The learning opportunities agreed will include a variety of opportunities as described above.

Industrial relations

All professionals and ancillary workers in the NHS and Social Services are entitled to be members of a trade union. Members of professions will be members of their professional body, each of which is also a recognised and registered, independent trade union. Ancillary workers may join any registered trade union that has been recognised by the employer for which they hold relevant qualifications. The pattern of recognition varies between NHS Trusts and Local Authorities, etc., but the largest trade union, Unison, is recognised universally and represents the greatest number of public sector employees of all professions and grades.

Recognised trade unions are entitled to be consulted about all organisational changes, and to collectively represent their membership in discussions about general organisational behaviour. This is normally achieved through standing consultative committees.

Trade union representatives have a statutory right to be involved in all actions between staff and management. These include:

- grievances, where an individual employee wishes to take action against a manager;
- disputes, where a group of individuals wish to take action against a manager;
- disciplinary action, where a manager wishes to take action against an individual employee.

For each of the above events, the organisation is required to have a formal procedure which has been agreed by the consultative committee, mentioned above. The Arbitration & Conciliation Advisory Service (ACAS) publishes guidance on each of the above procedures and this guidance forms the basis of local agreement. Each action is a staged process. Each stage allows the opportunity for resolution and a route for escalation if resolution is not possible. The procedure requires that a trade union official, or other representative for non-TU members, is notified at each stage and that the individual is appraised of his or her right to representation before each stage is conducted.

Procedures vary in detail, but the general pattern is as below:

Grievance procedure

Stage 1
The individual makes the grievance known, in writing and by interview, to the immediate manager, who has the opportunity to correct the situation. If resolution is agreed, then the action is recorded and discontinues.

Stage 2
The individual makes his grievance known, in writing and by interview, to the manager of the immediate manager, who has the opportunity to correct the situation. If resolution is agreed, then the action is recorded and discontinues.

Stage 3
The individual makes his grievance known, in writing and then by interview, to a panel drawn from the management board, who will decide the case. Generally, this panel will not include the CEO or the Chair of the Board of Directors of the organisation, as these will be held in reserve in case of appeal.

Appeal
If the individual is dissatisfied with the outcome of the hearing, then there will, normally, be the right of appeal to a more senior panel.

If failure of an appeal makes continued employment impossible, then the employee may leave the organisation, considering himself or herself to have suffered 'constructive dismissal'. Constructive dismissal may be taken to an industrial tribunal as a form of 'unfair dismissal'. However, this action is unlikely to succeed if the procedures have been clearly defined and scrupulously followed.

At each stage, the personnel department or their TU representative may assist the complainants. In some organisations, all cases are routed through the personnel department.

Disputes procedure
A grievance held by a number of employees is known as a dispute.

Stage 1
The group of individuals makes the dispute known, in writing and by interview, to the immediate manager, who has the opportunity to correct the situation. If resolution is agreed, then the action is recorded and discontinues.

Stage 2
The group makes the dispute known, in writing and then by interview, to the manager of the manager who has the opportunity to correct the situation. If resolution is agreed, then the action is recorded and discontinues.

Stage 3
The group makes the dispute known, in writing and then by interview, to a panel drawn from the management board, who will decide the case. Generally, this panel will not include the CEO or the Chair of the organisation, as these will be held in reserve in case of appeal.

Appeal
If the group is dissatisfied with the outcome of the hearing, then there will, normally, be the right of appeal to a more senior panel.

At each stage, the personnel department or their TU representative may assist the complainants. In some organisations, all cases are routed through the personnel department.

Disciplinary procedure

Preliminary counselling
Before a formal disciplinary procedure is commenced, the manager interviews the individual, alerts him or her to the problems and discusses the ways in which they may be corrected. It is required that the individual is advised that this is a counselling interview prior to and as a part of a disciplinary action. If this resolves the problem, then disciplinary procedure is not deemed to have been evoked.

Stage 1
If counselling has not resolved the problem, then the manager makes the unsatisfactory performance explicit, in writing and by interview, to the individual, who has the opportunity to correct the situation by agreeing a set of objectives with timescales. If these objectives are achieved, then the action is recorded and discontinued. The record should be deleted after a period of six months' satisfactory performance. This is often described as a verbal warning. However, this is a misnomer, because the warning is given verbally and in writing.

Stage 2
If the objectives are not achieved, then the manager reaffirms the unsatisfactory performance, in writing and then by interview, to the individual, who has further opportunity to correct the situation by agreeing a further set of objectives with timescales. If these objectives are achieved, then the action is recorded and discontinued. This is often described as a written warning. However, once again, this is a misnomer, because the warning is given verbally and in writing.

Stage 3
If the objectives are not achieved, then the manager will dismiss the employee or otherwise alter his or her employment terms.

Appeal
The individual will have the right of appeal about the outcome of any stage to a panel drawn from the Board of Directors of the organisation.

Gross misconduct
In prescribed cases, a manager may skip one or more of the stages in the procedure. In extreme cases, misconduct may result in instant dismissal.

Suspension
Where serious misconduct is alleged, but not yet decided, it may be necessary to suspend employment, with or without pay, while the allegations are investigated and decided. This is usually done where the allegations, if true, would suggest that the organisation or its clients are at risk from the employee, or the employee is placed at risk by continued practice without resolution of the allegations.

Industrial tribunal
If the individual and his or her representative consider the dismissal unfair, then they may ask that an industrial tribunal consider the case as a possible unfair dismissal. This avenue is available only to employees with over one year's employment and in a permanent position. A major indicator to the fairness of a dismissal, as assessed by a tribunal, is the care with which the manager has followed and documented the agreed procedures in arriving at a dismissal decision.

Burden of proof
In an industrial tribunal, as in all industrial relations panel decisions, the test of proof is the civil one that 'in the balance of probability' the misconduct occurred. This test of proof is far less stringent than that in criminal courts, in which conviction requires that 'beyond all reasonable doubt' the misconduct occurred.

If an industrial tribunal finds that a dismissal is unfair, it can order reinstatement. If the employer refuses to comply with this order, then the tribunal will order compensation for loss of earnings and other distress. It is important that any decision being appealed is examined against the evidence available to the manager at the time of the decision. If a dismissal is made and contested, the manager must show that the dismissal was fair with respect to the information held at the time of the dismissal. Further evidence that became known after the dismissal which may vindicate the decision cannot be cited as justification of a dismissal. Equally, evidence that emerges after the dismissal vindicating the employee would not render the dismissal unfair. However, in this case the manager might consider reinstatement a reasonable course of action.

Accountability
As has been described above a clinician may be called to account by:

1 the patient/client
2 the employer

3 the profession
4 the community

The response to this should not be defensive practice, because this inhibits good patient/client care, but good practice and good record keeping.

Professional good practice

To be defensible to any of the four stakeholders above, the individual has only to behave as an exemplary member of his or her profession. This is a very simple defence and liberates clinicians from defensive practice. If the clinician always practises properly, doing what a reasonable clinician or manager would do, and keeping good records, then he or she will have nothing to fear when called to account.

Paradoxically, if the clinician becomes too focused on the law and attempts to become an amateur lawyer, instead of a clinician, this will impinge on his or her ability to act properly within his or her profession and will weaken any defence. The nurse in charge during an armed raid reported the event as she imagined a lawyer would speak: 'When the gunman entered the room all of the patients evacuated themselves.' Although possible, it is doubtful that the meaning conveyed was the meaning intended. Attempting to use law-speak had prevented her from communicating clearly as a nurse (Andrews and Wheeler, 1997). 'Don't get involved, for fear of being sued' – common bar-room advice – will only result in being sued for your omissions. Omissions are as important as positive actions in deciding negligence. The only defence is to do what a competent clinician of your profession would do, and keep records accordingly.

Record keeping

A complainant will remember the events occasioning the complaint very clearly, because it has been central to his or her life for a long time. You as a manager or a clinician, on the other hand, will struggle even to remember consultations of many years ago, far less to recall the precise words that you used and the actions that you took. The judge decides the case on the balance of probabilities. Who has produced the best evidence? Your faint or non-existent recollection versus the plaintiff's total recall makes for a one-sided contest.

You can overcome this problem by the production of detailed records. With good, accurate and detailed notes, your answer can be compiled. Without these, however good your treatment practice may have been in actuality, it is very difficult for you to mount a defence.

Your records must show: what information you elicited by the various routes; what underlying theory explained your action proposed; what consents you obtained; what actions you took; and what consequences resulted. Sometimes Kipling's six serving men can help – 'Who? What? Where? When? Why? and How?' (Kipling, 1950) – but they must between them answer the points above.

Team working

Your work with patients and clients is inevitably conducted in teams in order to bring to bear the breadth of expertise necessary. Teams go through a predictable life cycle in reaching a stage of maturity. The stages that you will observe are often categorised as: forming, storming, norming and performing. You as a team member can usefully identify the current stage of each of the teams to which you belong and make contributions calculated to move your team forward.

Forming

Team behaviour
Making introductions and attempting to understand the other members of the team. Forming collegiate relationships and establishing communications.

You as a team member can help by
- facilitating communication;
- helping members to better understand each other as people as well as professionals;
- encouraging interaction between members on neutral issues as well as work problems;
- organising social events, etc.

Storming

Team behaviour
Establishing a pecking order, forming strategic alliances, gaining a comfortable position, agreeing leadership, establishing responsibilities and demarcations.

You as a team member can help by
- mediating conflict;
- drawing out the special contributions made by each individual;
- avoiding cliques;
- seeking win–win resolutions to power conflicts;
- ensuring that decisions reached meet all parties' needs rather that allowing one party to win at the expense of another;
- continuing to progress the endeavour to help team members to know one another as people.

Norming

Team behaviour
Settling down into workable patterns, agreeing protocols and procedures, establishing relationships and responsibilities that are comfortable to all members.

You as a team member can help by
- testing processes devised against client/patient need;

- ensuring that no members are disadvantaged or disenfranchised;
- ensuring that all skills and expertise have been considered and exploited.

Performing

Team behaviour
Getting the job done, running in line with agreed protocols, beginning the process of transcending the rules and allowing role blurring and overlaps for efficient cooperation.

You as a team member can help by
- testing performance against objectives;
- avoiding complacency;
- driving up quality;
- testing the rules devised above to find those that can be gradually relaxed.

Team roles

In any team, there are a number of roles that are performed, and each of us has a profile of strengths in these roles. It is important to know your strengths and perform team roles as are appropriate to you. You may perform different roles in different teams because of the roles dictated by the strengths and position of your colleagues. Your contribution in each situation will reflect the range of abilities across each team seen as a whole. Conflict in teams may arise where two individuals have similar profiles and are unconsciously seeking to take the same role. This conflict may be overcome by explicit recognition of profiles and aptitudes. Conflict may also arise between two team members whose profiles and roles, although necessary, are in conflict. Recognising why a colleague is performing differently to you can make your relationship easier. The 'shaper' may be in conflict with the 'completer finisher', because of the nature of the contributions each make. However, each needs the other for the team to work. If both can gain an explicit understanding of the relationship, then they can learn to value one another rather than simply be irritated by each other.

Inefficient team working may also arise where individual team roles are not being performed by those best suited to them. Again, to achieve an explicit understanding of the aptitude of each team member, and to allocate roles accordingly will enable the team to perform at its best level.

Belbin (1993) describes team functions as:

Company worker
The company worker is described as: conservative, dutiful, loyal and predictable. He or she will have organising abilities, common sense and discipline, and will be hard working. He or she may be inflexible and wary of risk.

Chair
The chair is described as calm, self-confident and controlled. He or she will have a strong focus on objectives, and will be unprejudiced and unconditionally welcoming. He or she need be of no more than average intellect.

Shaper
The shaper is described as: highly strung, outgoing and dynamic. He or she will have restless drive, and will be challenging towards inertia and complacency. He or she may be impatient and easily provoked.

Plant
The plant is described as: individualistic, serious minded and unorthodox. He or she will have genius, intellect, imagination and knowledge. He or she may be impractical, and disrespecting towards protocols.

Resource investigator
The Resource Investigator is described as: extravert, enthusiastic, curious and communicative. He or she will be good at contacting people, responsive to challenge and enthusiastic about exploring anything new. He or she may be able to sustain his or her interest in anything for only a short time, before pursuing something new.

Monitor evaluator
The monitor evaluator is described as: sober, unemotional and prudent. He or she will have judgement, discretion and hard-headedness. He or she may lack inspiration or the ability to motivate others.

Team worker
The team worker is described as: socially orientated, mild and sensitive. He or she will respond to people and promote a team spirit. He or she may be indecisive.

Completer finisher
The completer finisher is described as: painstaking, orderly, conscientious and anxious. He or she will have a capacity to follow a project through to the absolute conclusion and be a perfectionist. He or she may worry about small, unimportant considerations and be unable to let go.

Identifying your team function
You may be able to allocate team functions from the above descriptions. To get a more robust idea, you might make your own assessment of yourself and compare it with that of a close colleague. In order to gain a more considered assessment you might complete an inventory and derive a score that allocates you to a role. You may find that you are adept at more than one function and you can therefore make a varied contribution in various situations.

Negotiation

Negotiation divides into two types: affiliative and distributive. In affiliative negotiation both parties seek to achieve a 'win–win' outcome. As an affiliative negotiator, you will seek an outcome where each party is satisfied. This may result in a degree of compromise on both sides, with neither gaining everything they want. However, long-term benefits will ensue, because of the beneficial relationship established for future negotiation.

In distributive negotiation the parties are seeking a 'win–lose' outcome. Should you be obliged to act as a distributive negotiator, you will be seeking to achieve advantage at the expense of the other party. This may result in benefiting from the negotiation at the expense of the other. The immediate benefit of this (to the winner) is great but the other party will be seeking to redress the balance in future negotiations, or if this is not possible they may elect not to do business with you again. Distributive negotiation is inappropriate in long-term supply relationships, but may be inescapable where no future relationship is likely or where the other party is evidently operating according to a distributive paradigm.

Negotiating teams

Negotiating is commonly conducted between teams, and each member will have a specific role.

Negotiator

The negotiator takes the lead in discussions, described as 'making the running'. You will discuss the positions set out by both sides, introduce information as appropriate and make piecemeal steps toward agreement. You will start from a position demanding maximum benefit and give way on a series of points in exchange for reciprocal concessions until a point of agreement has been achieved. Each negotiator will, however, have a point beyond which he or she cannot go.

Figure 3.10 shows the range of acceptable outcomes for negotiators 1 and 2. Here the scope for agreement is represented by the overlap of the two lines. Each negotiator is seeking to agree an overlap position as near to his or her start position as he or she can achieve. In distributive negotiation, these positions are not revealed, and therefore the negotiation exercise is one of exploration and con-

Figure 3.10 The range of acceptable outcomes

trolled disclosure. The distributive negotiator may, however, reveal a false minimum point as a negotiating ploy.

In affiliative negotiation, the positions are both revealed at the outset of the negotiations and evidenced as appropriate, and a conclusion reached that allows equal benefit to both parties.

Co-negotiator

A team may employ a co-negotiator who works in tandem with the negotiator, by listening and chipping in throughout the discussions. The baton may even be passed from one to the other throughout the negotiation.

Recorder

The recorder is an analyst who knows and clearly understands what has been agreed and can quickly make comment when discussion backslides from this position or compromises an agreed position. The recorder does not keep minutes, but can at all times give a precise statement of what has been agreed and what remains outstanding.

Technical expert

A number of experts within their field may be present to advise during a negotiation. These might include clinicians, accountants, lawyers, etc.

Arbitration

If negotiation is badly conducted, overly distributive, or there is no overlap in the positions shown in Figure 3.10 then the parties may agree to arbitration.

Arbitration may be binding arbitration, in which case parties agree in advance to enact the arbiter's decision, or advisory, in which case the parties may still continue the discussion. Arbitration may be of a pendulum arbitration type, where the arbiter is obliged to decide in favour of one party or the other, or may be to find a compromise, in which case the arbiter seeks a solution to the satisfaction of both parties.

In the case of the NHS, where agreement between purchaser and provider cannot be achieved the law requires binding, pendulum arbitration to be conducted by the DoH Outpost.

Managing oneself

All employees are responsible for managing themselves to the best advantage. This represents consumption of a very significant resource.

Time

The management of your time is the most important aspect of life at work and elsewhere, and is discussed at length in Chapter 2, which you should read in conjunction with the material in this chapter.

Stress

Every modern work environment is a stressing one, but employment in health care is made more than usually stressful by the nature of the work to be done. The management of stress is essential, both to the individual and to the organisation. Stress and burnout may be a result of a mismatch between the degree of challenge experienced and the amount of support received. As the demand in a job increases, so should the support. It is healthy for a job to have periods of high demand interspersed with periods of lower demand allowing space for recuperation, tying up loose ends and creative reflection. When a job is in a demanding phase, it is appropriate for the employee to seek appropriate support. This might come from a supervisor, mentor, peer or counsellor. Stress may also arise from poor time management. Stress may increase insidiously, arising from indistinct or multiple sources and through difficulties taking on a greater than necessary importance.

The management of stress might be considered in causal or reactive terms and intellectual/emotional or physical terms. This can be represented as a grid, as in Figure 3.11.

	Intellectual/emotional response	Physical response
Cause-focused action	• Observe fluctuating stress levels. • Understand the causes of stress. • Reflect on whether the individual causes are very important. • Decide upon changes that can be made to reduce identified stressors. • Improve time management.	• Break into vicious cycle stress patterns. • Practice relaxation techniques in stressful settings. • Diminish environmental stressors such as poor seating, lighting, noise, etc. • Avoid long unbroken meetings, etc.
Reaction-focused action	• Gain increased support. • Set achievable goals. • Recognise and express feelings. • Maximise the benefit of social contacts for emotional release. • Question perfectionism: consider 'Good enough' outcomes. • Adopt empowering language and attitudes.	• Ensure suitable diet. • Take exercise weekly and daily. • Ensure a balance of work, domestic duties and recreation. • Practice active relaxation at some point every day. • Ensure deep relaxation periodically with holidays, short breaks and occasional days of indulgence.

Figure 3.11 Stress management grid

Personal and professional development through portfolios and profiles

In order to control and maximise your rate of professional progress, you need to have a clear picture of your present attributes. This may be achieved by drawing up a profile supported by a portfolio. A profile enables you to monitor your progress from novice to state-registered clinician or manager and throughout your career. It enables you to analyse the current position and, by reference to aspirations, decide and plan for your learning needs. It is sensible that you record your progress in discussion with a tutor, mentor coach or line manager at least annually.

The process of profiling provides an opportunity to reflect upon your professional and personal qualities. This can be a primary vehicle for addressing continuing professional development (CPD) needs, which will affect your progress on the career ladder.

It is good for you to discuss your progress with a colleague and agree a series of scores that best reflect your position. The insights gained will help you to maximise your rate of progress. It may be helpful to discuss your profile with course leaders when joining a course of study in order for them to tailor the learning opportunity to your best advantage. The same can be done with a new line manager in order that he or she tailors experience to your maximum benefit.

In a highly competitive environment, an explicit profile will show to prospective employers what skills, knowledge and understanding you have gained during your education and thereafter. This, alongside a curriculum vitae document (CV), enables you to describe yourself in the job market. It is acceptable at interview to say that you have been a sister on an elderly care ward. However, it is better to say that you have been a sister and that you have gained expertise in managing money, selecting, training and supervising staff, etc. To describe skills, knowledge and understanding is more persuasive than to simply refer to time served.

Figure 3.12 shows a practitioner skilled in health and safety (H&S) matters, highly professional, with good communications and teamwork skills. He or she describes lower ability in self-management and reflection. This profile is designed for a novice practitioner, covering those things necessary for the first year of practice. A clinician aspiring to a management career would have skills such as marketing, HR management, financial management, etc. on the profile. Each individual should decide how many sections to have in his or her profile. This may be influenced by published requirements from a professional body and personal preference for models of practice.

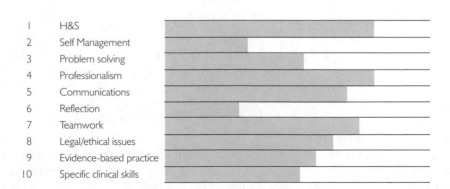

1	H&S
2	Self Management
3	Problem solving
4	Professionalism
5	Communications
6	Reflection
7	Teamwork
8	Legal/ethical issues
9	Evidence-based practice
10	Specific clinical skills

Figure 3.12 A personal profile

Portfolio

In order to substantiate the profile, clinicians collect evidence of ability from their professional and personal life. This evidence may include testimonials, examples of work, course marks and comments, reflective diaries, etc. and is called a portfolio. Your portfolio may take any of a number of forms. Perhaps the simplest is a concertina file with sections created to match the sections chosen for your profile. As pieces of evidence occur you can easily file them for future attention. Periodically, your portfolio should be closely examined and an assessment made of each section. You are advised to be continually alert to pieces of evidence of an ability or attribute to add to your portfolio.

Evidence

It is important to be flexible about what constitutes evidence for your portfolio. Some evidence will come in a conveniently fileable form, such as certificates from courses, but much will need to be canvassed: 'Would you write a brief appraisal of my communication with the next patient?' Evidence might also be the result of personal reflection. Reflections on an achievement can make rich evidence if captured quickly after an event, and particularly if seen in conjunction with other tangible evidence such as a certificate or testimonial. The question of what is appropriate might be answered by considering the uses for which you might use your portfolio. If it is to win you jobs, then consider what evidence a panel might want you to describe.

Uses for portfolios

Portfolios are mandatory for nurses and midwives as evidence for re-registration. This requirement is likely to be adopted by the other health and social care professions.

Portfolios and the profiles that can be deduced from them may be used for many purposes, including self-evaluation, obtaining a job or planning personal development.

Self-evaluation

This involves looking through your portfolio and improving your opinion about your attributes. This requires only that the evidence is honest and gives rich information from which a profile can be deduced. This calls for reports of experience, reflections, testimonials, colleague and client comments, etc. You will critically examine your portfolio in order to decide what your balance of attainments looks like.

Evidence for job interviews

Evidence for job interviews from this your portfolio must be persuasive and incisive. An interviewer is willing to hear about experiences, courses, achievements and accomplishments, where they clearly indicate a skill that helps them to match you up against a person specification. The portfolio is not normally physically present at an interview except in unusual cases. However, the interviewee is called upon, metaphorically, to delve into their portfolio and refer to or describe evidence that can persuade the panel of their match with the person specification and therefore their suitability for a position.

Evidence for supervision and personal development planning interview

The profile and portfolio form the basis of independent performance review (IPR) and personal development planning (PDP), discussed above. Here you are seeking to draw the interviewer's attention to evidence of which both may have prior knowledge. The interviewee may refer to individual cases and projects, citing the outcome as evidence of ability and achievement. Alternatively, the evidence may be offered to demonstrate an ability that is not yet satisfactory and indicate the need for further learning by any of a number of routes. There might be a discussion between interviewee and interviewer until a common view of the profile is achieved based upon the evidence in the virtual or physical portfolio. A similar process might occur in an interview to decide performance-related pay (PRP). Possession of a portfolio and explicit understanding of the profile enables the interviewee to be more in control of an interview of the types described above.

It is important that you have a sense of ownership of your portfolio. That way, you can ensure that it gives best benefit for the time that you commit. If your portfolio is compiled mechanistically, simply to meet the demands of your professional body, then the value will be far less than if you compile your portfolio for your own benefit and ensure that it, incidentally, meets the demands of your professional regulatory machinery.

Your personal development plan emerges from a study of your profile and portfolio. It may also be used as a vehicle for your PDP. Having stated a learning need, based upon study of the portfolio, it is possible to describe the learning in terms of the changes anticipated in the portfolio. Thus the evidence to be obtained is known, and from this the best type of learning opportunity is evident. This may help you to be more creative in recognition of learning methods. It may be more valuable to join a project team and thereby gain experience than to follow a course and gain knowledge. Commonly, however, it is the combination of theoretical input and experiential learning that proves to be most educational and persuasive.

Job hunting

The process of job hunting can mirror the processes described above for recruitment: job specification, attracting potential employers, researching potential employers, passing screening, being selected.

Job specification

The first task is to define the job sought. If the job is not defined, then the job hunter is vulnerable to eye-catching advertisements and may apply for attractive positions that will not adequately meet his or her needs.

There are a number of parameters to consider in your job specification. These are shown in Figure 3.13. It may appear that the candidate is in a poor position to define the position because the range is limited by availability. In this case, the parameters may be set wide. However, it is necessary to be explicit about the parameters in order to focus attention on to a manageable number of ideal jobs, and make a high quality application for these.

Quality	Essential	Desirable
Locality	Greater London	Inner London
Salary	£20,000	£25,000
Training opportunities	General support in principle	Funding for MSc
Client group	Mental health	Acute adult mental health
Assistance	Travel allowance	Lease car
Supervision	Weekly supervision meetings	Peer support group

Figure 3.13 Specifying job parameters

Attracting potential employers

Making contact with potential employers may be by response to an advertisement, introduction by current employee, or cold calling.

Responding to an advertisement has the advantage that the employer is anticipating applicants and has set aside time to respond to them. The disadvantage is that such candidates are reactive, and have to use other methods to prove their creativity. Introduction by employee is a good route, because the introduction carries some recommendation and there is some innovation demonstrated by not waiting for an advertisement. Cold calling shows the maximum initiative, but faces the maximum expectation of rejection. Cold calling is best by letter, allowing the recipient to respond in his or her own time. Cold calling by telephone is not recommended, because this is likely to inconvenience and annoy the recipient, although meetings and conferences may offer an opportunity for networking and informal enquiries, and responding to published research may create an employment prospect. The serious job hunter should consider all of these routes. When candidates have been generated by personal contacts it remains likely that a formal advertisement will be placed to ensure equal opportunity. However, those candidates who showed initiative in their approach will have an advantage in a position where initiative is important.

Once a desired employer has been selected, it is important to research the organisation. This research has three purposes: to confirm choice of employer, to persuade the employer of your enthusiasm, and to find out about the candidate qualities sought.

Information will be gained from the job pack sent to candidates, publications such as annual reports, personal contacts in the organisation and the traditional informal visit. It is important to collect as much information by paper research as possible before the informal visit. This will allow insightful questions to be asked and the maximum to be gained from the exercise. It is important to use the informal visit to collect information that will strengthen the application. Candidates should not spend this meeting talking about themselves, although the employer may be impressed by the knowledgeable and insightful nature of their questions.

CVs

The purpose of a CV is to ensure that you pass the screening exercise and obtain an interview. It may, at best, ensure you a high place on the candidate order, but cannot bring about an appointment. The CV should be written to demonstrate how well you match the person specification described above. It must be rewritten for each application. That is not to suggest that the CV is not entirely honest; in fact, it is important that it is scrupulous. However, a great deal can be said about a candidate and it is necessary to select that which interests this employer. For this reason, commercial pre-printed CVs are of limited value.

Your CV is an example of the quality of the work that you can deliver and for this reason it should be drawn up with great care over a number of days and finished to a very high quality. It is advisable to submit a number of copies of a CV in order that all panellists receive a top copy rather than a photocopied one.

The notion of an ideal CV is specific to each industry. For health and social care industries, a comprehensive CV is the norm. A good format is shown in Figure 3.14.

CV

Name

Address

DoB

Résumé or Personal Statement, summarising strengths and aptitudes, with some reference to experience and other evidence that might persuade the reader that these qualities are genuine. Max ½ page.

Education History in reverse chronological order, stating institutions and qualifications obtained. Add a script to a piece, if there is a particular point to make that is relevant to the position.
e.g. Uni of Keele: MBA Note: this is a specialist MBA for NHS Executives.
Employment History in reverse chronological order giving a list of responsibilities, achievements and skills learned in each. Allow greater space for recent posts diminishing, as the positions become older. Focus on giving information that demonstrates your match with the person Specification.
Other attributes, such as clean driving licence, first aid qualification, etc.
Hobbies and interests. This is to show a good balanced existence, but may also underline a desire to live in the locality and evidence some qualities claimed in the Résumé.

Figure 3.14 Curriculum vitae example

Publications
List all papers, presentations and exercises to make public the results of your research, experiences and thinking. This list needs to be creative. Do not just list journal papers, as these may be few, but also include other times when you made your knowledge public, e.g. conference presentations made, lectures given, work-based training offered, papers written for the Board, etc.

Interviews
The purpose of an interview is to allow the selection panel to match the candidates with the person specification. Panellists will want to know that you are making a thoughtful and well-informed choice of job and will therefore perform well. They will then want to know that you have all necessary abilities and aptitudes to perform well and they will test you in each of these areas. Consequently, you should expect all three questions, in a variety of forms. These questions are:

- Why do you want this job and what do you know of the job/organisation/industry/locality?
- Where do you want your career to go?
- What qualities have you that make you a suitable candidate, and what evidence can you offer for these qualities; what knowledge can you demonstrate? e.g. by case example.

A long list of questions can be generated from this base, and you might practise answers to each in informal role-plays with friends and colleagues.

Possible interview questions
It is worth your while to become fluent in answering any of the commonly asked questions. Not to have thought about these areas might be interpreted as lacking drive and initiative.

With a friend, rehearse the example questions listed in Figure 3.15. You will notice that they all amount to variants on the three questions above. You should do this until you are comfortable talking about yourself while under a spotlight. Give feedback to one another and ensure that your performance is as good as it is possible for it to be.

In answering questions, consider the three ways in which you are expressing yourself. Mehrabian (1971) has shown that audiences are persuaded by three factors in a communication. Least persuasive are the words spoken. More persuasive is the intonation and voice quality when presenting. Of greatest importance are the body communications given when speaking. Mehrabian observed the relative importance of these three factors in persuading an audience and, more critically, pointed out that maximum effect is achieved when all three devices are in harmony.

Other interview advice
At the interview, your research carried out before application will allow you to

1	WHY DO YOU WANT THIS JOB?
2	WHAT ARE YOUR STRENGTHS?
3	HAVE YOU ANY WEAKNESSES?
4	WHAT JOB DO YOU WANT TO BE DOING IN 5 YEARS?
5	WHAT JOB DO YOU WANT TO BE DOING IN 10 YEARS?
6	WHAT ARE YOUR MAJOR ACHIEVEMENTS?
7	WHAT DO YOU ENJOY DOING MOST?
8	WHAT EXPERIENCES DO YOU THINK MAKE YOU SUITABLE FOR THIS JOB?
9	WHAT ABILITIES DO YOU THINK MAKE YOU SUITABLE FOR THIS JOB?
10	WHAT DO YOU WANT FROM THIS JOB?
11	WHAT WOULD YOU WANT FROM YOUR MANAGER?
12	WHAT WOULD YOU OFFER TO THIS JOB?
13	WHAT DO YOU KNOW ABOUT THIS TRUST?
14	WHAT DO YOU KNOW ABOUT THIS AREA?
15	WHAT DO YOU THINK IS THE FUTURE FOR THE NHS?
16	IF OFFERED THE JOB WILL YOU TAKE IT?
17	HOW DO YOU THINK THAT OTs SHOULD WORK WITH PTs/Psych/Etc?
18	WHAT IS THE DIFFERENCE BETWEEN STUDENT AND BASIC GRADE OT?
19	HAVE YOU ANY QUESTIONS FOR THE PANEL?
20	YOU COULD BE GIVEN CASE EXAMPLES AS PROBLEMS TO SOLVE

Figure 3.15 Questions to expect

offer a very sophisticated match to the person specification and reassure the panellists that you really understand the organisation that you wish to join.

General points to note are:

1 Dress smart, but no more formal than the organisational norm.
2 Actively relax at the start of the interview, and smile.
3 Practice a firm handshake.
4 Rehearse answers. Research shows that the least influential component of your communication is what is said. Tone of voice is of medium importance, and general demeanour is of greatest importance (Mehrabian, 1971). Therefore to convince an employer, the candidate must not simply practise the right answers, but must learn to use convincing tone of voice and demeanour.
5 Know exactly where the interview will be held, arrive early, park and then find a restaurant in which to relax and freshen up.
6 Carry the name and telephone number in order to call if you are delayed. If you do arrive late, late ask for time to freshen up so that you can perform well. Do not be rushed into a poor performance.
7 Answer the question asked, not the one you hoped for. If unsure ask for clarification.
8 Ask questions when prompted that show insight and demonstrate other skills, e.g. 'Would there be an opportunity to use and further my IT skills?' Do not ask about salary or holidays at interview.
9 Do ask about training etc. at interview. The answer forms part of the contract.
10 Immediately after an interview make a reflective note. What went well/badly? What lesson have you learned? What will you do differently next time? In this way, interview technique will rapidly improve.

A salient warning

It is important that employers and employees are as honest as possible in the selection process. However, a degree of spin is to be expected and, as candidate, you should be cautions about what is said. Your broad knowledge of the situation should not be overwhelmed by a slick presentation. The following public domain case history demonstrates.

One day, a woman manager was suddenly killed. She arrived at the gates to Heaven, where St Peter met her.

'You are very welcome,' he said, but, after a pause, he continued, 'although, you do present us with a problem. As you might imagine, we've never had a manager make it to Heaven before and we're not really sure what to do.'

'Just let me in,' said the woman.

'I'd like to,' replied the Gatekeepcr, 'but I have my orders. What we are going to do is let you have a day in Hell and a day in Heaven, and then you can choose.'

'Actually, I prefer to stay in Heaven,' said the woman.

'Rules,' said St Peter, and he put her into an elevator to Hell.

She was surprised. She found herself on a beautiful paradise island. In the distance was a country club, and standing there were all of her friends and colleagues. They were all dressed gorgeously and cheering for her. They ran up and shook her hand and they talked about old times. They played every kind of sport, and that night went to the country club where she enjoyed an excellent steak dinner. She met the Devil, who was quite charming. She had a great time telling jokes and dancing and before she knew it, it was time to leave. Everybody shook her hand and waved goodbye as she got on the elevator.

The manager spent the next 24 hours on clouds and playing the harp and singing. She had a great time, and before she knew it, her 24 hours were up.

St Peter came. 'You have spent a day in Hell and in Heaven. Now you can choose,' he said.

The woman paused for a second, and then replied, 'I never thought I'd say this. Heaven has been really great, but I think I had a better time in Hell.'

Accordingly, St Peter escorted her to the elevator and back to Hell. When the doors of the elevator opened, she found herself standing in a desolate wasteland covered in all manner of filth. She saw her friends dressed in rags picking up garbage and putting it in sacks. Proprietarily, the Devil put his arm around her.

'I don't understand,' said the woman. 'Yesterday there was a country club and we ate steak and danced. I had a great time. Now all there is is wasteland and garbage. All of my friends look miserable.

The Devil looked at her and smiled. 'Yesterday we were recruiting you; today you're staff.'

Conclusion

Health and sservices are human resource intensive organisations. A very large portion of revenue is spent on people, far in excess of the proportion in most other sectors of industry. How well these resources are managed and how efficiently they are employed determine the efficiency of the service. Reduced staff turnover, increased activity, optimised cooperation and goal achievement lead to more and better patient/client care, so to achieve HR efficiency is an ethical imperative. You have a personal duty to enable maximum, harmonious performance for the benefit of the end user. Additionally, you are a human resource, and have a duty to ensure that you are delivering the best value that you can.

REFERENCES

Andrews, A. and Wheeler, N. (1997) Accountability and occupational therapy. *British Journal of Occupational Therapy*, 59(10), 483.

Belbin, R.M. (1993) *Team Roles at Work*. Butterworth-Heinemann, Oxford.

Handy, C.B. (1990) *Inside Organisations*. BBC Books, London.

IPM (1990) *Recruitment Code of Practice*. IPM, London.

Kipling, R. (1950) *The Just So Stories*. Macmillan, London.

The Home Office (1974) *A Guide to the Rehabilitation of Offenders Act*. HMSO, London.

Wheeler, N. and Grice, D. (1995) Generic or specialist: a model for contracting the professions. *British Journal of Therapy and Rehabilitation*, 3(1), 11–17.

FURTHER READING

Atkinson, J. (1989) Four stages of adjustment to demographic downturn. *Journal of Personnel Management*, August 20–24.

Handy, C.B. (1993) *Understanding Organisations*. Penguin, London.

Handy, C.B. (1996) *Beyond Certainty: The Changing Worlds of Organisations*. Arrow, London.

Wheeler, N. (1995) Whither the professions? *British Journal of Therapy and Rehabilitation*.

4 THE MANAGEMENT OF FINANCIAL RESOURCES

INTRODUCTION

The NHS and Social Services can never be adequately funded. Demand is potentially infinite and resources are finite. Financial demands escalate because of the progressively ageing population, technological progress and increasing consumer expectation. All of these developments are desirable, but they place a demand upon health and social care providers that cannot be entirely satisfied. There is a responsibility on society to make as much resource available as is possible, and then upon managers and clinicians to obtain the maximum benefit for patients and clients from this resource. Since only clinicians and some managers can know the real priorities in health and social care, they have an ethical duty to engage with the management of resources. This function cannot be delegated to management accountants alone.

THE THEORETICAL FRAMEWORK

The channels

The NHS is funded by central taxation. This comes in part from National Insurance payments, collected through payrolls. The balance comes from the general national taxation pool.

Funds are passed to District Health Authorities (DHA) according to a formula that takes account of population size, demographic make-up and social deprivation. DHAs apportion resources to Primary Care Groups (PCG) and work with those groups to enter into contracts with hospitals, other NHS Trusts and independent sector providers to deliver care to their population when this care is required. Contracts are set for one or more years. The nature of services to be purchased and the number of patients expected are based upon knowledge from previous years. If insufficient treatment is commissioned in this way, then waiting lists will be held until the DHA and PCG can fund further treatments. DHAs also act as payroll for general medical and dental practitioner services. NHS Trusts receive moneys in exchange for agreeing to provide services to patients through contracts.

Social care is funded in part from central taxation passed to local authorities through Social Services Grants and partly through local taxation: Council Tax. Local Authority Social Services Departments (LASSD) receive funds from the District or County Council according to the council's assets and as far as possible in line with 'Ratepayers' wishes'. Social Services departments employ staff such as social workers and occupational therapists to deliver services, but a minimum of 80% of their resources must be spent through contracts with independent contractors. This usually accounts for the provision of residential care.

Both the NHS and Social Services Departments add to their available resources by making means-tested co-payment charges. The burden upon the consumer in Social Services is generally far higher than in health care, although there is a trend to increase the contributions in both fields. Co-payments in the NHS include: prescription charges, ophthalmic and dental charges, and charges to insurers for treatment resulting from road traffic accidents, and further charges are periodically discussed. Co-payments in Social Services are levied on residential services, day care services and home care services. These co-payments can amount to 100% of the total cost and, as in the case of home care, may even exceed the market cost, leading consumers to elect to pay for private provision as a cost-saving exercise. Means tests seek to ensure that patients and clients are not prevented from receiving care on financial grounds.

Income and expenditure

NHS Trusts gain income by entering into contracts with DHAs, PCGs and other agencies, such as BUPA, to provide treatments to those patients who are the responsibility of the purchaser. The Trust is required by statute to match its expenditure exactly to its income. A NHS Trust is not permitted to run in deficit or to make a profit. This means that a NHS Trust is required to calculate how much it will cost to provide a service sought by a purchaser and this must be the price at which the service is offered. The NHS Trust is not permitted to cross-subsidise services, i.e. it may not make an accountancy loss on one service and make it up on another. Each contract must operate in balance. The calculation of cost, however, is a very complicated exercise.

Direct and indirect costs

Provision of a service will involve some expenditure directly on the service and some expenditure indirectly spent in order for the service to be provided. For illumination, this section will explore X-ray assessment services as a case example (Figure 4.1).

Direct costs include:	Indirect costs include part of the costs of:
Radiographers and receptionists Film Dedicated X-ray premises Maintenance of machinery	The Management Board General premises such as reception, car park, etc. Support services such as portering Public Relations Department

Figure 4.1 Direct and indirect costs

Fixed and variable costs

Fixed costs will be payable regardless of the amount of work to be done. Variable costs will depend upon the amount of work to be undertaken, i.e. they increase with every unit of production. See case example in Figure 4.2.

Fixed costs may include:	Variable costs may include:
Radiographers and receptionists on salaries	Film
Dedicated X-ray premises	Maintenance of machinery
General premises such as reception, car park, etc.	Support services such as portering
The Management Board	Staff on sessional contracts
Public Relations Department	

Figure 4.2 Fixed and variable costs

Clearly some items described as fixed may be variable in some circumstances, e.g. if the radiographer is employed on a session basis to attend only when needed, then he or she would constitute a variable cost. Alternatively, if the machinery was serviced and replaced at regular intervals rather then after a fixed number of treatments it would become a fixed cost.

Full and marginal costs

The full cost of a service is that calculated to account for all direct, indirect, fixed and variable costs in total. However, if a certain number of treatments were planned and a price agreed that recovered all of the fixed costs as well as the variable costs associated with those treatments, then thereafter to continue charging that unit price would result in a profit. The cost to the Trust would only be the variable costs, because the fixed costs had already been recouped. The marginal cost is defined as the additional cost of producing one additional unit of productivity. It would be appropriate, in that case, to offer further activity to the purchaser at the marginal cost, i.e. the cost of production. A difficulty arises if the additional activity is sold to a different purchaser. In this case, one purchaser may appear to be subsidising the other, i.e. the two purchasers purchased the same service at different prices. If this happens more than very rarely, it must be a failure of planning in that the Trust failed to predict accurately the volume of activity for the year. An accurate prediction of activity would allow for apportionment of the fixed costs over all of the activity and thereby achieve a consistent unit price.

Apportionment of overheads

Each service provided by a Trust must be priced at the true cost. This requires fair apportionment of overheads (indirect costs) to each service. How much of each overhead the X-ray department should bear may be calculated according to one of several methodologies. The simplest methodology is to apportion overhead costs according to the ratio of direct costs. If the X-ray direct costs amount to 5% of the direct costs for all of the Trust's services then the X-ray department would bear 5% of the costs of the car park, the management board, the reception, portering services, etc. This system is simple to calculate and therefore commonly applied. However, the drawback is that it carries no incentive to be frugal in the use of these services. If the charge were proportionate to use, then there would be an incentive to control usage and allow the overhead to reduce, thus releasing resources for other purposes. The alternative, therefore, is for X-ray to bear overhead costs in line with usage of each. Thus, the portering service overhead might be apportioned to X-ray according to the amount that they use it. A general reduction may be achieved, because it is not seen as 'free' and the resource deployed into direct services.

How Trusts apportion overheads will affect the prices charged for each service, and could be manipulated to reduce the prices in a competitive service area and load price where the Trust enjoys a monopoly. This, however, would constitute subtle cross-subsidisation. Internal and external auditors will examine the apportionment of overheads to prevent this practice.

Capital and revenue

Money consumed in producing a good or service and the income earned by selling the good or service are referred to as revenue. Money spent on an asset, such as a building or machine, is referred to as capital. Revenue is consumed in making a product or service and can only be retrieved by sales. Capital expenditure is matched by asset increase and the capital could be released by sale of the asset. Revenue purchases are generally recurrent, whereas capital spends are generally a series of one-off events.

The distinction between capital and revenue is indistinct at the margin. Is a treatment couch that is replaced every five years a capital asset or is it consumed in delivering care? Accountancy procedures in each organisation define capital and revenue for their own purposes leading to artificial but consistent boundaries. The NHS and Social Services define capital spends by amount. Any single item purchase more than an agreed limit is taken to be capital spend.

Capital charges

Holding capital has a cost. If the capital is loaned to an organisation, then there will be interest to pay. If the capital is owned by the organisation, then using it for purchase of assets means forgoing interest income. In order for this cost to be reflected in service prices, the NHS requires Trusts to pay a capital charge for the assets they hold. This allows fair competition with private sector service providers and encourages the Trusts to be frugal in their capital holdings.

Capital charges include a number of elements. These are a 'rent' on the money, a depreciation repayment and an inflation adjustment. The rent on the money is represented by a 6% payment to the DoH on the total value of the assets held by the Trust per annum. The depreciation component is calculated by assessing the life of the asset and requiring a payback to the DoH such that the amount will be fully repaid by the time the asset is completely depreciated and needs replacing. This calculation is made assuming straight-line depreciation, i.e. an asset with a ten-year life is deemed to lose one-tenth of its value each year. In reality most assets depreciation is on a curve, but at the end of the asset's life the effect is the same. Rather than paying the DoH money to compensate for inflation, as is the case with a bank loan, the value of the asset is periodically reassessed and the debt increased accordingly. Thus, capital charges include an interest component and a deprecia-tion component. Inflation is managed by revising the debt to reflect the changing value of the currency. This revaluation will also adjust the debt to reflect consider-ations such as fluctuating land values.

The net effect of capital charging is to make service providers see capital as having a cost. If they can minimise use of capital, then they pay less capital charges and release funds for other purposes, or reduce prices thus making it more likely that they win contracts in the future.

Pricing

The usual definition of price is 'whatever the market will bear'. Competition keeps prices to a minimum so long as there are enough suppliers; the services are com-parable and information about each is freely available to customers. In health and social care services, there is rarely good competition and services vary in how they are packaged. For this reason, it is required that price is cost. This seeks to min-imise prices, but presents two difficulties. The absence of competition in many areas fails to deliver the efficiency that was an objective of the purchaser–provider separation. The absence of a profit motive for a Trust removes a drive to increase activity.

QALYs

Many attempts have been made to assess the value of health care outcomes. A simple currency is the extension of life. Procedure 'A' adds on average 5 years to life. If the procedure costs £1000 then a year's life is purchased for £200. The value for money of a treatment (Rx) may therefore be measured in life years gained per £1. A clear failing of this notion is that there is no recognition of the quality of the life experienced. Quality-adjusted life years (QALYs) are an attempt to factor in the quality dimension. One year of life in full health is rated at one QALY. Life with disability or chronic pain may be given a discounted rate. This is not to dimin-ish the value of people with disabilities. All involved in health care recognise the mistake in that. However, the intent of health care is to reduce illness and disabil-ity as well as to increase life span. This methodology condenses quality and length of life into a single scale. Conceptually, a year of life with a profound disability is given a QALY value of less than one. Thus a procedure that extends life for five years but those years have a very poor quality achieves less than a procedure that extends life by five years and those years are in full health. A procedure that enhances quality of life but does not extend it at all may be seen as of great impor-tance when measured in QALY values although a measure of life extension would not rate it at all. Calculations might be as shown in Figure 4.3.

If a price for each intervention is given, then a cost per QALY gained may be cal-culated and this may be useful as a measure of how much good can be done with the moneys available to a health or social care purchaser (Figure 4.4).

This methodology provides a structure useful in prioritising health interventions with limited resources. It has the advantage of considering the life saving alongside

Intervention	Life expectancy before Rx	Life expectancy after Rx	Gained	Gained
Intervention A	0 year	5 years: full health	5 years	5 QALYs
Intervention B	0 year	5 years: poor health (50%)	5 years	2.5 QALYs
Intervention C	5 years: poor health (50%)	5 years: full health	0 years	2.5 QALYs
Intervention D	25 years: poor health (50%)	25 years: full health	0 years	12.5 QALYs

Figure 4.3 QALYs

Intervention	QALY gain	Cost	Cost/QALY gained	Rank order value for money
Intervention A	5 QALYs	£2000	£400	2nd
Intervention B	2.5 QALYs	£1500	£600	4th
Intervention C	2.5 QALYs	£1000	£400	2nd
Intervention D	12.5 QALYs	£3000	£240	1st

Figure 4.4 QALY rank order

the life enhancing. Difficulties are encountered in two areas. Setting the level of discount for less than perfect health is very subjective and agreement is difficult to achieve. Allotting a reduced QALY value to a life with profound disability can imply that the person is less valued as a consequence. Although this is not the intention, the suggestion makes the measure difficult for some managers to employ.

Regulations

The management of money is highly regulated. This is particularly the case with money from the public purse. Regulation is achieved with a series of Standing Financial Instructions (SFIs). SFIs regulate behaviour when receiving or spending moneys. Each Trust and Local Authority has its own SFIs but they have much in common. Most include the following examples.

1　Any purchase worth more than £5000 requires receipt of at least three independent price quotes and the lowest is chosen, provided the goods/services are of equivalent worth.
2　Any purchase requisition must be made by an authorised officer and countersigned by a more senior officer.
3　No employee may receive gifts of any nature from clients/patients.
4　Cash deposited by resident patients/clients must be received by two officers together and the record signed by both.

SFIs in any organisation will run to many pages and it is the responsibility of individuals to acquaint themselves with them as appropriate.

Audit

Each organisation has a duty to conduct audit annually. This will involve internal and external auditors at the expense of the organisation. Audit will cover three areas: audit of accounts, probity audit and value-for-money audit.

Audit of accounts

Each organisation is required to submit two types of accounts: ledger accounts, showing the flow of moneys in and out of the organisation, and profit and loss accounts, which show cash flow and also take note of debtors and creditors, stock level changes, etc. An NHS Trust is required to show both of these accounts in balance. Fluctuations from year to year are permissible, but in the long term there can be neither profit nor loss.

Probity audit

Auditors will ensure that no improper appropriation or use of money has occurred. This will amount to policing of the SFIs, and thereby ensuring that the moneys passed to an Authority or Trust are used for the purpose intended.

Value-for-money audit

Auditors will assess whether the organisation has obtained the very best value for the money that has been allotted to it.

THE PRACTICE

Budgetary control

NHS Trusts and Social Services departments generally work to fixed expenditure budgets, reviewed annually. Your department may be allocated a budget based upon an expected income from the contracts to which it contributes. Alternatively, it may be given an income and expenditure targets. In either case, your annual spending allowance is then derived.

An annual spend is not manageable as a whole. Budgetary control requires that an annual expenditure target be subdivided into manageable units. These units are known as budget lines. A line might represent a staff group, treatment materials, transport costs, etc. Resources are allocated to a line and expenditures are coded to particular lines in order to ensure that actual spends accord with budgetary target spends. The next step is to divide annual spend targets into monthly targets, and monthly reports will show budget targets and actual spends to allow the manager to see whether their spend is as required. In months 2 to 12, there will be an accumulated effect from previous months. Therefore the statement will also show budget to date figures and actual spend to date figures so that the manager can know the emerging position. Many budget statements show the position projected to month 12. This effectively tells the manager the anticipated year end position if he or she continues at the present rate of spend. The budget statement, therefore, appears as in Figure 4.5.

Line	Budget total	Budget this month	Actual this month	Variance this month	Budget to date	Actual to date	Variance to date	End-of-year projection
Senior staff								
Basic Grade								
Assistants								
Admin. staff								
Total: staff								
Material								
Transport								
Stationery								
Energy								
Telephones								
Total: non-staff								
Total								

Figure 4.5 A budget statement

Virement

Where there is a surplus under one budget line, the budget manager may be permitted to overspend on another line so that the totals remain in balance. This movement of resource between lines is known as virement. The rules regarding virement vary between Trusts and the manager should not assume that virement is permitted. Virement from non-staff lines to staff lines is rarely permitted because staff are a long-term, recurrent expenditure commitment and cannot therefore be funded by a short-term virement. Virement from staff to non-staff lines may be permitted, but the organisation may wish to consider other priorities for the resource released by a staff vacancy. Virement between staff lines is generally permitted, because it is a necessary condition for skill mix revision. If the skill mix revision is long term, then virement will be permitted for the current year and the future year budget will show the correct target figures. Virement between non-staff lines may be acceptable, but there is a need to explain an underspend before deciding to reallocate the resource. There may be outstanding invoices or stock reduction, both pointing to imminent expenditure. Additionally, the Trust may have greater priorities for the resource released by an underspend than to simply move it to another line in the same budget.

Month 13

At the end of month 12, there will be credits and debts associated with a budget year which remain to be resolved. It may not be appropriate to allow these receipts and spends to appear on the first month of the following year. In this case the catching up of a year's accounts may be noted on a statement called month 13 which usually runs alongside month 1 of the following year.

Zero-based budgeting

Budget plans for a year may be based upon the previous year with alterations to reflect inflation and the changes expected in performance. However, in zero-based budgeting, each budget is reconsidered annually and built up from scratch according to identified need. Clearly, some resources must roll forward from previous years, e.g. salaries and rents, but others may be reconsidered in the light of emerging priorities. Zero-based budgeting is necessary to facilitate change in a volatile market. Zero-based budgeting also allows for correction of lines where the actual expenditure is necessarily different from budget, such as staff who are paid more than budget because of long service or merit awards, etc.

Costings: staff and non-staff

Adding a new member of staff to a department requires new moneys in the budget. It is important that these costs are estimated accurately. The salary will normally be subject to incremental or PRP variance. This means that the post may attract a salary anywhere from £x to £y. The normal protocol is to set the budget at the midpoint. Therefore if the scale is £15,000–£19,000 according to experience, then the budget line will show (15000 + 19000) / 2 = 17,000. The assumption is that some staff will be below the midpoint and others above and that this will allow the budget to balance. However, if your department has low staff turnover, either because of economic conditions or regional variance, then you will find all of your staff occupying the top of incremental scales. This will overspend your budget through no fault of yours. In this situation, you should argue for your staff to be budgeted at the top of the scale.

A staff member receives an annual salary, but this is not the cost to the employer. Your budget must also allow for your employer's contribution to National Insurance, currently 6%, and Superannuation (Pension) contributions.   This results in an 'on cost' to salaries, usually set at 12% or 15%.

A staff member may use secretarial time, travelling expenses, stationery and telephone costs, etc. which must also be factored into the cost of a new employee. A bid or another member of staff might, therefore, look as shown in Figure 4.6.

Item	Annual cost (£)
Salary (at mid point):	17,000
On costs:	2550
Secretarial support (0.1 WTE):	1000
Travelling costs (est. 2500 miles @ 50p):	1250
General:	1200
Total revenue:	**23,000**

Figure 4.6 The cost of an employee

The vacancy factor

Staff lines will show salary for 12 months' employment. However, staff move positions and it is rarely possible to replace them immediately they leave. There will be a period when the salary is not being spent. Managers may enjoy using this resource by virement, as above. However, turnover of staff should not be treated as a surprise or as an individual event. A large budget centre is likely to have a number of vacant lines at any time. This should be seen as a standing situation where a regular percentage of revenue expenditure is not spent each year. This factor, if not allowed for, will result in repeated underspending. A budget holder may account for this vacancy factor by including it as a line in the budget statement. The money represented by the vacancy factor might be deducted from the totals, so that it is expected that managers will spend less than the full budget may suggest. Alternatively, plans may be made annually to spend this vacancy factor on developmental work to advance the service.

Case studies

There follow a number of case study budgets. Each tells a story with some exaggeration to make the point. Each should be studied and conclusions drawn.

CASE STUDY 4.1   GENERAL UNDERSPEND

Line Month 3	budget total	budget this month	actual this month	variance this month	budget to date	actual to date	variance to date	end-of-year projection
Senior staff	28000	2333	2000	–333	7000	6000	–1000	–4000
Basic Grade	26000	2167	2100	–67	6500	6300	–200	–800
Assistants	21000	1750	1500	–250	5250	4500	–750	–3000
Admin. staff	15000	1250	1000	–250	3750	3000	–750	–3000
Total: staff	**90000**	**7500**	**6600**	**–900**	**22500**	**19800**	**–2700**	**–10800**
Materials	31000	2583	60	–2523	7750	180	–7570	–30280
Energy	1990	166	150	–16	498	450	–48	–190
Telephones	2345	195	209	14	586	627	41	163
INCOME	–2300	–192	8	200	–575	24	599	2396
Total: non-staff	**33035**	**2753**	**427**	**–2326**	**8259**	**1281**	**–6978**	**–27911**
Total	**123035**	**10253**	**7027**	**–3226**	**30759**	**21081**	**–9678**	**–38711**

In this budget all staff and non-staff lines are underspending. The failure to earn income as budgeted appears as an overspend on that line. Telephone use is overspent. The 'to date' lines show that this situation has persisted for some time. There is an accumulated underspend. The projected year end figure is one of significant underspending. The manager may have bulk or seasonal material purchases planned, which could consume the £27,911 material costs. The manager may be saving staff moneys for winter pressures. The budget year is April–March. Therefore, the final three months may be expensive because of weather etc. If these explanations do not apply, then the manager needs to act to make best use of the resources available.

CASE STUDY 4.2   GENERAL OVERSPEND

Line Month 3	budget total	budget this month	actual this month	variance this month	budget to date	actual to date	variance to date	end-of-year projection
Senior staff	28000	2333	2400	67	7000	7200	200	800
Basic Grade	26000	2167	2345	178	6500	7035	535	2140
Assistants	21000	1750	1000	−750	5250	3000	−2250	−9000
Admin. staff	15000	1250	3000	1750	3750	9000	5250	21000
Total: staff	**90000**	**7500**	**8745**	**1245**	**22500**	**26235**	**3735**	**14940**
Materials	31000	2583	4008	1425	7750	12024	4274	17096
Energy	1990	166	1509	1343	498	4527	4030	16118
Telephones	2345	195	209	14	586	627	41	163
INCOME	−2300	−192	−1	191	−575	−3	572	2288
Total: non-staff	**33035**	**2753**	**5725**	**2972**	**8259**	**17175**	**8916**	**35665**
Total	**123035**	**10253**	**14470**	**4217**	**30759**	**43410**	**12651**	**50605**

In this budget there is a small overspend on staff totals this month arising from an excess of administrative staff, which is partially compensated for by the underspend on assistant staff. There is also an overspend on non-staff. The failure to bring in £191 income presents as an additional overspend. The 'to date' columns show that this situation has persisted for three months. The projection is for a large overspend. It may be that the material overspend is accounted for by bulk purchasing and therefore that line will be correct by the year end. However, there is need for a significant reduction in staff if the overspend of £14,940 is to be averted.

CASE STUDY 4.3 VIREMENT

Line Month 3	budget total	budget this month	actual this month	variance this month	budget to date	actual to date	variance to date	end-of-year projection
Senior staff	28000	2333	2300	−33	7000	6900	−100	−400
Basic Grade	26000	2167	2100	−67	6500	6300	−200	−800
Assistants	21000	1750	160	−1590	5250	480	−4770	−19080
Admin. staff	15000	1250	1000	−250	3750	3000	−750	−3000
Total: staff	**90000**	**7500**	**5560**	**−1940**	**22500**	**16680**	**−5820**	**−23280**
Materials	31000	2583	4521	1938	7750	13563	5813	23252
Energy	1990	166	170	4	498	510	13	50
Telephones	2345	195	200	5	586	600	14	55
INCOME	−2300	−192	−200	−8	−575	−600	−25	−100
Total: non-staff	**33035**	**2753**	**4691**	**1938**	**8259**	**14073**	**5814**	**23257**
Total	**123035**	**10253**	**10251**	**−2**	**30759**	**30753**	**−6**	**−23**

This budget appears to be performing correctly when attention is given to the totals (known as the 'bottom line'). In fact, there has been underspending on staff lines for some months, and the manager has taken advantage of the opportunity to make a large materials purchase. Although the budget is in balance (£2 underspend), the projection to end of year is misleading. In the absence of further material overspending, the budget will underspend because of staff shortages, such as of assistants. Assuming that the work of these assistants is necessary to patients, they need to be recruited to the level allowed by the budget.

CASE STUDY 4.4   MISLEADING BALANCE

Line Month 3	budget total	budget this month	actual this month	variance this month	budget to date	actual to date	variance to date	end-of-year projection
Senior staff	28000	2333	2450	117	7000	7350	350	1400
Basic Grade	26000	2167	3100	933	6500	9300	2800	11200
Assistants	21000	1750	3000	1250	5250	9000	3750	15000
Admin. staff	15000	1250	2000	750	3750	6000	2250	9000
Total: staff	**90000**	**7500**	**10550**	**3050**	**22500**	**31650**	**9150**	**36600**
Materials	31000	2583	0	−2583	7750	0	−7750	−31000
Energy	1990	166	0	−166	498	0	−498	−1990
Telephones	2345	195	0	−195	586	0	−586	−2345
INCOME	−2300	−192	−300	−108	−575	−900	−325	−1300
Total: non-staff	**33035**	**2753**	**−300**	**−3053**	**8259**	**−900**	**−9159**	**−36635**
Total	**123035**	**10253**	**10250**	**−3**	**30759**	**30753**	**−9**	**−35**

This budget initially appears to be in balance. This month's total shows an underspend of just £3. The 'to date' columns and projection columns support this interpretation. However, the staff expenditure lines are heavily overspent and this is masked by underspends on materials etc. Since energy, material and telephone costs will eventually need to be paid, it is inevitable that this budget will overspend before the year end. Additionally, the budget holder appears to have vired resources from non-staff lines to staff lines, which is generally prohibited. There needs to be a swift reduction in staff expenditure in this budget.

Financial business planning

Your business plan shows the projected activity, income and expenditure for future years. It is common for the business plan to extend for five years with general statements of the direction to be followed during the subsequent five years. Income and expenditure projections will be based upon an understanding of the marketplace and a realistic estimate of the business that can be won. The financial plan will show the viability of the organisation, based upon that assumed activity. A business plan is commonly devised when an organisation is seeking new capital. It projects the financial position demonstrating the ability of the business to service and eventually repay the debt.

Your business plan, therefore, shows the growth of your part of the organisation. A number of non-financial sections appear in a business plan. These are the implications of the planned growth for other aspects of the organisation. They show the reader that the infrastructure will be brought into place at the right time for planned developments to occur.

A typical business plan will have the following components:

Mission statement

This is an unambiguous statement of the reason for the existence of the organisation, e.g.

To maximise the health of the catchment population, by promotion of health and prevention, treatment or relief of illness.

Strategic direction

This is a long-term indication of future developments for the organisation, usually over ten years, e.g.

To reduce dependence on institutional care business and develop community-based provision for ...

Summary of current business

This section describes any current business of the organisation. It shows what is done, how quality is assured and what the volume of output is. It indicates who the customers are, and the nature of the consumers if these are different.

Market analysis

Audit and analysis of the external and internal factors affecting the organisation's prospects in the marketplace. This analysis must demonstrate the feasibility of the planned developments. Market audit and analysis devices appear in Chapter 7.

Assumptions and contingencies

Many assumptions are made in writing a plan. This is acceptable if they are explicitly recognised. e.g.

It is assumed that government legislation will allow an increase in private beds in an NHS Trust.

Where appropriate, contingency plans should be shown for deployment if the assumption proves incorrect, e.g.

If private beds are not permitted, then the new beds described in 'Developments planned' will be: (1) offered to the PCG purchasers, (2) offered to BUPA purchasers or (3) mothballed until needed.

Developments planned

This section contains detailed description and explanation of each of the developments planned. It will show the human and other resources required, the demand, the details of the activity planned with quality and volume measures, etc.

Financial projections

This section shows income and expenditure projections for the next five years, based upon current business and the developments (increases and decreases) above. These demonstrate the viability of the organisation with adequate revenue surplus to service and repay existing and any new capital investment. Year 1 projections will be highly detailed and precise; subsequent years become progressively imprecise. The latter will be updated yearly informed by experience. In a rolling plan these pages are rewritten annually, so that the next year is made firm and a new year 5 is added.

In any health or Social Services business plan there will be a pro forma for these pages. This will show exactly the form in which the information is to be given. With some additions for special details, the pro forma will look as shown in Figure 4.7. Additional pages may be drawn up to show the detail of income and expenditure for each year.

	Year 1	Year 2	Year 3	Year 4
Income				
Income 1	1400K	2000K	2000K	2000K
Income 2	1000K	1100K	1100K	1100K
Income 3	2000K	2000K	2000K	2000K
Income total	44000K	5100K	5100K	5100K
Expenditure				
Expenditure 1	2000K	2000K	2000K	2000K
Expenditure 2	2000K	2000K	2000K	2000K
Expenditure 3	900K	900K	1900K	900K
Expenditure total	4900K	4900K	4900K	4900K
Balance	(500K)	200K	200K	200K
Cumulative balance	(500K)	(300K)	(100K)	100K

Figure 4.7 Business plan financial proforma

Human resource plan

This section shows the way in which any changes to the human resources will be made. It demonstrates that the necessary workforce will be in place at the best time for the developments to be achieved. The plan will include workforce projections and demonstrate the expected availability of suitable recruits. There may be necessary training and/or retraining, and lead times must be adequately considered. There will also be consideration of redundancies. The costs of all of these developments will appear in the financial section.

Estates plan

This section shows the way in which any changes to the physical resources – buildings, equipment, etc. – will be made. It demonstrates that the necessary premises and equipment will be in place at the best time for the developments to be achieved and that the costs are realistically reflected. It will also show the effects of disposal of plant and buildings. This section must, additionally, show the maintenance and routine replacement of existing buildings and plant. Lead time for problem solving and staff training will be considered. The costs of these developmental and maintenance activities will appear in the financial section.

Marketing plan

This section shows the marketing activity that will be employed to ensure that the planned developments and continuance of current business are achieved. It will also show ongoing market research to evaluate any developments in demand for the services/goods to be and being marketed. For operational marketing practice see Chapter 7.

Management of your own financial resources

The above principles of budgeting and even business planning are as applicable to your own finances as they are to management of a major industry. Revenue budgeting will enable you to gain the very greatest benefit possible from your income, without need for unplanned (and very inefficient) debt or fear of financial difficulty. Sensible budgeting will ensure that you are in a position to have holidays, replace your car, etc. when necessary without feeling the pinch. Personal business planning will enable you to decide exactly how much you can afford to spend on a mortgage, car loan, private yacht, etc.

A personal budget statement might look like that shown in Figures 4.8 and 4.9. You might take this framework and put in your own figures.

Expenditure	2000/1	1,2	2,3	3,4	4,5	5,6	6,7
Education	**5000**	**10000**	**10000**	**5000**	**2000**	**2000**	**2000**
House	**18062**	**18062**	**18062**	**18062**	**18062**	**18062**	**18062**
Mortgage	10184	10184	10184	10184	10184	10184	10184
Endowments	1116	1116	1116	1116	1116	1116	1116
Phone	1200	1200	1200	1200	1200	1200	1200
Gas	1500	1500	1500	1500	1500	1500	1500
Electricity	800	800	800	800	800	800	800
Insurance	612	612	612	612	612	612	612
Rates	1650	1650	1650	1650	1650	1650	1650
Maintenance	1000	1000	1000	1000	1000	1000	1000
Other	**12984**	**12984**	**12984**	**12984**	**14484**	**13484**	**12984**
Presents	1000	1000	1000	1000	1000	1000	1000
Parties	500	500	500	500	500	500	500
Visits	1000	1000	1000	1000	1000	1000	1000
Holidays	1500	1500	1500	1500	3000		1500
Groceries	3000	3000	3000	3000	3000	3000	3000
Clothes	1000	1000	1000	1000	1000	1000	1000
Cars	3000	3000	3000	3000	3000	5000	3000
Animals	500	500	500	500	500	500	500
Children's trips	500	500	500	500	500	500	500
Memberships	192	192	192	192	192	192	192
Sky	312	312	312	312	312	312	312
CPSM	204	204	204	204	204	204	204
BMA	276	276	276	276	276	276	276
Exp. total	**36046**	**41046**	**41046**	**36046**	**34546**	**33546**	**33046**
Income	**41700**	**41700**	**41700**	**41700**	**41700**	**41700**	**41700**
1	20000	20000	20000	20000	20000	20000	20000
2	21000	21000	21000	21000	21000	21000	21000
Other	700	700	700	700	700	700	700
Surplus	**5654**	**654**	**654**	**5654**	**7154**	**8154**	**8654**

Figure 4.8 A personal budget statement

	2000/1	Month 1 budget	Month 1 spend	Month 2 budget	Month 2 spend
Education	**5000**	**417**		**417**	
House	**18062**	**1505**		**1505**	
Mortgage	10184	**849**		**849**	
Endowments	1116	**93**		**93**	
Phone	1200	**100**		**100**	
Gas	1500	**125**		**125**	
Electricity	800	**67**		**67**	
Insurance	612	**51**		**51**	
Rates	1650	**138**		**138**	
Maintenance	1000	**83**		**83**	
Other	**12984**	**1082**		**1082**	
Presents	1000	**83**		**83**	
Parties	500	**42**		**42**	
Visits	1000	**83**		**83**	
Holidays	1500	**125**		**125**	
Groceries	3000	**250**		**250**	
Clothes	1000	**83**		**83**	
Cars	3000	**250**		**250**	
Animals	500	**42**		**42**	
Children's trips	500	**42**		**42**	
Memberships	192	**16**		**16**	
Sky	312	**26**		**26**	
CPSM	204	**17**		**17**	
BMA	276	**23**		**23**	
Exp. total	**36046**	**3004**		**3004**	
Income	**41700**	**3475**		**3475**	
1	20000	**1667**		**1667**	
2	21000	**1750**		**1750**	
Other	700	**58**		**58**	
		0		**0**	
Surplus	**5654**	**471**		**471**	

Figure 4.9 A personal monthly statement

Conclusion

The expert management of financial resources is critical to the effectiveness of health and social care. There is a constant debate about how much resource can be allocated to health and social care. However, although increases are possible, these are at the margin. There is finite revenue that can be collected through taxation because above a certain percentage tax avoidance and evasion exceeds the returns from an increased taxation rate. How the resources are distributed between health, education law, etc. may be debated, but it is agreed that all are necessary. Health and social care provision is maximised by the most efficient use of the available resource. The management of financial resources is not restricted to budget holders. All clinicians expend resources when they prescribe and deliver treatment and care. Seen in aggregate, these expenditures are far more important than financial control attempted by managers. It is partially for this reason that successive governments have sought to bring together clinical and financial management through Clinicians in Management initiatives. You, as an individual clinician or manager have a duty to ensure the most efficient use of resources in order to maximise the amount of care and treatment available to your patients/clients.

FURTHER READING

Mellett, H.J. (1993) *Financial Management in the NHS: A Manager's Guide*. Chapman & Hall, London.

Hofstede, G. (1968) *The Game of Budget Control*. Tavistock, London.

McAlpine, T.S. (1976) *The Basic Arts of Budgeting*. Business Books, London.

Pyhrr, P.A. (1978) *Zero-Base Budgeting: A Practical Management Tool for Evaluating Expenses*. Wiley, New York and London.

Wheeler, N. (1992) The principles and methods of capital charging and their value to the functional manager. *British Journal of Occupational Therapy*, 54(12), 444–448.

5 THE MANAGEMENT OF QUALITY

INTRODUCTION

Optimising quality is an essential component of management, and is the responsibility of all employees. Those who directly relate to patients and clients exert the greatest influence on service quality. Standards can always be improved by the allocation of additional resources and there is a duty to make maximum resources available. However, the management of quality requires the maximisation of standards with whatever resources can be made available. Many quality improvements require no additional resource. Quality improvement may be achieved simply by taking time to consider the services delivered and improve empathy with the recipients. Management of quality is frequently a revenue-saving exercise when the cost of making-good after errors is added into the equation. Additionally, achieving the very best quality is progressively important in winning contracts, customers or clients and thereby remaining in operation.

Service quality in the health and social care industries has always been sustained by the dedication of the professionals involved. However, attention to consumer wishes was for many years subjugated to a paternalist paradigm and it was only with the 1983 Griffiths Report that consumerism began to be respected. This was reinforced by the reforms of the 1990 NHS and Community Care Act and 1998's *The New NHS: Modern and Dependable*.

THE THEORETICAL FRAMEWORK

Quality

A service is of acceptable quality if it satisfies a number of criteria:

1 It must do what the customer wants and needs it to do.
2 It must be reliable.
3 It must represent good value for money.

Meeting the customer's agreed wishes

In health care, the issue of meeting customers' wishes has become progressively prominent since 1980. However, there remains a responsibility for the clinician to interpose his or her expertise, thus modifying patient/client demands and reaching an intervention decision acceptable to both. This may be an informal negotiated contract if only one intervention is involved, but where the therapeutic relationship is a long-term one the process becomes iterative, as in Figure 5.1. The patient/client makes a request of the clinician. The clinician responds, adding his or her clinical expertise in the context of service provision. This service better informs the patient/client. There is a new situation and the patient request is informed by the previous iteration. Each party is modified by the other and by the outcome of former interventions. If this cycle is handled well, the requests and provision become ever more harmoniously aligned. In the final analysis, however well meaning is the clinician, if service provision is not what the patient or client wants for his or her life, subject to resource limits, then it is not good quality. However, the customer cannot be 'king', as marketplace doctrine requires, because of the gradient of expertise. Progressive alignment of clinician and consumer is essential.

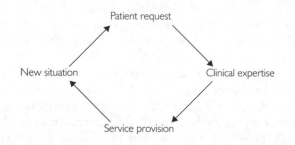

Figure 5.1 An iterative model for service definition

Entirely reliable

Many providers of goods and services maintain a reputation for quality based upon an unquestioning willingness to replace faulty products. Therefore, in the final analysis, the customer always gets a good product or service. This is not possible in health or social care, where the consequences of unreliable service are generally irreparable and always unacceptable: 'We regret that the operation was performed badly, but come back in a week and we will do it again completely free of charge.' 'I am so sorry that the stair rail came off the wall when you rested on it, but never fear, we will be back in the morning to put it right.' Health and social care providers must get the provision right first time or the consequences can be very serious. Again, in many industries there is an acceptable fail rate: '98% is pretty good'. In health and social care, no level of quality failure can be acceptable. 'We usually perform this operation properly' will not do. Nor will 'We usually place our frail elderly clients in a suitable residential home.' Therefore, services must be right first time and every time.

Costing no more that it must

Quality must include the notion of value for money. Services and products in all price brackets may achieve high quality. A factor in quality is that the standard is very good considering the cost. Conversely, if the standard is fixed, then quality may require the notion that the cost is no more than it needs to be. If a product is unnecessarily expensive for what the customer is getting, then the quality is poor. A quality product is therefore at the lowest possible price for a defined standard.

If we allow that a service can cost more than the minimum, even if it carries charming extras, then that extra resource will not be available for other treatments. This is not good quality health or social care when seen in aggregate.

Therefore, a quality service in health and social care may be defined as one that meets the client/clinician agreed need, first time every time, at the lowest possible price.

Quality control

In industry, an acceptable standard is defined with reference to customer demands and any product not reaching that standard is scrapped before the sales stage. That is why every radio purchased has a label attached indicating where, when and by whom it was checked before dispatch. The quality control approach is acceptable in many industries because the cost of a failing percentage is lower than the cost of ensuring perfect success. In health care, a quality control approach is not considered sufficient because the cost of any unnecessary failure is unacceptable.

Quality assurance

Quality assurance (QA) is a multistage, iterative process that sets, monitors, assures and continually improves standards. The stages in the process match the definition of quality, above, and are:

1. Ensure that the service really does address the agreed need of the patient/client.
2. Define the standards to be achieved, according to specific, measurable, achievable, relevant and timely (SMART) criteria.
3. Audit these standards and take measures to assure that they are always attained.
4. Improve the standards.
5. Evaluate the process.

As this is an iterative process (see Figure 5.2), there is no requirement that it be initiated at stage 1. In fact, it may be initiated at any stage, and it is when the cycle has revolved a number of times that it is really effective.

Figure 5.2 QA cycle

Total quality management

Total Quality Management (TQM) is a development of QA, attempting to reinforce the responsibility of the individual for a satisfactory outcome. The QA process, above, is retained, but every individual is encouraged to hold the outcome of the intervention paramount at all times. It may be that simply meeting agreed standards is not sufficient and that the need for exceeding or adapting standards is evident from observation of the results. In TQM, employees are expected to follow the spirit of the standard, going beyond the letter of the standard where necessary, and to ensure the best affordable outcome. This is to correct the possibility that a focus upon adherence to standards and policies moves the focus away from the idiosyncratic needs of patients. TQM prevents complacency where standards are attained but the service is self-evidently poor.

CASE STUDY 5.1   TQM

A family goes on holiday leaving the neighbour to water the prized plant. The standard is 1.5 litres of water at 6.00 p.m. every day. However, there is a heat wave and the soil dries out more quickly than predicted. The QA focused standard is observed at 1.5 litres per day and the plant dies of dehydration. A TQM approach would have explained the degree of moisture required in the soil or the general health of the plant and the neighbour could have adapted the watering volume to maintain moisture levels and plant health, thereby protecting the plant. In a TQM approach the neighbour is enabled to relate to the end result, plant health, and understands the requirements for this. He or she can therefore adjust the process standard to assure this quality outcome.

Audit

Audit was learned from the accountancy discipline – checking that agreed financial procedures have been adhered to, that no impropriety has occurred and that resources are well used.

This discipline was first adopted clinically by the medical profession, and thereafter by all health and care professions. It involves examination of processes employed in health care to ensure that procedures are followed, standards achieved, no impropriety occurs, stakeholders are optimally treated and best value is obtained from the resources consumed. The auditing process may be self, peer or supervisory colleague, internal or external, informal or formal, and formative or judgemental in its nature.

Audit procedures are iterative. It is essential to close the cycle by ensuring that lessons learned from an audit inform and directly influence future practice (Figure 5.3). That means that there must be a system to ensure that the findings of any quality audit are systematically fed back into a forum that can change practice in response to what is found.

Figure 5.3 The audit cycle

Clinical governance

Clinical governance is a sharpening of the focus of quality management introduced as part of the 1998 NHS reforms, *The New NHS: Modern and Dependable*. The development formalised, and made statutory, quality management in a number of areas. These are:

1 More formalised clinical audit. These are placed on NHS Trusts and Primary Care Trusts, who will have to initiate continuous quality improvement, recognition of all national standards, procedures for reporting concern about practice, etc. This is the personal responsibility of the Chief Executive Officer (CEO) of all NHS Trusts. Quality reports to the Board of Directors are required to be treated with the same rigour as financial reports.
2 Establishment of guidance to clinical best practice based upon sound evidence emerging from the evidence-based medicine (EBM) movement. The National Institute for Clinical Excellence (NICE) publishes this information and fosters research where the evidence is inadequate. Further guidance is promulgated in the form of a National Service Framework (NSF) for each area of NHS endeavour.
3 Establishment of more rigid protocols for the supervision of individuals by each profession. This is to give substance to the self-regulation of health and social care professions.

THE PRACTICE

Quality assurance and total quality management

The best choice of provision
Identifying the choice of provision for patients/clients and other stakeholders is a

multifaceted exercise. The parties to be consulted may be broadly divided into consumers and customers of services, although in health and social care services there are many other groups who might call themselves stakeholders. Customers and consumers may for convenient examination be categorised as in Figure 5.4. Many players might appear under either or both headings and others exist who are not listed. A service is meeting customer and consumer wishes when the wishes of all such as those listed in Figure 5.4 have been addressed.

Customers	Consumers
Purchasing DHAs and PGGs	Patients/clients
The employing NHS Trust of SS department	Carers
Private sector purchasers, e.g. BUPA	Family
Fee-paying patients/clients	Referring clinicians
Society in general	Society

Figure 5.4 Customers and consumers

Ascertaining the wishes of these groups is uncomplicated where they have formed an explicit expectation, and know how it is appropriate to convey it to service providers. In this situation, it is only necessary to make it clear to stakeholders that their views will be well received and to explain where and when they can be most effectively conveyed. This, at an individual patient/client level, means specifically asking each what they want to achieve from the intervention. In order to redefine the service offered, as required by QA, these expressions of demand have only to be aggregated and then modified to reflect your professional expertise and the services are then delivered accordingly. It is possible to devise complex mechanisms to learn what patients/clients want, but in some cases service providers overlook the simple route of asking articulate people what they would like to see happen.

For many different reasons, however, interested parties may not find it easy to articulate their demands. In this situation, there are a number of devices that you could employ to access your stakeholder views. It is usual to employ a range of mechanisms in order to obtain a rich spectrum of information. Some deliver a better response rate than others, and some deliver richer information than others. A high response rate is preferred, not simply for the quantity of information, but to ensure representativeness of respondents. If a low response rate is achieved, then there is a risk that those moved to respond have more extreme views than others. This is known as a self-selected, and potentially skewed, sample. To base service decisions on this sample alone may be undesirable. For the opinions collected to be valid, the department needs to employ a variety of collection devices and maximise the response rate achieved by each.

Suggestion boxes

Strategically placed boxes will allow service users to make comments and suggestions as they occur to them. It is essential that everything is available for the suggestion to be made spontaneously, as good intentions to make a comment are lost very quickly. A pad of paper and a pen must always be near a suggestion box. Boxes must be placed cautiously so that while they attract attention they also allow respondent anonymity. Therefore, a box must be sited so that it is eye catching but allows contributions to be made without direct observation from staff. Emptying must be routine, not in response to a specific comment. Good siting and resourcing of a suggestion box will make a significant difference to the response rate. Notices calling for suggestions and comments are valuable, but have a very poor response rate because by the time the respondent has accessed writing materials their spontaneous good intentions may have been lost. The best response rate is achieved if respondents have the wherewithal to comment when issues are fresh and time is on their hands, e.g. in waiting rooms. The respondent using a suggestion box is self-selected, but the consequent bias is diminished if the box is very easy to use and the response rate is maximised. The measures described above to improve response rate will therefore also improve the representative nature of the comments made.

Suggestion boxes are the focus of hoax and humorous comment and this is often cited as a reason not to provide them. However, these comments take little time to deal with and the serious information gained has the great advantage of immediacy. As soon as an idea arises whereby the service might be improved, the respondent has the opportunity to report it. Any delay will risk their forgetting or losing resolve.

Questionnaires

Before, during and after intervention, questionnaires offer the patient, client, carer, etc. the opportunity to say exactly what service would be or have been preferable. The questionnaire may be closed, having questions needing yes/no answers or answers chosen from a preset choice of answers, or open, allowing the respondent to express their opinion in their own words. Closed questions in a questionnaire give quantitative information that is easy to collate and from which it is possible to draw conclusions that may be cautiously generalised to the whole population. Open questions give qualitative data that may be more informative and allow scope for unexpected responses. However, the conclusion drawn from open questions cannot be so easily generalised to the whole population. Service quality questionnaires, therefore, need to be a mixture of open and closed style. A combination of open and closed questions gives a range of information. The two types may be combined in one of two ways:

1 Open->closed: open questions are asked of a small population in order to establish the agenda, followed by closed questions to a larger sample to ascertain how many people share the views expressed.
2 Closed->open: closed questions establish the common areas of concern to

respondents and open questions are then asked of a small number of respondents to better understand those issues identified as important.

For detailed guidance on constructing a questionnaire, see Chapter 2.

Interviews

Patients, clients and other interested parties may be interviewed before, during or after treatment. Interviews have the advantage of a very high response rate – few people refuse – and therefore a more representative sample is achieved. Even if the sample number is low, as long as selection is randomised, the results will be valid if the rate of cooperation by approached respondents is high. In order to assure validity, however, it is necessary to ensure that a high proportion of those approached do agree to the process. If the interviewer simply keeps approaching respondents until a target number is achieved, but the refusal rate is high, then the results will be potentially skewed. That is because those who responded are a self-selected group and may be willing to answer because they have extreme views.

Interviews may be to collect quantitative data, based upon closed questions, or quantitative, based upon open questions. It is usual practice to include closed questions followed by open questions, in order to satisfy the need for a range of data types, and to ease the frustration felt by respondents if faced with a string of closed questions. Interviewing is an expensive exercise and will therefore be used sparingly as a part of a broad strategy. For detailed guidance on constructing interviews, see Chapter 2.

Focus groups

Respondents may offer richer information if allowed to discuss the chosen issues in a small group. The patient who tells the interviewer 'Nurse was wonderful; they are all so kind' might be more willing to identify areas that could be improved if sat in a small group, with tea, to talk generally about the care given in the presence of an interviewer. Some focus groups involve the researcher simply making notes of the conversation as an observer or a participant observer, or they may go further and ask the group to form a consensus statement about possible improvements to the service. Conclusions of a focus group might usefully be checked out through a questionnaire to the whole population or, at the least, a representative sample. For detailed guidance on conducting focus group investigations, see Chapter 2.

Consultation meetings

Some interested parties, such as referring clinicians, are difficult to consult. However, it is dangerous to assume that their collective view is understood, or that the views of a vociferous minority are representative of the majority. Such parties might usefully be canvassed in meetings for that purpose. These may or may not take the form of a focus group. It is important to know your audience. In each locality and for each profession, there will be a different method recommended for gaining cooperation in this endeavour. You are advised to approach senior members of your target group and discover the best way to canvas their views about the service that you provide. There can be a temptation to entice an audience with gifts and meals, etc. However, although hospitality may be in order, you want your audience to recognise that this is an opportunity to influence your service to their advantage. This should be the motive for cooperation and a free meal should not be allowed to obscure that point.

Writing standards
Having established the service most favoured by your stakeholders and moderated this with your knowledge of your service's capabilities, you must set the standards that are acceptable and affordable. This exercise is a team exercise. Standards should be owned by all stakeholders. This will include service deliveries from all professions and non-professions, users, purchasers, etc. The standards must be explicit and precise. They have to be written in a language that allows for no ambiguity in their auditing. This is a four-stage process: aim, measure, criterion and quality standard.

1 State the overall aim of the standard. This is a clear statement of what is to be achieved, e.g. 'To ensure good note keeping'.
2 Choose the measure to be employed. What scale is to be employed? e.g. 'Frequency of entry on patient records'.
3 Set the criterion. What score is required? e.g. 'After every treatment'.
4 Write the quality standard, e.g. 'There will be an entry made in the case notes after every treatment session.'

The standard is reached through this four-stage sequential process. Although it might be possible, in this example, to write the standard without stages 1–3, the process makes the standard more comprehensible. In areas that are more complex, the process may be essential to ensure that a representative standard is achieved.

The standard should be specific, measurable, achievable, relevant and time bound (SMART). It is helpful to apply this SMART test to any standard in order to ensure that it addresses the right area and is subject to unambiguous audit.

Specific
A specific standard specifies precisely to what it refers.

Measurable
A measurable standard is one that you feel you will have no difficulty in scoring, and to which any observer would award the same score. It is important to avoid words such as 'appropriate' which are subjective in their interpretation. If the standard were to require that content be appropriate the notion might be sensible, but the evaluation would be entirely subjective. As such, it could not be measured and earn a score that all would accept.

Achievable

A standard must be achievable. However, when setting a standard it is important that it stretches the service provider to achieve the best quality possible. An excessively high standard will soon be abandoned as a lost cause and a low standard will be achieved without effort. Writing a standard, therefore, involves a balancing act so that the standard drives performance as high as possible but is achievable.

Relevant

Standards must be demonstrably relevant to the service involved and, further, must be the most important area possible, allowing that not all areas can be audited at one time.

Time bound

Timeliness is important, because if a standard is to be achieved then it is essential to know by when this achievement will be made. If the time allowed for achievement is not stated, then there can be no audit point at which compliance or failure may be evaluated.

Detail

The above standard, 'There will be an entry made in the case notes after every treatment session', would ensure that you as a clinician write up records at what you consider the appropriate times, although the word 'appropriate' is not included in the standard. It might appear that this does not ensure that the record made is a satisfactory one. The clinician could perhaps write gibberish and yet meet the standard. You might consider a second standard defining the content of the record. However, it is unlikely that you as a qualified health or social care professional will write rubbish in the case record. What is possible and probable is that time pressure might lead you to put off writing notes until later, and in reality never get around to it. The standard suggested above would suffice if it were accepted that when clinicians are sat down in front of the case notes they will write appropriately. The risk that you will fail to write at all is addressed by the standard, and the risk of poor writing is too small to require policing. If nothing is left to trust, then the quality standard list will be very long and a very big rule book will be devised that is very unlikely to be read and followed. This is an example of TQM, where the spirit is clear and some discretion is permitted, rather than QA or QC, where everything is defined and the intellect of the individual is not exploited.

By writing a small number of key standards, a great deal can be achieved at an acceptable cost. There is a cost to writing, observing and auditing quality standards. The resource put into this exercise must be justified by results in terms of improved quality of services. A number of key standards may be seen to be cost effective, but there will come a point where your exercise becomes bureaucratic and costs more than it delivers. Thus, you may feel that a standard ensuring note writing is justified where a string of standards dictating content is unproductive for a qualified health professional (Figure 5.5).

Aim (To ensure ...)	Measure	Criterion	Quality Standard
Good note keeping	Frequency of entry on patient records	After every treatment	There will be an entry made in the case notes after every treatment session
Prompt handling of telephone enquiries	Number of rings	Four	The telephone will be answered during the first four rings
Patients are interviewed promptly	Time from admission to interview	One day (working)	All newly admitted patients will be interviewed within one working day of admission
Client/patient privacy	Availability of private place	Available and offered	A private place is available for all initial interviews and this is offered to all patients

Figure 5.5 Writing a quality standard

In some areas, 100% achievement of the target score may be impossible. In these cases, a standard might be expressed in terms of a target score and secondarily a target for the percentage of patients for whom this target will be achieved (see Figure 5.6).

Patient satisfaction	Scale of 0–10	8	90% of patients score 8/10 on a self-rating satisfaction scale

Figure 5.6 A percentage success target

Auditing standards

You audit your standards in order to evaluate the success with which they are being achieved and to inform your planing for future services. There are a number of approaches to audit. Audit may be:

1 continuous, in which case all standards are audited continually;
2 random, in which case standards are selected randomly and then audited;
3 focused, in which case an area is selected for special attention for a particular period of time, and audited in detail;
4 retrospective, involving examination of records and other evidence of quality.

Continuous audit is expensive but guarantees compliance with standards. It may be adopted in areas where the consequences of any failure are unacceptable. The 'care plan approach', required by government as part of discharge from a mental health hospital, might be subject to continuous audit as may the procedures in an operating theatre.

A random audit is less expensive and yet all practitioners are aware that any of their standards might be scrutinised at the next audit cycle. This will inevitably focus the mind on high level achievement. The results may be generalised, resulting in a statement about quality which could be taken as an indicator of achievement throughout the organisation. The validity of any generalisation will depend on the number of standards audited and their representativeness within the organisation. Random audit may be conducted at any interval. It is common for a service to randomly select an area for audit every month.

Focused audit is used in an attempt to improve performance in a chosen, critical area. Repeated, detailed attention through several audit cycles rapidly improves the achievement of standards. When the area has achieved a performance plateau, then the focus is moved on to another area. This has the advantage of focusing the energy and resources of audit on to one area that is considered most in need of development. This may be a most efficient use of resources. However, the results are not generaliseable, because the audited individuals were aware of the area of interest and would have paid particular attention to it.

A retrospective audit may be random or focused and can involve examination of evidence from a variety of quantitative and qualitative sources.

The auditor
Your audit may be carried out by any of the following:

Self
You should monitor achievement of standards and ensure maximum performance at all times. This is intrinsically beneficial and ensures no surprises in the event of an external audit.

Peer
You can ask non-supervisory colleagues to check your standard compliance. This has the advantage of offering a critical audit without fear of penalty for failure, thus enabling free and open scrutiny.

Supervisor
Your line manager might examine achievement of standards as a part of the supervisory process. This would, ideally, be conducted in an attempt to assist you to achieve the very best cost-effective standards of service. If it is seen as a disciplinary scrutiny, then you will be less open to improvement through this route.

Internal auditors
Your organisation might employ auditors who have access to all work areas who periodically produce reports of achievement for the benefit of departmental managers, customers and senior management. Again, this will be a more productive exercise if it is conducted as a means to help individuals to continually improve rather than as a policing exercise.

External auditors
The NHS Purchaser, the Social Services Inspectorate and the DoH, etc. employ auditors who can examine any aspect of care and report on the standards achieved.

The Audit Commission

The Audit Commission is a national body with the remit of auditing all aspects of public sector activity. Much of their audit focuses on the proper use of money, but they also report on value for money spent and can comment on quality standards.

You are recommended to employ all of these auditors in a mixed strategy. Your standards are of paramount importance to you, above all others. Consistent good practice is your ticket to success, promotion, etc., and you should take every opportunity to gain feedback about your standards. Every comment is an opportunity to improve, and every improvement is to your advantage. Therefore audit of your work is in your interest. Others will wish to audit you as well, but although this might appear threatening you should recognise that you also want these results and should support the process as far as possible. External audit is an opportunity to improve your service and thereby remain in employment/business.

Improving standards

Whatever the type, frequency or means of audit, it is essential that the results are used to effect change in future performance. Therefore it is essential that a systematic, iterative loop feeds audit findings into the provision and management of services. An ideal audit mechanism has this feedback as an automatic process. For example, the performance-related payment (PRP) for a manager might be directly linked to audit results. This will ensure that all managers closely monitor results and make improvements immediately a poor result is known. These mechanisms should feed results into any forum that can effect improvement. The primary focus in this is the individual clinician who is delivering the service. Feeding results back to this individual allow him or her to act for continuous improvement. Some service improvements require management action and consequently the audit results should appear at relevant management meetings. It is important that action plans are always made in response to audit reports and that the usual protocols of 'Matters arising from the previous meeting' are employed to ensure that planned action is carried out. It is not enough for an audit report to be made to the Board of Directors if it is to be welcomed and commended but not acted upon.

A broader audit may, also, be carried out to collect information about the service which goes beyond simple compliance with standards. Such an audit might consult staff, customers and consumers about services in general or may ask questions about value achieved for money. Auditors may seek to make comparisons with other service providers, making general enquiries or applying national standards resulting in a benchmark that shows how an organisation lies on a nationwide spectrum ranging from poor to excellent.

Evaluate the process

Audit of the service may itself be audited. An analysis might be made of the appropriateness of the standards adopted and the extent to which they are owned by employees and valued by patients/clients. Examination should be made of the representativeness and rigour of the audit mechanism. Special attention will be made of the extent to which the findings from each audit exercise are used to improve performance. This is known as closing the audit loop. Assessment of the process would involve following an audit trail. This would involve assurance that the conclusion from an audit was thoroughly examined. There should be clear plans made for improvement, perhaps at a management meeting, and there should be clear evidence of the implementation of the plans with evaluation of the effectiveness of this implementation. This examination of the audit process should result in continuous improvement.

Some external auditors will be adequately reassured by the presence of a valid and robust internal audit system, with clear audit trails, thus negating the need for external audit. For example, it is common for DHAs to audit the audit procedures of NHS Trusts rather than the quality standards themselves. If the audit procedures are believed to be robust, and audit loops are closed, then Trusts' audit results might satisfy purchaser enquiries into the quality of the services provided.

Quality circles

A number of people with a shared interest in an aspect of quality, but with different skills, may come together to consider possibilities for quality improvement. These groups may be called quality circles, quality improvement teams, etc. They may be set up for long-term or short-term operation. The performance of a quality circle is similar to that of a focus group. It is important that they take a creative approach to the area under discussion and build upon the ideas expressed by one another until an optimum proposition is arrived at. This may be achieved in a small number of meetings, or a standing committee may exploit the creative ideas occurring to participants on long journeys, on holiday, in the bath, etc. The group may conduct a brainstorm exercise in which ideas of tangential relevance to the subject are shared and participants build upon peer suggestions until a creative way forward is achieved.

It is important for quality circles to employ a creative, divergent-thinking phase in their deliberations before converging on to a solution. There is often benefit in examining quite impractical solutions in order to draw out useful lessons for application.

CASE STUDY 5.2 QUALITY CIRCLE

A group of hospital staff formed a short duration quality circle to consider their very poor waiting facilities. Initially, convergent, problem-solving techniques said that they should improve the décor, the seating, the quality of reading material, etc. Although valuable, all of these solutions would be expensive to implement, and would have only limited benefit. A divergent-thinking phase was introduced. What was the best experience they could quote of good waiting facilities? They quickly agreed that one such was the airport lounge, where passengers wait for, on average, two hours and rarely express distress. Hospital patients express dissatisfaction if kept waiting for half an hour. Initially, team members felt reservations about the lessons that could be learned from that source. The hospital could not replicate the happiness of anticipated holidays, or the excitement of an atmosphere filled with Jumbo Jets. Therefore they thought that could learn little from considering an airport lounge. However, there were many factors at work in the airport lounge.

Customers in an airport do not sit and wait in one place for several hours. They spend a short time in one lounge and are then called to check in, after which they can move to another lounge. They spend time here and then they are called to a departure lounge. From here, they move to another lounge where they embark on the aeroplane. This process of movement gives the customer the feeling of progress. Sitting in a hospital waiting room denies any feeling of progress, which causes unnecessary distress.

Customers in an airport are given clear information about the time for which they will wait, and they adjust accordingly. They engage in other activities commensurate with the time that they know they have to spend. Even when the delay time alters, appropriate information is given to customers and they adjust their expectations again. Hospital patients are simply asked to sit, and often have no information about whether they will be there ten minutes or several hours. When they ask receptionists, 'How much longer?' the receptionist is rarely in a position to answer, and may be too overburdened to find out. This can cause more irritation in the waiting room.

Customers in an airport have the opportunity to browse shops and spend money. This is possible because the facilities exist, and they know how long they have to wait. In hospital, little is available near the waiting rooms and patients will not visit the shops that do exist for fear of missing the call when it comes.

This conversation lasted for less than two hours and lead to three improvements that with minimal financial outlay improved the patient experience dramatically. The waiting rooms were made sequential. Patients on reception were directed to the first waiting room area. The nurse weighed them and they returned to a different part of the waiting room; they underwent a clerking process and returned to another part of the waiting area, from where they were called by the consultant. Throughout this experience they knew how long they had to wait because they had a fixed appointment time and, although clinics generally ran late, the delay was known and shown on a blackboard. Thus, patients could calculate the time when they would be seen, e.g. 10.20 appointment; clinic running 45 minutes late; patient expects to be seen at 11.05. It was preferred that patients did not wonder off to shops, so vendors were given shelf space in the waiting areas, and self-funding diversion was thus provided.

Interestingly, these devices benefiting the airport were not a result of airport staff ingenuity. Rather they were essential actions to make management of travellers possible. It was largely fortuitous that they improved customer satisfaction. However, when transferred to a hospital setting, they were exclusively for the achievement of customer comfort. This exercise was highly successful. Dissatisfaction because of waiting facilities decreased significantly and there were almost no cost implications.

Conclusion

Quality in health and social care is dictated by those who deliver services. The appointment of a Director of Quality or a quality-minded manager may assist in this process, but good or bad service is the responsibility of the clinician. It is essential for you to set the highest standards commensurate with patient/client numbers, have a robust means of assuring those standards and seek to constantly improve what is done. Always look for creative changes that will improve standards in your blackspots and ensure that quality audit is transparent and directly linked to your planning processes. Be open to feedback and audit wherever you can get it. That will enable you to continually improve. The excellence you will achieve is the best possible route to recognition, promotion and job security.

REFERENCES

DoH (1998) *A New NHS Modern and Dependable*. HMSO, London.

FURTHER READING

Appleby, J. (1995) *Acting on the Evidence: A Review of Clinical Effectiveness: Sources of Information*. NAHAT, Birmingham.

Baker, R., Lakhani, M., Fraser, R. and Cheater, F. (1999) A model for clinical governance in primary care groups. *British Medical Journal*, **318**, 779–783.

Dewar, S. (1999) *Clinical Governance under Construction: Problems of Design and Difficulties*. King's Fund, London.

Ellis, R. (ed.) (1989) *Professional Competence and Quality Assurance in the Caring Professions*. Croom Helm, London.

Lugon, M. and Secker-Walker, J. (1999) (eds) *Clinical Governance: Making It Happen*. Royal Society of Medicine Press, London.

Parsley, K. and Corrigan, P. (1994) *Quality Improvement in Nursing and Healthcare: A Practical Approach*. Chapman & Hall, London.

Parsley, K. and Corrigan, P. (1998) *Quality Improvement in Healthcare: Putting Evidence into Practice*. Stanley Thornes, Cheltenham.

Peters, T.J. (1985) *A Passion for Excellence: The Leadership Difference*. Collins, London.

Riely, R. (1987) *Evaluation of Therapeutic Recreation through Quality Assurance*. Venture Publishing, Pennsylvania.

Royal College of Nursing (1987) *Nursing Quality Measurement: Quality Assurance Methods for Peer Review*. Wiley, Chichester.

Royal College of Nursing (1998) *Guidance for Nurses on Clinical Governance*. RCN, London.

Shaw, C.D. (1986) *Introducing Quality Assurance*. King's Fund, London.

Sinha, M.N. and Willborn, W.W.O. (1985) *The Management of Quality Assurance.* Wiley, New York and Chichester.

Walshe, K. and Ham, C. (1997) *Acting on the Evidence: Progress in the NHS.* HSMC, University of Birmingham, Birmingham.

World Health Organisation (1982) *Quality Assurance in Diagnostic Radiology.* WHO, Geneva.

6 THE MANAGEMENT OF CHANGE

INTRODUCTION

The UK NHS has changed steadily since its inception in 1947. Successful management in this arena requires the successful management of change. For that reason, the management of change is given close attention in this text. The chapter analyses and collates published comment and research and draws conclusions. This understanding will enable the reader to become an effective manager of change. Insight into the processes of change are generally considered to be necessary for a change agent, as a formulaic approach is not always sufficient. However, the reader wishing to simply refer to 'what to do' will find ample instruction in 'The practice'.

This is a critical review of the literature collating material and identifying and evaluating emergent themes that may prove helpful to the clinician or health care manager and the management of human resources in change.

Inertia in enormous organisations such as the NHS is well described by writers from March and Simon (1958) to Pettigrew (1993a), and effecting change takes strong, active management action. There are many sources of guidance to the management of change and these, although divergent, have a number of common features. These are examined and discussed in this thematic, critical review of the literature.

Many writers on change seek to describe a model that enables those involved to predict the future, control the present and make sense of what is occurring (Hogan, 1997).

The discipline of organisational development (OD) suggests formulaic actions that may aid in change. OD may be described as being based in rationalism, pragmatism or existentialism. Rationalism and pragmatism based approaches allow for a degree of formulaic recipe exercised within an organisation to aid change (Freidlander, 1976). Existentialism suggests a great reliance on individuality, context and environment, with the consequence that managing change is a far more intricate and difficult process. A postmodern approach to management theory might say that formulaic change paths seen in isolation could offer little of value. Pettigrew (1985), without abandoning the notion that good management practice is important in change, argues that change in organisations is a consequence of contextual pressures more than internal action and in many cases occurs with a significant fortuitous component.

There emerges a diverse spread of views about the ability of managers and management consultants to control change. Buchanan (1997), studying change in business process re-engineering (BPR) in the hospital arena concluded that BPR might not be as context sensitive as has been recently claimed so that local drives can be very effective in changing an organisation. At the other extreme end of an emergent 'formula–no-formula' continuum, White and Jacques (1995) suggest that application of postmodern theories of organisational behaviour to a post-industrial community must cast doubt, almost by definition, on the validity of any business organisational theory. Taking a middle way, Mabey and Mayon-White (1993) write that an approach to change management based upon a recipe of necessary and sufficient ingredients will fail because it can never take adequate account of the individuality of people, organisations and their external environment. However, they comment, certain process elements can be identified as necessary ingredients for successful management of change. This chapter identifies and explores those necessary, but not sufficient, elements that are relevant to health and social care management.

In considering this subject, it is necessary to recognise that the UK NHS, and to a lesser extent Social Services departments, are not typical of UK industry, for a number of reasons. Two particular idiosyncrasies are the absence of a profit motive, and the indistinct line relationships between managers and senior clinicians (Ham, 1991). The notions of clinical freedom and hegemonic control enjoyed by the medical profession described by Crozier (1976) illuminate the limitations of line-managerial control over medical and other health and social care practitioners. For these reasons, it may be the case that approaches to change management devised for traditional industries need to be modified in order to be effective in this setting.

The nature of change

The nature, as well as the rate, of change has radically altered in the past two to three decades. 'Thirty years ago, the company saw the future as predictable ... more of the same only better' (Handy, 1995, p. 5). The altered nature of contemporary change is arguably more significant than the increased rate of change. 'Incremental change suddenly becomes discontinuous change' (Handy, 1995, p. 7). It is discontinuous change that is at work in modern industry to lift organisations out of their old tramlines and on to wholly new paths. Certainly, it is discontinuous change has been evident in the UK National Health Service (NHS), particularly since the NHS and Community Care Act (DoH, 1990). This discontinuous change has been reinforced in major legislation since that time.

Burnes (1996) describes the replacement of planned change, defined by Lewin in 1951, by emergent change which is perpetual, open ended and not predictable and therefore not amenable to incremental planning as a continuous sequence. In apparent agreement with Handy, Burnes describes emergent change as taking the organisation away from the route that continuous change would have devised.

A string of incremental, planned changes were made to the NHS since its origins in the NHS Act of 1947 (DoH, 1947). These include the NHS (Amendment) Act 1949 (DoH, 1949), the NHS Act 1951 (DoH, 1951), the NHS Act 1952 (DoH, 1952), the NHS Reorganisation Act 1973 (DoH, 1973) and the NHS Reorganisation 1982 (DoH, 1982). All of these changes sought to provide more and better patient treatment, through streamlining and decentralising responsibility while reinforcing central accountability. These changes did not, however, alter the fundamental way in which health care was managed.

The NHS and Community Care Act (1990) may be seen as the first emergent or discontinuous change, since it saw a total revision in the administration and management of health care. This was moving the service away from its 44-year-old line management tramlines on to the completely new ground of management by marketplace economic forces. This is a good example of the process described by Johnson:

> *Typically, organisations go through long periods where strategies appear to be developed incrementally. There occur infrequently more fundamental shifts in strategy as major readjustment of the strategic direction of the firm takes place. (1993, p. 60)*

The movement between steady progression and periodic radical change is explained by Johnson (1993) as a consequence of strategic drift. Strategy exists as part of a cultural history and the inevitable drift leads to periodic major strategic redirection that needs a dramatic unfreezing in order to occur. This redirection becomes a far more frequent experience in the context of the current rapidly developing cultural environment.

Pettigrew *et al.* (1992) in their study of the effect on the pace of change of general management following the NHS Reorganisation (1982) found that there was substantial acceleration of pace of change in the NHS by the late 1980s. They also report that institutions may be intentionally transformed through the process of radical shock. The Thatcher experiment, they comment, may be considered an example of radical shock. In this they are suggesting that, in addition to a radical redirection of strategy and management, there may have been a deliberate intent to shock the organisation throughout in order to facilitate unfreezing (described below; Lewin, 1951), rethinking and redirection. This notion is supported by the literature and promotional media appearances in which both the Prime Minister and Secretary of State for Health repeatedly described the reforms as 'Effecting root and branch changes to the NHS' (DoH, 1989a).

Thus, rather than reassuring employees, there was an intent to maximise the perceived effect on individuals and thereby, perhaps, to prepare them to change working practices radically.

THE THEORETICAL FRAMEWORK

The process of effectively bringing about change in the behaviour of people has been contemplated and researched for a very long period, with a great volume of important published work. This study considers publications from 1951, which saw the publication of Kurt Lewin's *Field Theory in Social Science*. Change management theory generally requires that a number of components be in place. Each is well described by commentators and to varying degrees has been tested by empirical examination. Empirical research in this field is predominantly of a case study nature, since there is limited opportunity or demand for controlled experiment in changing large organisations. Even the Hawthorn Studies, which could be described loosely as a longitudinal A–B–A–B design, emerged as a fortuitous case study.

Studies reported tend to be either cross-sectional or longitudinal. Cross-sectional studies compare different management units, inferring relationships between inputs and outcomes, which may be causal. However, it is impossible to eliminate the effect of individual idiosyncrasies and external factors. Any relationships demonstrated cannot be assigned certain causality (Easterby-Smith *et al.*, 1991). Longitudinal studies, focusing on small samples over a long period, seek to use time series data to unearth the complex patterns that explain organisational behaviour. This process does not compare the wide range of possible relationships achieved by cross-sectional study, but delivers a more robust model, particularly if the whole environmental and political context is taken into account (Pettigrew 1985).

Authors do not often claim generalisability and all studies are unrepeatable because they relate to events that occur once only in conditions that cannot, by definition, be caused to reoccur. None the less, the lessons drawn can be applied to future situations if active adaptation is continually made to bring about best fit.

Thematic analysis of this descriptive theory and empirical literature sees the emergence of a number of clear areas for consideration, as are discussed below.

Conditioning and gestalt

Pavlov (1927), in classical conditioning theory, described a system for changing behaviours through linking external stimuli in order to modify subjects' reflexes. A reaction normally produced reflexively in response to one stimulus might be progressively induced in reaction to another stimulus if those two stimuli are consistently experienced together by the subject. This discipline transfers from animal to human subjects, and is used to explain a phenomenon such as motion sickness when it occurs as a response to the vehicle before motion commences. However, little success has been achieved in using classical conditioning to alter more than the most basic of human behaviours.

Skinner (1974), in operant conditioning theory, describes systematic rewards for desired behaviours and ignoration of undesirable behaviours modifying future behaviour in animals. This discipline, as behaviour therapy, has been demonstrated to be very effective when used with human subjects, with some very complex behaviour being altered in this way.

However, in gestalt field theory the manipulation of external stimuli described in conditioning theories is considered insufficient. The notion of gestalt is that the whole organism or system is more than simply the sum of its component parts. This leads some observers to consider that the reductionist approach used in behaviour therapy, which reduces complex behaviour to simple components that may be modified, is insufficient to alter a complex being. A lasting change in behaviour requires a change of the subjects' understanding of themselves and the context in which they exist as well as simply a change to stimulus/response through rewards. The effect of a change of stimuli through reward and ignoration as described by Skinner is considered important in gestalt. However, there must also be attention to cognitive functions, and the place of the individual in a community, before change can be effective at more than a cosmetic level (Smith *et al.*, 1982).

The need to consider change in terms beyond reward for desired behaviour is developed by many theorists on the change process. Nadler (1993), echoing Smith *et al.*, points out that the forces of equilibrium tend to work against any localised change. Only when the change considers the stimuli on individuals, the conceptualisations of individuals and the manner in which individuals make up an organisation-wide system will changes become permanent.

In all, there are many approaches recorded to managing stimuli in order to bring about alterations to individuals' understanding in order to effect a change in behaviour. These have formed a part of change management and organisation development theory.

Theories of the management of change

In the study of general, and NHS-specific, change management theory there is considerable divergence in approach to be found; however, there are also a number of constant themes and large areas of agreement.

Participative leadership and involvement of employees

Employee ownership of the unsatisfactory nature of the present and desirability of the proposed future is generally reported to be critical in gaining enthusiasm and cooperation. This was described by Beckhard and Harris (1987) in the 'change equation': $D + V + S > R$, where D is dissatisfaction with the present, V is a vision of a better future, S is step 1, and R is the resistance to change expressed by employees. This is an important component of change management theory. It suggests that where change is not accelerating at the desired rate, then the situation may be improved by increasing D, V or S rather than simply attempting to eliminate resistance R, which is commonly the first line of approach. This model complements the force-field analysis described by Lewin (1951) (see Figure 6.1).

Figure 6.1 Force-field analysis

Lippitt *et al.* (1985) report that involvement in the planning of change gives employees confidence and enables them to understand what is being done. It exploits the insights of those intimately involved with the processes concerned and consequently results in improved planning. Also, they comment, if managers make it possible for subordinates to own and solve problems, and then supply the new conditions that the subordinates have prescribed for themselves, this is more effective than offering a *fait accompli* change. They consider that it results in employees effecting change because they wish to and believe that it is right rather than because they have been instructed to do so.

Vaill (1982) pointed to this notion, commenting that the whole system must be the object of change. All employees must be involved, in order that the entire system has been taken into account in change design and also in order that the whole system is actively changed. Change of a single facet, involving only a small part of the work force carries the risk that the remaining unchanged rump will undo the change effected in the minority

Burnes (1996) describes the need for the level of involvement of the individual to be proportionate to the extent that he or she will be affected.

Mabey and Mayon-White (1993) describe the emphasis on participative change management as the most important change to change thinking over recent years. In the same year, Nadler said that one of the most consistent findings in his research on change is that participation reduces resistance, builds ownership of solutions and motivates people to make changes work (Nadler, 1993).

Van de Ven (1980) and Quin (1980) both describe involvement of employees as essential to assist them to see issues in a wider context and enable a natural process to occur which leads to institutionalisation of new management ideas and a natural move over to new working practice. This supports the notion of change as a complex, contextually based occurrence and yet offers simple practical means of manipulation. At a simple level, employees are able to see the reason for change, and so cooperate. At another level, the individual is exposed to the difficult-to-conceptualise, context-based rationale for change and by sophisticated behaviours will steer the change through an environment too complex for a single manager to manipulate.

Michael Walton, a clinical psychologist and organisational development (OD) consultant in the NHS, considers that in that setting a significant determinant of the outcome of a change exercise is the agreement among staff that the changes are needed. He also expresses the view that it is essential that they have been involved in the decision to change as well as the choice of path to be followed (Walton, 1997).

Nadler (1993) says that the first action step has to be to identify and bring to the surface dissatisfaction with the current state of things as perceived by the workforce. Upton and Brookes (1995) report on the need to bring to the surface any dissatisfaction with the present situation and also with the planned changes, if any exist. In a case study of an NHS community resettlement scheme for patients, they found that passive resistance to change was more difficult to deal with than active resistance. Where a workforce is involved with the process and will voice concerns and state reasons for preferring not to alter practices, then these can be the subjects of negotiated settlement. Where resistance is not expressed but simply results in failure to cooperate, then it is far more difficult to find acceptable avenues of compromise. A common reason given for the recognition of trade unions is the desire to bring concerns into the public arena and thereby to begin the process of reconciliation. The NHS, through its Whitley Council Committees for staff recognition, has strong machinery to facilitate this dialogue.

Burnes (1996) reported finding infrequent exceptions to the need for comprehensive communication. In fact, he occasionally found that changes are adopted very rapidly without careful management preparation. Burnes and James (1995) also note this phenomenon and suggest that cognitive dissonance might explain this phenomenon. In cognitive dissonance theory, individuals will alter their perceptions of the world in order to resolve paradoxes and contradiction between the various models, or even the total paradigm by which they explain their beliefs and behaviours (Festinger, 1957; Jones, 1990). Burnes and James (1995) suggest that, on occasion, detailed involvement of staff is not required to effect change, because if staff perceive a dissonance between their underlying beliefs and their behaviours then they experience discomfort and intrinsically are motivated to change either their behaviour or their beliefs. This intrinsic motivation replaces the extrinsic motivation achieved by high level involvement and explains occasional cooperation with profound change in the absence of adequate involvement

However, in a cautionary note, Vrakking (1997) points out that consultation is time consuming and this time lag may reduce the success of the change drive. Studying change in The Netherlands, taking account of the health service reforms based upon the Dekker Report (Dekker, 1987), Vrakking considered that there was an inverse relationship between the time taken to implement a change and the extent of change ultimately achieved (see Figure 6.2).

Preparations must be made during the innovation phase to ensure that the target level can be achieved as soon as possible. This requires well-planned and irreversible actions, which are implemented in big steps (Vrakking, 1997, p. 37).

Figure 6.2 The relationship between time and change

Therefore, although involvement and ownership are universally valued, time is a qualifier. These conditions are not of necessity contradictory, but the time concern might temper the enthusiasm for endless consultation.

Participative leadership is tested empirically by research conducted in a variety of studies. Peter Langseth was management consultant to the World Bank, leading its major restructuring and redirection which concluded in 1982. His longitudinal case study is reported extensively in Lippitt *et al.* (1985). In this study, Langseth describes the importance of employee participation as a major lesson that was derived from the exercise. Participation, he found, identified needs, created trust, generated ideas, and offered expertise specific to the industrial area concerned. However, the tendency to raise unrealistic expectations was noted and a need for guarded realism was advocated. This is the informed report of a commissioned project. Findings are the considered conclusions of expert deliberation. However, the project cannot be described as a formal experiment, control of outside factors would not be appropriate and the study is not repeatable. It is not claimed that the population studied (bank employees) is representative of wider populations and in particular is not very similar to a health care population.

Participation requires reciprocal communication regarding the need to change, the consequent proposed changes and progress towards the chosen condition. Many analysts describe the importance of this communication.

Communication and feedback

There is a crucial need for change managers to continually reiterate the superiority of the vision of the future and the way in which the change process will bring the organisation to the desired state.

> *One of the first and most critical steps for managing change is to develop and then communicate a clear image of the future ... resistance and confusion frequently develop during organisational change because people are unclear about what the future might be like. (Nadler, 1993)*

Nadler describes the importance of multi-channel communication, repetition and variety in this communication. This, he observed, might include small group meetings, large group briefings, newsletters, videotape presentations, etc. Lippitt echoes this observation, commenting that it is crucial to inform individuals about the change effort before it commences and to ensure that they understand the intended result and the mechanism by which this change will bring it about. In addition, there is a need for managers to hear responses in order to modify the process as appropriate and to permit expression of concerns and catharsis. These concerns might otherwise lead to resistance. In catharsis, employees feeling aroused and distressed by proposed changes release this energy constructively, in this case through dialogue. Even when dialogue is heated, it may perform a constructive part by enabling release of strongly felt emotions.

Changes may be usefully modified to become more acceptable to employees who have legitimate concerns. Interactive communication elicits concerns not otherwise evident to change managers. Lippitt proposes a situation where reasonable change might be resisted, merely because it moves an influential individual away from a window thereby reducing his or her enjoyment of the working environment. It, therefore, may be critical to successful change management that such issues are brought to the surface and resolved.

Nadler reports the importance of developing feedback mechanisms specifically targeted on the effectiveness of change initiatives in train. Steady-state feedback mechanisms often break down under the turbulence of change, particularly in response to the increased influence of the grapevine.

Michael Walton observed that change leadership is effective only if it addresses a number of communication components. The need for change must be made clear and evident to all; the practical scope for change must be made clear and evident to all; the resources must be identified and transparently allocated to the process; an explicit commitment to change must be obtained from all affected.

The communication process will expose conflict. Failure to acknowledge this conflict and to allow its expression will prevent individuals from resolving tensions and restructuring their personal models and paradigms. This exercise requires an allocation of time in which employees make the journey that has already been made by the change agent in arriving at the need to change. The exercise also shows up the need for internal communication opportunities among subjects of change as well as hierarchical communications between change agents and subjects of change (Marris, 1993).

Empirically, the part played by complex communication in effecting change is comprehensively explored. In the World Bank study, Lippitt *et al.* (1985) reported the importance of communication before and during change. It was found necessary to establish new mechanisms, and even language for communication under the new conditions, with reference sources for individual access, and constant feedback about achievements.

Price and Murphy (1987), in a longitudinal case study, reported the effect of their work on OD in British Telecom, Western London District. The study was with a broad skill mix of employees, in a technically demanding field, working in a multi-million pound organisation with a workforce of 6000 plus. As such the subject group had something in common with a larger NHS Trust. The report is, as described by Mabey and Mayon-White, 'Anecdotal and unsystematic ... but realistic' (1993, p. 153).

The study found that that there was a need to simplify and publicise information. This, they observed, needed to be comprehensive and multi-channelled. A simple information cascade used in isolation, they found, could not give adequate coverage or clarity. They observed that meetings for idea formulation and information needed to be visible within normal working circumstances. They found it to be damaging when decisions happened mysteriously, e.g. out of hours, through an awayday in a hotel, etc.

The importance of recognising the inevitability of conflict was found by Burnes (1996) when in a cross-sectional case study he examined the merger of five colleges of nursing and/or midwifery into one large college of midwifery and nursing. This 1993 study was of a longitudinal, descriptive and analytical nature and involved academic members of the health service. As such, Burnes considers the lessons relevant to the NHS and other public sector industries in the UK. The five colleges were drawn together under one management and in partially new premises. There was conflict described between the two professions and between the various management teams. This conflict was inevitable, and it was necessary to recognise this and make it explicit in order for it to be addressed. This explicit attention to conflict made resolution possible. Failure to recognise and address conflict led to continuing resistance at various formal and informal arenas in the organisation and an increase of inertia and resistance. The critical importance of addressing conflicts through sophisticated and robust communication is reported as the main lesson from the study.

The importance of devising and communicating a clear strategy was found by Burnes (1996) in his case study of GK Printers Ltd as they made radical changes throughout their organisation to deliver dramatically improved quality and flexibility in their product. The longitudinal study tested a variety of inputs over a number of change phases, with some clear conclusions. Significant among the conclusions is the importance of success through attention to the customer and the critical contribution of communicating a well-constructed strategy.

> *The company had a strategy for the future ... and therefore was able to take an overview in all areas of its business in relation to future objectives. Because the company was strategy driven it was able to establish not only where problems lay, but also whether the problems were high, medium or low priority. (Burnes, 1996, p. 258)*

Tom Peters (1989), from anecdotal study of a very broad spectrum of US organisations, observed the same point, commenting that 'Communicating a strategic mindset, focused on skill building, is more important than ever' (Peters 1989, p. 394).

Buchanan (1997) studied BPR in hospitals using a case study design. He found that where there was not an adequately precise definition of focus and methodology, politically driven actors manipulate the exercise to subvert the outcomes. This, he found, was compounded by the absence of a clear and well-understood strategic direction for the organisation.

The issue appears to reduce to a requirement for reciprocal and open communication over a sustained period of time to allow employees to adjust their models, adopt a new strategy and contribute to a proposal to such an extent that they can own the change effort. Many organisations use formal and informal education opportunities in part as a vehicle for this time and communication based personal development to occur.

Education

Change agents will have assimilated changes and reformulated their models so that the proposed system makes sense to them. This may have occurred over a long period. Subjects of change need to hear this new vision clearly and, crucially, to be given the opportunity to actively reform their own constructs before they can work positively towards a changed model. Many observers and managers recognise the value of educational opportunities in facilitating this developmental process.

Walton (1997), in examining NHS change, observed that understanding the emotionality of change is critical to outcome. Staff need the time to reassure themselves that change is worthwhile and that it leads to a future in which they are needed and in which they are able to be influential. This process requires time and may be enhanced by the opportunity for detached education.

There is reference in the literature to the importance of time out and an opportunity for contemplation to help employees to move through the threshold represented by major change.

Handy (1995) observes that there has been an explosion in MBA degrees as part of a rush by organisations to link their development plans to some form of qualification.

Plant (1987) argues that the learning process is the key to the self and organisational change. Handy (1995) and Marris (1993) describe time for reflection and development, associated with educational opportunities. The impact of educational opportunity on the ability to change is more than anecdotally demonstrated. In the World Bank project report (Lippitt et al., 1985), Langseth reports the importance of direct education in change management, observation and various technical specific areas.

Goodstien and Burke (1991) in the British Airways study found that many training programmes were required to enable staff to generally improve their understanding of the industry. This was an example of the benefit of more general educational opportunities, not simply to inculcate skills but to change insights and attitudes to work. In the movement phase of the exercise, a very heavy emphasis was placed on manager training in management and leadership. As part of their refreezing exercise, the organisation has adopted executive 'Academies' leading to MBA awards.

Graham Benjamin (Benjamin and Mabey, 1990), reporting his work as consultant to Billton International Metals in The Hague during their major reorganisation, drew a number of conclusions around the nature of time needed to change attitudes. A major reorganisation will require individuals to question their vision. This, he found, required time for individual values, attitudes, beliefs and behaviours to be worked on participatively, alongside business and organisational imperatives. Leaders needed to change their behaviour in a visible form in order to model the required behaviour.

Burnes (1996) in his study of the Rover Group between 1989 and 1994 found success firmly based in a belief in education of the workforce. Through the creation of the Rover Learning Business (RLB) as an independent organisation within the Rover Group, a situation was achieved where at one time over 50% of the workforce are engaged in learning activities. Burnes found the RLB to be a dynamic and very effective device for bringing about change. The introduction of the Land Rover Discovery range was managed by the RLB and described as 'the smoothest and quickest change project ... ever' (Burnes, 1996, p. 248).

The Chair of British Aerospace during the period building up to their purchase of Rover, Sir Austin Pearce, had already expressed his recognition of the essential part of education in industry by accepting the position of Pro-chancellor of the University of Surrey and Chair of the Science Museum (Ezra and Oates, 1989)

Lawler and Hearn (1997), in a cross-sectional case study examining the rise of managerialism in Local Authority Social Services Departments, found manager training to be a major predictor of successful change. They did not, however, encounter the organisation-wide learning culture described by Burnes (1996) in his study of the Rover Group.

Leadership and trust

The critical nature of the communication, involvement and education process leads to examination of the nature of the leadership involved.

Nadler observes the importance of using leader behaviour to generate energy in support of change. Change needs to consider formal leaders, deriving power from their position, and informal leaders, whose power derives from one of many other sources. Concert of leaders is essential.

Sets of leaders working in coordination can have a tremendously powerful impact on the informal organisation. (Nadler, 1993, p. 96)

The importance of symbols and energising language to support leadership is reported by Peters (1978), and this, he observes, may be an essential adjunct to the energising behaviour of leaders.

It is not possible to ensure that the reasons for every component of a change are explicitly understood by all parties affected. Therefore, successful leadership requires that some management actions can be taken on trust. Equally, leaders will benefit if they can be seen to trust employees to make decisions and act in the best interest of the organisation without the need for tireless supervision.

Lippitt *et al.* (1985) express the importance of trust and observe that mistrust arises when information given is incomplete or misleading and that trust might be earned by open and candid communication.

Burnes (1996), in a longitudinal case study, looked at Process Control, Inc., which employs 395 staff of various skill levels in management, technical and support roles as they restructured in response to business expansion. Strong conclusions are drawn in relationship to the leadership role. The study concluded that strong and directive leadership was essential to the change achieved and that this leadership needed to display consistency and continuity. Managerial changes were found counterproductive. Commitment from the team was found essential in promulgating the leadership message, and emergent/iterative strategy development was found unhelpful. Therefore direction, which does not preclude participation, from managers was found essential. Burnes found that no new ingredients were required to effect change. Rather a fortuitous coincidence of factors can sponta-neously lead to desirable outcomes. This reflects the comments of Pettigrew (1985, 1989) when he observes that chance and opportunism play major parts in effect-ing change. These findings must be tempered by the limited similarity of the Mid-lands-based organisation to the UK NHS.

Attention to the impact of change on individuals

Change to the processes, outputs and outcomes consequent upon an organisation's new endeavour will have profound effect on the lives of those concerned with it. Careful attention to the effect of change on what, how, where, when people work with whom and to what personal benefit is described as critical to the success of a change effort.

Lippitt *et al.* (1985) point to the need to consider disruption to congenial work-ing groups and the consequent impact on issues such as vacation possibilities, dining groups, etc. Fear of alteration to commuting arrangements, car pool deals, etc. can result in resistance that is hard to bring to the surface and therefore hard to address. Upton and Brookes (1995) point out that staff will be concerned about the possibility of their becoming a part of a different group. They might be con-cerned about their status and influence in the new setting. They may also have con-cern about the acceptability of the change agents in relationship to the current informal hierarchy.

Changing to a new model of operating requires abandoning an old model, and may amount to letting go of a former way of life. For many individuals, this con-stitutes a distressing loss. An experience similar to bereavement is often described. The feelings experienced in times of dramatic change are often categorised into the stages of shock, denial, bargaining, acceptance and performance. These are the same stages described by people experiencing other forms of bereavement and some commentators propose similar support mechanisms. Nadler (1993) observes that change frequently creates a feeling of loss that is 'not unlike death'. He sug-gests that people need to mourn for that change. Plans might usefully allow the time for mourning to occur and the various stages of bereavement to be recog-nised. In a transition stage, bereavement can obstruct progress and there may be benefit from permitting it to follow its natural course to resolution before expect-ing active change.

In health and Social Services, the scope for loss of power and status for leaders of individual professions or other groups that will be fragmented by change is con-siderable. This potential for the feeling of loss may be of great importance. Marris goes further, suggesting that bereavement is the paramount consideration:

> *We need to recognise the element of bereavement, above all, in the process of a*
> *major reconstruction. (Marris, 1993, p. 218)*

Major effects on the individual may be anticipated or experienced early in the process and successful change management requires the careful management of this experience.

Recognition of the importance of the impact of change on individuals and groups is supported empirically by Iles and Auluck (1990), who, in a longitudinal study of a health and social care teams, concluded that team-building exercises considering the meaning of proposed changes for individuals contribute to diagnosis and problem solving in OD. It is essential, they observed, that the team achieves personal commitment and consensus on mission and vision with consequent commitment to objectives. The study involved small teams of between ten and fifty people, and a full range of health and social care staff. Although the numbers were small and the case reports anecdotal, the study is particularly valuable because it is specific to the health and social care industries.

The early experience of benefit

In many settings, the early experience might be one of benefit if management effort was exerted to ensure this end. As change begins to deliver results, it may become possible to ensure reward for those who have been affected. Alternatively, the change process can last for a considerable time, and the promised end benefits can appear to be a long time away. Many writers advise change managers to ensure that some small benefits and successes are achieved in the early stages of a change process.

Clearly, early experience of benefit fits well with Skinner's notion that reward encourages the repetition of desirable behaviours. In this case desired behaviours are change-supporting behaviours and these might be amply rewarded. Nadler (1993) echoes Skinner, in describing the importance of rewards for desired behaviour in the early transition stage of a change process. He observes that reward systems devised during relatively static phases of an organisation's existence may be ineffective or even obstructive in the enactment of change; that rewards 'need to be carefully examined during major reorganisational changes and restructured to support the direction of the transition' (Nadler, 1993, p. 93).

Lippitt *et al.* (1985) say that managers should facilitate early implementation of a tangible component of the change and reward those who contributed. This is an example of extrinsic reward, in that the reward is applied externally to recognise contributors. An intrinsic reward, i.e. one that is a direct benefit of the change, can be shown to have an even greater value. Thus, if the change is manipulated to be to the direct benefit of change subjects, then this will better ensure future cooperation than a reward applied by a manager. However, if an intrinsic reward is not possible, then an extrinsic reward should be applied as a very good second best.

Unmodified reward systems can contribute to the cultural factors that hold individuals' loyalty to the present system of practice and thereby hold back change. The change of reward systems is therefore a factor in freeing up a structure in order to allow it to change. This should include consideration of official formal rewards such as bonus schemes and informal rewards such as peer recognition. All rewards should be considered for their possible effects in locking up the present or motivating a change to a future state. New reward systems are needed, to confirm and establish a new way of working. The notion of manipulated reward appeared in a number of change models, particularly in Lewin's field theory.

Models of change management

There have been a number of models of the managed change process, which although different, have much in common. Many models derive from Lewin's field theory. Lewin describes the need to unfreeze, change and refreeze the organisation. Lewin, in force-field analysis (see Figure 6.1), also described the notion of examining the forces at work and manipulating any or all to achieve movement. In particular, force-field analysis shows how change can be aided by reducing resistive forces as effectively as progressively increasing driving forces.

Johnson (1993) describes unfreezing the paradigm by making explicit the constructs within the paradigm. He points out that people who are not part of the system to be changed more easily do this. This supports the need for employment of formal change consultants from outside the organisation. Once a new process has been established, Johnson observes, it is necessary to refreeze by adjusting infrastructure and systems to ensure that it is easy to continue with the new system, and to prevent backsliding. In addition, he considers it necessary to extend any new process to other parts of the organisation rapidly and thereby to maximise the benefit achieved while minimising the risk of reversion to the old.

The refreezing component is described by Lippitt *et al.* as critical and prone to being overlooked:

> *Perhaps the most critically overlooked and vital part of change is that of timely assembly of a human support system dedicated to maintaining the new. (Lippitt* et al., *1985, p. 101)*

The implementation of new systems will not always receive the support of the workforce. Hogan (1997) observes that, in the NHS, poor usage of a revised or new system can often be seen. This has the effect of preventing stabilisation and a failure to refreeze the system. This rejection of the new, or regression to the old, radically reduces the efficiency of the organisation and may be taken as a failure of the implementation process.

The steady-state model for before and after the change may or may not be the same, but it is inevitably unsuitable for the change period. Consequently, special structures to manage the change need to be developed. Further different structures may be needed for employment after the change, to institutionalise the new structure (Nadler and Tushman, 1979).

Pettigrew (1985) reflects the unfreezing process, expressing the need to delegitimise the ideas associated with inertia. The old model will have had legitimacy in the past and this legitimacy must be removed rather than simply countered. This supports the model of force-field analysis, where removing a force supporting inertia is as important as adding a force for change and demonstrates unfreezing in action.

As is made clear by gestalt theory (Smith *et al.* 1982), the management of change cannot be conducted at single points in the organisation. Nadler (1993) says that multiple and consistent leverage, recognising the interdependence of the components of the organisation, brings about successful alterations. Therefore, he considers, the unfreezing and refreezing process needs to be considered throughout the organisation.

Walton (1997) describes a process in NHS change which mirrors field theory while recognising the medical model of intervention. Change, he observes, requires diagnosis, building a basis for collective change action, enabling change and maintaining changed systems.

Systematic manipulation of the paradigm employing models such as force-field analysis is identified in field research by Goodstein and Burke (1991), who used it as a model to evaluate the restructuring of British Airways between 1982 and 1987. The study is of a very large organisation having 60,000 employees. The organisation was in the service sector, had a skill mix similar to the NHS and like the NHS was experiencing the change from bureaucratic state control to market control.

The study was able to match occurrences in the reorganisation closely to the Lewin force-field model, with unfreezing involving a 37% workforce reduction and a change of CEO and Chairmen. A broad range of educational opportunities were introduced to allow staff to develop a better understanding of the industry and to facilitate unfreezing.

The movement phase of the Lewin model again involved education, this time for senior and middle managers in the area of management and leadership. This phase was characterised by the use of diagonal-slice task forces and extensive team-building activity. Support for individuals at all levels was reported and involvement of the new CEO in formal and informal contact was found critical. This echoes the comments made by Peters in 1989 and 1994 when he observed the importance of 'managing by wandering about' in his studies of the USA's most successful organisations. Refreezing was achieved by human resource management changes, including the promotion of those who exemplified new practices into higher management levels. Refreezing was further achieved by the instigation of new performance appraisal mechanisms based on behaviour and results in line with new practices. This clearly demonstrates the value of introduction of new human resource practices to refreeze the system as described by Lippitt *et al.*

Goodstein and Burke express a strong belief, following the lessons from the BA reorganisation, that an understanding of the social psychology of change through models such as those of Lewin assists in achieving the desired outcome.

Price and Murphy in their British Telecom (BT) study (1987) noted the critical nature of the refreezing after change, establishing processes and systems capable of institutionalising an entire new paradigm. They observe that a steering group was an effective venue for spotting the time for refreezing, thereby identifying a comprehensive yet efficient means of fixing the new.

Burnes, in his study of the Midshires College of Midwifery and Nursing, pointed to the importance of considering the stage at which the process is, because 'A style of management suited to a stable state may, as in this instance, be totally unsuited to a more dynamic situation' (Burnes, 1996, p. 228).

Thus, different behaviours need to be consciously adopted during the unfreezing, moving and refreezing phases of a change.

Upton and Brookes in a case study of an NHS community resettlement scheme found the destabilising exercise to be crucial, even where the acceptance of change was suggested by superficial observation:

While change may be agreed on the surface, it will not happen unless there is some real dissatisfaction felt within the staff team. (Upton and Brookes, 1995, p. 44)

Since Lewin, theories have evolved in a number of directions. A distinction exists between the more internally and systematically focused pragmatic and rational schools of OD, with a choice of rational, linear, longitudinal analyses, and the far richer but less manageable, expanded focus model as described by Pettigrew (1985). Pettigrew considered that change is not simply a prescribed management action but a natural process resulting from external and internal elements acting in often fortuitous combinations. Changes may not be a systemwide planned exercise but the result of the action of a small subset of people in the organisation responding to perceived mismatch between environmental demands and organisational performance. Some attempt to reconcile these views exists in open systems thinking in work by Spurgeon and Barwell (1991). They consider that, whatever the personal belief preferred, successful management requires the existence of a personal model of the organisation which is dynamic enough to explain current performance and the continuous changes that it is undergoing. The degree of simplicity or holism of this model may depend on the individual and the situation. Schwenk (1988) describes models as 'schemata' that are devised personally and applied diagnostically to situations. Schwenk points to the tendency to adapt old models to new problems, using metaphor and analogy. This practice is natural, but may result in faulty diagnosis. It is helpful to be explicit when a proven model is adapted to an untried situation and thus to exercise caution and guard against false assumption.

Change as a process consumes energy over and above routine management of the organisation, which is frequently continuing alongside the change process. Nadler (1993) finds that resources such as financial, human, training, consultative input, etc. must be provided for the transitional stage in order for change to occur. However, it is not assumed that these are entirely new resources. Resources may be redirected for this purpose and short periods of exceptional managerial productivity are frequently harnessed for the change process.

Nadler points to the stark need for new resources to be applied to the change process, since it constitutes activity over and above the routine of operational management. Johnson (1993) considers that the extra resource should take the form of a change agent from outside the organisation, which can therefore recognise a separate role as well as a new function and new human resource. The effectiveness of change agents has been richly examined, although the rigour of the evidence offered is limited.

In the World Bank project, Lippitt *et al.* showed that a separate change management project group was essential to effect a reorganisation, but this group, they found, needed to be closely linked to operations management. This was found necessary to support operations managers as well as in order that operations managers might operationalise new systems to refreeze after changes. The use of internal and external consultants is helpful, but these must be controlled and integrated (Lippitt *et al.*, 1985, p. 153).

Price and Murphy (1987) in their BT study reinforced this concern, finding that too much reliance on change consultants worked against sustainability in changes achieved. Where they are not working in close concert with operational managers, the effects of the change cannot be sustained in the absence of the consultant. Additionally Price and Murphy report the importance of early recognition of the time requirement and the need for injection of resource for this period.

Vrakking (1997) went a stage further in quantifying this resource with his X 2X formula. This formula said that whatever the cost of planning and designing the change, the cost of implementation would amount to double that figure. This conclusion was drawn from studies of a number of organisations in The Netherlands, including some health service changes.

In the NHS, however, although the planning resource is frequently provided as an extra to operational costs, the resource for enacting the change is commonly achieved by redirection of normal revenue.

Subsidiarity, and levels of interference: breadth and depth of intervention

Many writers discuss limiting the scope of change to that which is necessary. Destabilising an organisation is essential to enable change. However, the relationship between reduced stability and increased ability to effect change extends only to a limited point. Just as the stress curve relates stress positively to learning performance but recognises a critical point where performance falls away (see Figure 6.3; Walton, 1997), so stress can be related to change performance, with a critical stress level at which the ability to change is adversely affected. Nadler (1993) recognises that the increased anxiety associated with destabilisation, while initially beneficial, may reach a point where it has a detrimental effect. Therefore, Nadler points to the need for protected sources of stability through systems that do not change. Walton in examining NHS change considers that it is crucial to limit disruption,

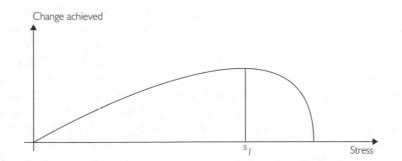

Figure 6.3 The stress curve

confusion and consequent anxiety in order to secure positive commitment from the staff involved. Thus the unfreezing phase involves destabilisation, but this needs to be tempered in order not to disable the workforce.

Change managers need to alter swathes of an organisation, but they are advised to consider that this is an invasion and intervene only where there is clear benefit anticipated, and in any event not to the extent that constructive cooperation is disabled.

Harrison (1970) suggested that managers should interfere at a level no deeper than that required to produce an enduring solution. In addition, he observed that it is pointless to interfere at a level where change energy is not available. To do so would not achieve results and may discredit the change process by setting about a task that was not to be completed.

Senior management within an organisation should not make change decisions for lower levels of the organisation which could have been made at that lower level. Subsidiarity suggests that no decisions should be made at a level of an organisation that could have been made at a lower level. Handy (1995) considers it an injustice for an organisation to arrogate to itself a decision that could be made efficiently by a lower body.

Pettigrew (1993b) observes that intervention needs to take account of all internal and external levels in an organisation in order for changes to be effective. Smith *et al.* (1982) reinforce this point, observing that multipoint leverage is needed to bring about directional change. Goodstein and Burke (1991) in the BA study concluded that multiple level management-led intervention was essential, with many leverage points and multifaceted support including maximum contact between the CEO and all levels of the organisation. However, Burnes (1996) identified the importance of allowing decisions to be managed at appropriately low levels in the GK Printers study. The company was moving to a state where change was the norm.

Without devolving responsibility to those affected, change either would not take place, or would not be successful; 'When the MD went back to taking decisions ... the company failed to maintain behavioural changes' (Burnes, 1996, p. 266).

This suggests a need for comprehensive intervention, but with constraints around unnecessary interference. Although Handy and Harrison define conceptual cut-off points, little evidence exists to answer the question of how much and how deep. In addition to consideration of the above local intra-organisational cause and effect considerations, it is critical to address the context and the environment in which the individual department exists as part of an open system. Therefore, it may be argued that no change process can have enduring benefit unless it works at all internal levels. Pettigrew (1985, 1989) says that there is a tendency to attend to the content of changes and consequent outcomes at the expense of consideration of context and process. Context and environment affect the behaviour of all levels of the organisation. Formulaic change management must be insufficient if it fails to account for individuality, and much benefit is gained from chance and opportunism when individuals make inevitable responses to the wider environment in which they exist. It is evident that insight into the broad organisational context and attention to processes that occur at all levels in an organisation can have a substantial benefit.

Pettigrew (1987) makes it clear that although it is not practicable to integrate the operational context of change into a prescriptive formula it is essential to have a good understanding of context in order to effect lasting change. This is reinforced by a study of Oticon in which Burnes (1996) found that a deep understanding of the marketplace in which they operated was central to their effective reorganisation. The Oticon organisation is a small international organisation described by Peters in 1994 as having visionary leadership which enabled it to change the rules of their endeavour. The significance of context is powerfully expressed by Burnes. It is further emphasised that understanding and exploiting societal values has played a major part in the success of this reorganisation.

Burnes, in his study of GK Printers during their radical change, found that the context in which the organisation operated was central to its successful transformation:

> ... *understanding what the customers wanted and were willing to pay for. In speaking to customers, GK also identified what competitors were offering.* (Burnes, 1996, p. 264)

There is only limited similarity between these organisations and the UK NHS, and transferring this conclusion requires caution.

Summary of the theory

The literature is complex in nature. It ranges from simple opinion, through anecdotal observation to soundly constructed case study analysis. It appears that the necessary but not sufficient conditions that consistently emerge are as follows.

Reward

Ensuring that participants see rapid personal benefit and are thereby rewarded for their cooperation is consistantly advised. This recognises theories of learning through conditioning and is demonstrated through recent and applicable case studies. The change manager could usefully engineer early opportunities for those affected to experience advantage. It may be advantageous if the benefit were focused upon those whose part in the change process was of a high profile nature. It is also important to ensure that participants are not adversely affected if possible. This will involve close examination of the situation to uncover and address possible areas for personal inconvenience and disadvantage.

Communication systems

Much is said about the importance of communications. The machinery in place for steady-state communications will need to be dramatically upgraded in order to meet needs during a change event. Informal communications will immediately accelerate and it is necessary for the formal routes also to accelerate to keep pace.

The machinery introduced needs to be varied in nature; this could include all media and a full spectrum from highly formal to spontaneous and very informal.

The communications need to be reciprocal, so that concerns can be identified and addressed, and so that those involved may develop a perception of ownership of the decisions that emerge from the planning exercise. Ownership of the unsatisfactory present and the improved future sought among the workforce is essential. Change is rarely gratuitous, but unless the workforce is allowed to recognise the need for change, through this protracted communication exercise, then they are unlikely to be intrinsically supportive of the development.

Time, and time out

Managers partake in awaydays and interminable executive meetings, through which avenues they will have made the developmental journey that enables them to recognise the unsatisfactory components of the present and the need for the proposed developments. The other members of the workforce have not had this advantage. Therefore, all of the workforce will need time to digest and accept the development proposals if they are to give active cooperation. Thus, a period is needed to allow the ideas to germinate and develop to the point where the change manager can harvest the benefit. This will happen naturally if the issues are held current in employees' thinking and patience is practised. However, the process can be accelerated if active opportunities are created for discussion and exploration. The literature refers to the adoption of educational exercises to facilitate this development. Exercises reported range from short study sessions in the workplace to facilitation of long courses such as university-based degree study. A note of caution is introduced, however, since there may be a time when the iron is hot and the benefits of action may decay if the initiative is not swiftly grasped.

Leadership and trust

The importance of credible leadership is clearly demonstrated in the literature. Leaders need to earn the trust of employees if they are to cooperate without needing to know the reason behind every move. The literature suggests that trust is earned by consistent open communication and that it may be lost rapidly and permanently if a manager is found careless with the truth. A perception of fairness will also develop trust.

Subsidiarity

There is a paradox to consider when deciding the extent to which a change should permeate the whole organisation. It may be that a change effected in one part of the organisation will not take hold if the bulk of the organisation continues to operate unaltered. This suggests that the more wide-ranging the change, the more likely is the success. However, there are repeated observations that it is unhelpful to alter portions of the organisation from above where that change was not directly needed or where that change could have been managed internally. To make gratuitous change is ethically questionable and results in a destabilisation that causes unnecessary stress to employees. This is ethically unsound and may result in stress levels sufficiently high to disable more vulnerable individuals and detract from patient/client care.

Models

The Lewin model may be seen at the heart of more current change management protocols. This model is also identified at work in current research. There are examples cited where the force-field model can be recognised in successful change exercises and others where the model was not respected in exercises that were not successful. Clearly, these are associations only and the evidence is not powerful enough to definitively demonstrate a causal relationship. The necessity to respect the stages of unfreezing and refreezing as well as changing is repeatedly reported. Failure to unfreeze is given as a cause of failure to effect change, and failure to refreeze is given as a reason for reversion to old ways of working when the change driver is removed.

Discussion

Is the literature advocating an outmoded county club approach to management in a sector where hard-nosed management is essential in a ruthless environment? The health and social care sectors are managerially driven and operate under ever tighter constraints. The responsibility of the manager is to use the system to achieve the best quality and value for patients and clients. NHS Trusts and Social Services Departments are not sheltered employment schemes for the benefit of staff. Clearly, this is so, and management practices should be adopted only if they result in the maximum benefit for patients and clients as end users of the service. Applying this principle to the conclusions of the literature search results in discussion, but it can be argued that in general good behaviour from managers will result in optimum services to users.

Staff must feel benefit from changes. However, changes may not be to the benefit of staff and this must be recognised. Employees can always be coerced to cooperate with change by threat of greater disadvantage if they do not. This results in a coercion paradigm in which developments occur only where they cannot be avoided. This will minimise the amount of change that is achieved and demand a large amount of management effort at all stages. Alternatively, benefits can be identified and made evident to individuals, thereby maximising their recognition. Disadvantage can be identified and actively negated wherever possible. Positive rewards can be engineered for those who actively drive change or the entire workforce where a point is to be made. Redundancies may be unavoidable in change, but if these are seen to be managed with scrupulous fairness and individuals are given all of the help possible, then the effects on residual and future personnel will be considerable. If perception is all there is (Peters, T.J., 1985), then there is benefit for the change manager to be careful to be seen to be minimising disadvantage wherever possible, maximising benefit wherever possible and rewarding loyalty religiously. Then he or she will be seen as caring for the workforce and may expect more support. This costs very little in terms of management effort or other resources and might be rewarded by cooperation based on loyalty. The output in terms of achievement is maximised and the input in terms of management resource is minimised. Therefore, taking a ruthless economic approach, this approach is the most efficient.

Communication systems and time out, even sponsorship of courses, are advocated in the literature as a means of achieving ownership of the change exercise among the workforce. Is this necessary, when employees would cooperate out of fear, or out of a wish to ingratiate themselves with their managers? The benefit of ownership appears to be that the workforce that owns the problem and the solution will actively cause it to happen rather than passively allowing it to happen. They will want the exercise to succeed and might be expected to find creative ways to enhance the project or solve problems rather than simply following received guidance.

Earning the trust of the workforce is advocated, which requires care and attention. The workforce can be caused to cooperate through fear of redundancy or discipline, and it is easy to find anecdotal examples of this style of management. However, this again is an example of gaining cooperation through coercion and that paradigm has been shown inefficient as well as unethical. It is largely because of the inefficiency of this approach to management that so many organisations have published anti-bullying policies that refer as much to bullying managers as other grades. This prevention of bullying has an efficiency driver as much as an ethical one.

The Lewin model may be seen as arcane and overly fussy in the prevailing fast-moving culture. However, there is strong evidence supporting its effectiveness in practice. The logic of removing the factors that wed us to the way things are done now is clear in freeing us to consider other ways of being. This often requires managers to undermine and discredit old ways of thinking in order to allow new ones to develop currency. This is an exercise in destabilising the system in order to allow it to move, because a stable system, while very secure, is unable to change. The inherently unstable fighter aircraft has far more manoeuvrability than the very stable passenger airliner. The business of undermining an old paradigm risks causing damage to those individuals who hold them dear. However, the discrediting can be seen in the context of current developments and not in terms of the environment when that paradigm was prevalent. It may also be important to ensure that it is the paradigm that is undermined and not its proponents. Thus any conflict can be around issues and not around people. The refreezing argument is a mirror to the unfreezing argument. Just as it is necessary to release the ties in order to permit movement, it is equally essential to create new ties once the new model has been achieved in order to keep it at work. Thus, the gardener takes great care to release the roots of a plant before attempting to move it and then firmly to bed them in the new location in order to hold it there. Any other approach will damage the plant.

Why is it that the pace of change has accelerated so dramatically in recent years?

Virtually all commentators observe that the pace and nature of change have accelerated and altered dramatically over the past one or two decades. Little discussion satisfactorily explains this phenomenon. It may be that the pace of technological advancement has accelerated and organisations are moving ever faster to exploit this environmental change. Additionally, there is the move from an industrial age to an information age, and this may be causing a change similar in impact to the industrial revolution of the 19th century. Alternatively, perhaps the rapidly expanding population and explosively improving communications and mounting expectations are at the heart of this drive. One explanation, less frequently discussed, is to look at the individuals who are now running the major industries and services in the Western world. The 1960s and 1970s saw the emergence of an unusually challenging cadre of post-war youth, perhaps facilitated by mass communication, who did not accept the ways of life of their forebears, questioning and changing the entire nature of adolescence. That generation is now in its fifth and sixth decade and there are many anecdotal examples of this very turbulent generation holding very influential national positions. In developmental terms, we do not leave behind earlier developmental stages, but transcend and integrate them. Therefore the adult still has the adolescent within. This explanation might be paraphrased 'The hippies and punks are now running the world!' If that is true, and it is difficult to see how it cannot be so, then a turbulent period can be no surprise.

Limitations

No scrutiny of theory can be truly comprehensive and this one does not claim such. Case study and anecdotal evidence does not lend itself to meta-analysis as do quantitative data and therefore the aggregation of information must be imperfect. The greatest limitation of this chapter, however, may lie in the attempt, through reductionism, to identify a list of instructions for the successful management of change. This chapter, therefore, claims only to have discussed necessary but not sufficient conditions in change management – i.e. those that must be considered – but will not guarantee success. The intent is to highlight areas where insight and consideration would benefit the manager.

Conclusion

In conclusion, if there are recipe ingredients, a clear list emerges. These are: staff involvement, communication, education, leadership, attention to the impact of changes on individuals, the early experience of benefit, a systemwide model, care about the breadth and depth of intervention, and integrated consideration of the context in which the organisation operates. These might be condensed into rewards, communication, time and time out, leadership and trust, subsidiarity and the application of models.

Attention and thoughtful insight into each of these factors may be seen as a necessary condition for successful change, although they are not proposed as always sufficient. The additional factors in success are the open system in which the organisation exists, the unique individuality of the players, and sheer chance. The extent to which formulaic practice alone will lead to a desired outcome is questioned by the postmodern trend towards longitudinal, open systems attention to the widest possible contextual model. However, this uncertainty is not a licence for inactivity. Rather, there is an imperative to ensure that all components are in place and dynamically addressed and then to maintain constant vigil to understand and reflect the part played by the additional factors.

THE PRACTICE

If you are going to bring about change in the area under your control, you will need to do a number of practical things for and with the staff who are to be part of that change. These are 'necessary, but not sufficient' conditions. That is to say that they are essential if your organisational change is to be effective, but they will not of themselves guarantee success. They cannot be treated as a recipe that will always gain a consistent outcome, but should be in place before you address the more idiosyncratic concerns of individuals and the way that they interpret the environment in which they operate. In addition to the issues below, there are contextual issues that will influence the open system that is your workplace. These will have a significant bearing on outcomes. There will be benefit to you in being well informed about the context in which you operate and taking such account of this context as you are able. This will allow you to understand better why outcomes are not as you expected even though you have done everything according to the book.

Models of change management: force-field analysis

Good change management requires sound internal logic. This gives credence to the process and allows you to understand why the process may not have gone as you expected. The Lewin models have passed the test of time and retain considerable currency.

Force-field theory suggests that you use a three-stage process: unfreeze, change and refreeze. Two commonly found errors in change management are to attempt to change without unfreezing, and to fail to refreeze the system and lock up the new situation afterwards, thereby allowing backsliding to the previous state.

Unfreezing

Unfreezing requires the change manager to remove those forces that hold the present practices and processes in place. Many possible forces encourage a workforce to remain with an existing mode of practice. These may include:

1 Administrative processes that ensure the present arrangements persist, i.e. because of the way the infrastructure of the organisation operates it is easiest to continue with existing practices. These processes must be removed in order that they do not encourage inertia.
2 Reward systems will have been established to encourage operation in a particular way. If a new way of operating is to be established, then the old reward systems may be unhelpful and may need to be dismantled. This may include

alteration of formal rewards such as bonus and overtime payments, or informal rewards such as deals regarding leave opportunities.

3 Satisfaction with current processes militates against change. Therefore, it is necessary to establish an agreement that current working is not delivering the best possible results for patients and clients in order to enable the workforce to contemplate changing.

4 Loyalties to groups other than the employer may result in resistance to change if those groups are to be disrupted by the change. This is countered by asking employees to consider that they are a part of another group alongside the existing one. It can be achieved in most cases only with patient attention. A number of phases of the various NHS reforms have involved breaking down tribal loyalties to professions and encouraging new loyalties to client-related groups. This process has operated over a long time frame with some success, allowing professional clinicians to consider themselves part of a group serving for example people with learning disabilities as much as a group of people who are speech and language therapists.

Many other factors may be implicated in freezing the current situation and thereby preventing change. It is your responsibility as a change agent or as a professional involved in a changing service to identify and unfreeze these forces.

The force-field analysis shown in Figure 6.1 may be useful in identifying and describing some of these pressures. You can use the force-field analysis to show the direction and strength of all of the forces freezing the paradigm. These can then be examined explicitly and removed, or undermined, wherever possible. The diagram also shows the forces supporting the change, such as each of the benefits anticipated for patients or clients.

You will achieve change when the forces for change outweigh those for stasis from the perspective of all employees. However, it is a mistake to force change by simply building the change forces so that they overwhelm the forces for stasis. In such a model, as you will see, the forces may become massive and the organisation can become very volatile with unsatisfactory results for employees. Reducing the forces for stasis will allow change to be effected with only small change-driving forces. This change will be more harmonious.

The change equation, $D + V + S > R$, will also allow you to balance the positive and negative forces and decide when you are in a position to effect change. When the positive forces D, V and S in the change equation exceed the resistive forces R then change is to be expected. However, reducing resistance will create a better change than simply escalating the forces for change.

Changing

Once freedom to change has been achieved through careful unfreezing of the existing paradigm, you can bring about change. This requires a sequential plan that is well understood by all stakeholders. A sound and robust plan can be developed by a process of divergent and convergent thinking involving stakeholders. The divergent phase of the plan might involve exercises such as brainstorming in which all possible angles and opportunities are expressed. A brainstorm may be conducted by inviting all participants to offer ideas, which are recorded on an open display such as on a flip chart. Participants should not judge the comments of peers, since it is often the quixotic suggestions that can point to the most creative developments. However, colleagues should be encouraged to build upon one another's comments and in this way help creative plans to emerge.

If, for example, there is a need to change arrangements for notifying a plethora of community colleagues about frequent changes to responsibilities in the department, a quixotic suggestion might be, 'We could always try sky-writing.' Nobody expects that to happen, but the build might be, 'Of course we couldn't do that, but we could post it on a secure intranet site, and put the address on all referral forms.'

Thus, a creative but impractical suggestion has led to a creative and very practical solution. This ability to build on the suggestions of colleagues, rather than seeking to solve all problems individually, can be a mark of an effective team.

The plan

The change plan must cover all aspects of the change in order to proceed smoothly and not to involve frequent redirecting, thereby losing the confidence of the participants. Aspects to consider include the following.

Mission statement
A reminder should be given of the purpose of the organisation, showing how the proposed change will advance that mission.

Strategic direction
It should be made clear how this change will advance the agreed strategic direction of the organisation. This will reassure those concerned that the change is not a whim of the manager, but a logical move in the already agreed direction.

Summary of business
The plan should show what is achieved now with current systems, and what will be done after the change, demonstrating clear benefit.

Market analysis
Where appropriate, the plan should show the evidence for a belief that the customers, purchasers, clients, patients, etc. want these changes.

Assumptions and contingencies
The plan will involve assumptions. If these are proven wrong by developments, then you do not want the workforce to see this as a mistake. If assumptions and contingencies are made explicit at the planning stage, then when they are enacted as a result of environmental changes, it will be seen as good planning, rather than correcting an error.

Details of the changes planned
Each move must be described in careful detail. If it is possible to delegate these choices, then the objectives and outcomes required might be detailed and the subordinate department allowed to devise careful plans that will achieve these targets.

The plan should be checked and challenged through wide consultation before publication in order that it is seen as robust. Responsiveness to comment at the design stage will be perceived as flexibility, but alterations after the launch will appear as incompetence.

Financial implications
How changes will alter the financial position must be made explicit, and where any new resources will be accessed must be agreed before publication of a plan. New resources must include short-term resources to drive the change as well as new resources to run the organisation in its future state.

Human resource plan
The plan must consider and explain negotiation, retraining, redeployment and recruitment of workers. Each of these actions will have different lead times and the plan should show when they are to be initiated so that the necessary workforce comes on line at exactly the time for the service needs. A hold-up in a plan, while staff are recruited, although common, will demonstrate incompetent planning.

Plant and equipment
The plan will show any changes needed to equipment and buildings. These developments must be initiated so that they are delivered at just the right time for service needs. This is simply a matter of advance planning, and reduces the resistance from employees based upon absence of needed resources.

Critical path analysis and plan
In order to visualise and communicate a plan a critical path analysis (CPA) might be drawn up, showing the relationships between the various components of the plan and indicating when each task should be initiated. The critical path is the sequence of activities dependent upon one another that decide the length of time needed for the change. Items on this path must occur exactly to schedule or the change will be delayed. Other activities will have some allowance for slippage. The CPA in Figure 6.4 shows when each activity is to occur. Working backward from

Jan	Feb	Mar	April	May	June	July	Aug	Sept	Oct	Nov	Dec
						Recruit					
Consult	Audit plant		Devise Systems								Train
							Install Equipment				

Figure 6.4 A critical path analysis

project completion in December and allowing the known lead time for each component will enable you to calculate start times for each aspect of the change.

Refreezing

Once the new paradigm has been established, action must be taken to lock it into place, and thereby prevent backsliding to the old systems. Refreezing requires consideration of a number of issues. These might include the following.

Administrative procedures

You may need to alter reporting arrangements, referral arrangements, etc. if you are to prevent employees, colleagues and patients/clients reverting to the old arrangements because they are accessing their old administrative contacts.

Rewards systems

Rewards such as grading structures may have been put into place to support the old paradigm. If salary depends upon how many subordinate staff you had, then moving to a system of collegiate working will disadvantage you and you will be at risk of trying to rebuild your empire. The grading structure will need revision to reward the new collegiate working.

Informal networks

If employees choose exclusively to interact socially with a former team, then the new team will not adequately gel. You may benefit from organising social events, such as informal sport meetings, barbecues, treasure hunts, etc. in which new colleagues may form loyalties.

Make explicit the benefits enjoyed by all stakeholders. A newsletter might regularly focus on the benefits of the new paradigm, thereby creating an ownership of the new arrangements.

Tactical endeavours to enable change

When applying a change process as described above, a number of broad conditions will help. The following considerations have been shown to help and may play an essential part in your planing.

Communication and feedback

The quality of communication within your service and between services needs to be even more effective during a period of change than at other times. Change plans make the grapevine for communication become more than usually active and convincing. Incomplete information promulgated by informal routes will create anxiety about the changes, leading to unnecessary stress and resistance. The counter to the grapevine is good accurate and timely communication. This must be readily available, multi-channel and comprehensively understood. Devices to consider include:

Team briefing

Here you create a formal updating message, containing accurate and simple packages that are passed from the top to the bottom of the organisation, thereby dispelling the most alarming of the rumours that abound. Team briefing should be short and swift. Information is cascaded through agreed channels very rapidly. The briefing exercise involves ensuring that everyone knows and understands the message, but it must not become a discussion forum, because that will make the exercise too time consuming to be effective, and the message may become distorted.

Newsletter

A special edition of an existing newsletter might be introduced to carry change information, or it might be necessary to create one for the purpose. A newsletter has the advantage of being the result of careful thought and attention to wording and it has permanence. If departments are encouraged to keep a file copy, then individuals can refer back as appropriate and can take some responsibility for dispelling incorrect information that is the subject of rumour.

Bulletin boards

Where a new project is established, it may be helpful to establish a shortlived notice board through which information can be disseminated. For multisite organisations, several will be needed. The intranet for your organisation may be able to offer a virtual bulletin board for public display of information. You may even want to allow the board to carry staff questions as well as management answers. Such a process allows the entire workforce to see the dialogue that surrounds the change and therefore better understand the decisions that emerge. This is particularly effective in the case of virtual bulletin boards on the intranet. It is important, if you develop this system, that it is frequently serviced and questions do not go long unanswered.

Suggestion schemes

Offering your staff the opportunity to make suggestions and contribute to the exercise will make the process seem far less remote. You may be concerned about the less constructive contributions that such schemes attract. However, these are easy to bin and should not prevent your harnessing the goodwill that exists. It is important to attract a high response rate, perhaps by offering a prize, and to find suggestions to adopt publicly, demonstrating the value of the communication exercise.

Roadshows

As a leader in change, you need to get among the people affected. This involves travelling to the involved sites, if more than one is involved, and setting aside time to explain the plan and hear reactions. You might also address the various constituencies involved. For instance, domestic staff may be unwilling to raise concerns at meetings where medical consultants lead the questions. They might be more forthcoming at meetings dedicated to ancillary employees. This communication exercise enables the workforce to feel valued and involved and may supply you with useful information and insights. Be willing to hear trivial as well as substantial comments because both can explain resistance to change. In a smaller department, this might involve no more than time in a staff meeting and in larger settings may become a vast semi-public meeting. Whatever the scale, the rule is that you must make yourself visibly available to explain and listen. You must be seen to be putting yourself out for staff benefit, and must couch your communications in terms relevant to the audience. You must also talk about benefits that are applicable to the staff group, not simply the organisation.

Management by wandering about (MBWA)

It will be helpful if you can make informal time to talk and listen to affected staff. You might also encourage managers from higher in the organisation to accompany you on some tours. This partnership will show the workforce that they are respected and valued in the process, because managers at all levels take the trouble to visit. Wandering about with senior managers will reassure staff that you have access to more influential management tiers and that they hear you. This will encourage your staff to confide in you, because you are seen to be able to act on their behalf.

Ownership

For enthusiastic cooperation with change plans, employees need to know that they have been consulted about plans and have played a part in their development. Thus, they are implementing plans that they constructed. Achieving ownership will require involvement of staff at all stages of the process. As soon as change is anticipated, it may be appropriate to commence a dialogue, so that staff are able to work through the issues and accept the need for change, before the planning stage is reached (unfreezing).

Once the need for change is accepted, the nature of the objectives can be discussed. Once the objectives are agreed, the means by which they can be achieved can be discussed. Clearly, these stages are sequential. It is a common error to be trying to gain acceptance for one stage when the previous stage has not been agreed.

If you have authority to design your own solutions, you can work with interested staff to produce a solution. This change will be very easy to implement, because the workforce owns it. If you write your own solution and then try to sell it to the workforce, you can expect resistance, even if the solution is the one that the staff would have chosen had they been given the chance. If you are going to be required to implement a solution from another tier of the organisation, over which you have little influence, then the consultation process should be conducted as a fact-finding exercise, with small groups. Thus, if an idea is offered that, although sensible, is not in line with orders then you must not be in the position of failing to honour what staff may perceive as an agreement.

Wherever possible, be seen to make or modify plans in line with staff suggestions and thereby to maximise the impression that it is their solutions that are being implemented. Do this at the planning stage if possible. To do it at the implementation stage might appear indecisive.

Education

Education gives a perspective that cannot easily be achieved at the workplace. You are advised to increase the opportunities for key staff and yourself to become involved in short or longer courses. This may appear to be diverting a resource when there is extra work to be done, but achieves valuable benefits in terms of improved perspective and insight, as well as ensuring that individuals feel valued. Elevated loyalty can improve the prospects of success, and justify the investment.

Leadership and trust

You will need to show strong leadership in a time of change. Your staff are to follow you into a situation that is unknown. Therefore you must be informed, confident and decisive in your actions. You will consult throughout the process, but this is out of courtesy and respect for their insights, and must not appear as indecision. Trust is achieved by open, comprehensive and candid communication. Some messages will be carefully planned in order to demonstrate decisiveness, and surety, but it is important that information is consistent and honest. Where a change in direction occurs, this should be admitted and explained, rather that shrouded in vagueness. Information that is incomplete, dishonest or inconsistent will lose trust in you and develop a local grapevine that will convey harmful ideas.

Attention to the impact of change on individuals

Very few people are truly altruistic. They cannot easily accept a change that is for the greater good when it causes them considerable personal disadvantage. You will effect change more easily if you can recognise simple disbenefits affecting individuals and counter them. This may be alteration of working relationships to protect successful teams, or funding additional home-to-work transport. However, there may be far more difficult issues to resolve, such as redundancies. How these are handled will affect the remaining workforce as much as the redundant individual. All of the assistance described in Chapter 3 should be offered and the individual helped in every imaginable way.

Some disadvantages affecting individuals may not be immediately evident. Fears and inconveniences must be brought to the surface in order for you to help. Therefore you will need to create an environment where individuals can raise concerns, however trivial or foolish they may appear. If you fail to realise that a change is depriving a staff member of some small but cherished benefit, then you may encounter incomprehensible resistance which could have been avoided by better insight.

The early experience of benefit

Reward those who contribute to the change. Also, contrive to ensure that the early stages of the change bring benefit to all staff. Thus, they may gain enthusiasm for the process and help it to continue. Generally, the higher you rise in an organisation, the longer will be your time focus. Therefore, although you may be happy to know that there will be advantages in two years, staff lower in the organisation might need far swifter evidence of benefit.

There may be benefit that is missed by some staff. The newsletter or staff meetings should be used to ensure that all benefits receive maximum publicity. For instance, patients might be receiving better services because of the early stages of a change, but this may not be obvious to those staff without patient contact. Ensure that this becomes well known and discussed, while, of course, respecting the need for confidentiality.

Subsidiarity, and levels of interference: breadth and depth of intervention

Devolve responsibility for designing and implementing change to as low in the organisation as possible. This will minimise resistance and respects the autonomy of staff members. A manager taking this approach will gain respect from staff and build a healthy organisation. It is essential that the objectives are agreed and that the plans drawn up will be acceptable to the wider organisation. However, there are frequently a number of ways to achieve one objective and if individuals can chose their own solutions they will implement them with greater enthusiasm and strive to ensure that they work well.

Conclusion to tactical endeavours to enable change

Health and social care provision is in a state of permanent change. It may be tempting to look forward to the time when it all settles down; however, there is no reason to believe that it will and, therefore, good clinicians must perform in a constantly changing environment. Additionally, clinicians and managers must strive to make change as smooth, positive and patient/client friendly as possible. That requires sound knowledge of the issues above, in order to contribute to an environment delivering the necessary although not sufficient conditions for smooth transition. This is the personal responsibility of the change manager, all other managers in the system and all professionals operating in that arena.

REFERENCES

Beckhard, R. and Harris, R. (1987) *Organisational Transition*. Addison Wesley, London.

Benjamin, G. and Mobey, C. (1990) A case of organisational transformation. *Management and Educational Journal*, 30 (1), 34–38.

Buchanan, D. (1997) The limitations and opportunities of business process reengineering in a politicised organisational climate. *Journal of Human Relations*, 50 (1), 52–72.

Burnes, B. (1996) *Managing Change*. Pitman, London.

Burnes, B. and James, H. (1995) Culture, cognitive dissonance and the management of change. *International journal of operations and production management*, 15(8) 334.

Crozier, M. (1976) *The Bureaucratic Phenomenon*. Tavistock, London.

Dekker, W. (1987) *Willingness to Change*. DOP, The Hague.

DoH (1947) *NHS Act*, HMSO, London.

DoH (1949) *NHS (Amendments) Act*, HMSO, London.

DoH (1951) *NHS Act*, HMSO, London.

DoH (1952) *NHS Act*, HMSO, London.

DoH (1973) *NHS Reorganisation Act*, HMSO, London.

DoH (1982) *NHS Reorganisation Act*, HMSO, London.

DoH (1989a) *Working for Patients*, HMSO, London.

DoH (1990) *NHS and Community Care Act*, HMSO, London.

Easterby-Smith, M., Thorpe, R. and Lowe, A. (1991) *Management Research*. Sage, London.

Ezra, D. and Oates, D. (1989) *Advice from the Top*. David & Charles, London.

Festinger, L. (1957) *The Theory of Cognitive Dissonance*. Stanford University Press, Stanford, CA.

Friedlander, C. (1976) OD reaches adolescence. *Journal of Applied Behavioural Science*, **12**(1), 241–244.

Goodstein, L.D. and Burke, W.W. (1991) Creating successful organisational change. *Organisational Dynamics*, Spring, 151–164.

Ham, C. (1991) *The New National Health Service: Organisation and Management*. Radcliffe Medical Press, Oxford.

Handy, C. (1995) *The Age of Unreason*. Business Books, London.

Harrison, R. (1970) Choosing the depth of organisational intervention. *Journal of Applied Behavioural Science*, **6**(2), 118–201.

Hogan, K. (1997) Change in the NHS. In: *Management for Nurses and Health Care Professionals* (ed. Clark, J. and Copcutt, L.). Churchill, London.

Iles, P. and Auluck, R. (1990) Team building, interagency team development and social work. *British Journal of Social Work*, **20**(2), 151–164.

Johnson, G. (1993) In: *Managing Change* (ed. Mabey, C. and Mayon-White, B.). Oxford University Press, London.

Jones, E.E. (1990) *Interpersonal perception*, Freeman, New York.

Lewin, K. (1951) *Field Theory in Social Science*. Harper & Row, New York.

Lippitt, G., Langseth, P. and Mossop, J. (1985) *Implementing Organisational Change*. Jossey-Bass, London.

Mabey, C. and Mayon-White, B. (eds) (1993) *Managing Change*, Oxford University Press, London.

March, J.G. and Simon, H.A. (1958) *Organisations*. Wiley, New York.

Marris, P. (1993) The management of change. In: *Managing Change* (ed. Mabey, C. and Mayon-White, B.). Oxford University Press, London.

Nadler, D. (1993) In: *Managing Change* (ed. Mabey, C. and Mayon-White, B.). Oxford University Press, London.

Nadler, D. and Tushman, L. (1979) Feedback and organisation development using data based methods. *Journal of Human Relations*, **50**(1), 52–72.

Pavlov, I.P. (1927) *Conditioned Reflexes*. Oxford University Press, London.

Peters, T. (1978) Symbols, patterns and settings: an optimistic case for getting things done. *Organisational Dynamics*, **3**, 23.

Peters, T. (1994) *Crazy Times*, Harper and Row, New York.

Peters, T. (1989) *Thriving on Chaos*, Harper and Row, New York.

Peters, T.J. (1985) *A passion for excellence: the leadership difference*, Collins, London.

Pettigrew, A.M. (1985) *The Awakening Giant: Continuity and Change in ICI*. Blackwell, Oxford.

Pettigrew, A.M. (1987) Context and action in the transformation of the firm. *Journal of*

Management Studies, **24**, 649–670.

Pettigrew, A.M. (1989) Longitudinal methods to study change. In Mansfield, R. (ed.) *Frontiers of Management*, Routledge, London.

Pettigrew, A.M. (1993a) In: Tilly, I. *Managing the Internal Market* (ed. Tilly, I.). Chapman & Hall, London.

Pettigrew, A.M. (1993b) In: *Perspectives on Strategic Change* (ed. Luca, Z., Zambon, S. and Pettigrew, A.M.). Kluwer Academic Press, London.

Pettigrew, A.M., Ferlie, E. and McKee, L. (1992) The leadership role of the new health authorities. *Public Money and Management*, April, 39–43.

Plant, R. (1987) *Managing Change and Making It Stick*. Fontana, London.

Price, C. and Murphy, M. (1987) Organisational development in British Telecom. *Training and Development*, July, 45–48.

Quin, J. B. (1980) *Strategies for Change*. Irwin, Homewood, IL.

Schwenk, C.R. (1988) The cognitive perspective on strategic decision making. *Journal of Management Studies*, **25**(1), 41–52.

Skinner, G.E. (1974) *About Behaviourism*. Cape, London.

Smith, M., Beck, J., Cooper, C.L., Cox, C. Ottoway, D. and Talbot, R. (1982) *Introducing Organisational Behaviour*. Macmillan, London.

Spurgeon, P. and Barwell, F. (1991) *Implementing Change in the NHS*. Chapman & Hall, London.

Upton, T. and Brookes, B. (1995) *Managing Change in the NHS*. Kogan Page, London.

Vaill, P. (1982) The purposing of high performing systems. *Organisational Dynamics*, **2**(2), 23–39.

Van de Ven, A.H. (1980) Problem solving, planning and innovation. *Human Relations Journal*, November, 10–11.

Vrakking, W. (1997) The implementation game. *Journal of Organisational Change Management*, **8**(3), 31–46.

Walton, M. (1997) *Management and Managing: Leadership in the NHS*. Stanley Thornes, London.

White, R. and Jacques, R. (1995) Operationalising the post modernity construct for efficient organisational change management. *Journal of Change Management*, **8**(2), 45–71.

FURTHER READING

Wilson, T.A. (1994) *A Manual for Change*. Pitman, Aldershot.

7 MARKETING

INTRODUCTION

Marketing may be defined as succeeding in business by providing goods and services that best satisfy the demands of customers. This involves the four components of the marketing mix – see Figure 7.1.

The Marketing Mix (Product, Place, Price, Promotion)

1) identifying from and with future customers the goods/service that will best satisfy them;

2) creating, packaging and delivering these services/goods to the best location for the customers;

3) ensuring the best price;

4) advertising the fact that they are available and describing their qualities; and then

1) return to customer to discuss product enhancements, etc.

Figure 7.1 The marketing mix

The marketing mix is an iterative exercise. A marketer does not go through the process once and then consider the task complete. Rather he or she cycles around the loop throughout the product's or service's life cycle. All stages are under constant consideration, and yet there is a sequence in which one aspect of the mix clearly informs the next, in a continuous loop.

The marketing function has an important place in the health and social care industries in achieving all of the four targets of the marketing mix; without it the organisation would exist in isolation from an essential understanding of consumer aspirations. The critical role in marketing health care is performed by the clinician, who has access to consumers and is in a position to make decisions for them far beyond anything achievable by managers. This is discussed at length in this chapter.

Customers and consumers

The notions of 'customers' and 'consumers' are important in marketing. It may appear that these are foreign notions in health and social care, where 'patients' and 'clients' are the normal terms. However, it is important to distinguish between customer (who pays for the service) and consumer (who receives the service), and use this framework to better conceptualise and understand how to help patients/

clients. To be successful in the marketplace, of course, the organisation must please both customer and consumer simultaneously. If there is a conflict between the aspirations of these two parties, then it may be the responsibility of the service provider to act as intermediary and develop a service to the satisfaction of both. If only one party is satisfied, then the product/service will not succeed. Dog food will not sell unless the customer (dog owner) thinks it is good value and quality. However, sales will not continue for long if the consumer (dog – hopefully!) is unwilling to eat it. Children's shoes must satisfy the parent and the child. Thus, we see advertisements for a shoe in hard-wearing leather which comes in six width fittings and has a star on the sole that will grant wishes. Similarly, if the GP did not think out-patient speech and language therapy locally is good value, he or she would not commission it, but if it is purchased as being excellent value but patients refuse to attend because it is in the wrong location, then the GP will not purchase it again. Marketing health care must satisfy the demand of purchasing Health Authorities / Primary Care Groups, referrers and patients/clients/carers.

When customers and consumers choose a product, they do so on their perceptions of the information and services available. Therefore it is not sufficient to have an excellent service. That will not assure custom. The service must be perceived to be excellent. That requires marketing effort by all involved. Additionally, benefits appreciated by one customer may not be appreciated by another. The best advice is that the more benefits there are the more customers and consumers will perceive the service to be desirable.

The history of getting goods on to the market

The marketing of goods and services may be seen as having passed through a number of distinct phases. It is helpful to see former stages as developmentally transcended rather than simply discarded. Early developmental stages have been subsumed into new stages, and associated behaviours or values remain active, but enhanced by developments. The way in which goods have been marketed in the past gives insight into current practice. It is helpful, therefore, to know the historical progression in understanding current practice.

The product-orientated approach

Build a better mousetrap and the world will beat a path to your door.

In the 18th century and 19th century, great emphasis was placed upon engineering innovation, with a creative elite developing better products and an intelligent consumer, also from an elite minority, naturally buying that product in preference to an inferior product from another source.

The production-orientated approach

As the 19th century progressed, industrialisation created a far wider consumer class; then in the 20th century the notion of mass production emerged, most famously, but not exclusively, from Henry Ford. This approach sought to minimise production costs by efficient production and thereby to make goods available to a far deeper consumer constituency. Production became possible by a less skilled workforce and consumption became possible for a far less elite consumer group. Mass production by production-line organisation did not replace the drive for ever better products, but introduced a greater cost awareness and accepted a degree of trade-off between the two considerations of excellence and price. In actuality, mass production has resulted in increased quality and reduced prices in many manufacturing areas.

This period of manufacturing history is often retrospectively described as the Fordist era. That era has been associated with 'modernist' thinking, and provides a focus for discussion of a 'postmodernist' approach to industrial and economic thinking.

The sales-orientated approach
With the advent of high quality mass communications accessible to all of the franchised population, the era of sales-focused marketing emerged in the mid 20th century. The power of communications to persuade the consumer that a product was the best one at the best price became more important than the drive to achieve the reality of both or either. This era emerged as a result of accessible communications on paper and TV, but was supplemented by a significant increase in face-to-face sales staff, both in retail outlets and on the doorstep.

The marketing approach
As a result of progressively more sophisticated consumer behaviour the industry focus has moved from the importance and ascendance of the supplier to that of the consumer. It remains essential to have the best product at the best price and to advertise that fact to potential consumers, but it has became necessary to see those definitions from the perspective of the consumer. The discipline of market research has gained ascendance in this period. The easiest way to make consumers want a product is to develop the product that consumers have said they wanted in the first place. Many models emerged to define products from a progressively wider perspective always viewed from the consumer's standpoint. The marketing mix, introduced above, is described below.

The holistic (green) and postmodern approach
In the 1980s two new perspectives began to emerge.

Firstly, consumers started to make demands about the product which went beyond its direct function. They began to view products holistically. Washing powder had not just to be effective and inexpensive, but also had to perform without causing harm to the environment. Eggs had to be free range in the interest of chickens. This gained momentum in the 1990s with lead-free petrol, recycled paper, and timber from sustainable forests.

Secondly, there has been a rejection of the consequences of mass production. The post-Fordist era has consumers wanting not to keep up with the Joneses but to differentiate themselves from the Joneses. Thus a large proportion of motor car sales involve sales of mass-produced models disguised as individual ones by offering an unusual combination of extras and calling them 'limited editions' or 'specials'.

All of the above phases are evident in current marketing practice and in the health and social care industry, regulated in part by market forces, they can be clearly seen at work. The clinician and service manager have a duty to use marketing practice to ensure that patients and clients enjoy the very best service affordable. This chapter sets out to equip the reader with the insights and abilities necessary to perform to an optimum level.

THE THEORETICAL FRAMEWORK

Strategic and operational marketing

Marketing practice is often divided into strategic and operational marketing. Strategic marketing involves making long-term plans for the organisation based upon macro analysis of the marketplace and the position of the organisation therein. Operational marketing involves looking in detail at individual goods or services and ensuring that they gain the best possible market share. It may be argued that these functions are stages of the same process and that to divide them is artificial. To see the items as separate is untenable and to see them as linear is misleading. Although strategy informs operational plans, it is also the case that operational marketing collects information that is necessary for strategic analysis to take place. It is helpful to see the relationship as an iterative process in which strategy and operations are continually informing each other. Although this is a persuasive argument, it is convenient to conceptualise the functions separately for explanatory purposes, provided that the practitioner recognises the interdependence that exists.

Strategic marketing: analysis and planning

Marketing planning involves a number of stages:

1 market audit
2 market analysis
3 making assumptions
4 generating strategy
5 implementation plan

This planning process is conducted in close association with business planning. See Chapter 4.

Market audit

Market analysis and planning are intertwined practices. The first stage in devising a market plan is to conduct an audit of the organisation and the marketplace. This involves collecting information external and internal to the organisation. External information includes information about:

- growth, reduction or redirection of the market;
- influences on and interplay between consumers and customers;
- the legal, economic and sociological environment;
- competitors;
- workforce supply;
- other supplies, such as buildings equipment and materials;
- technological advances.

Each of the analysis areas is capable of generating threats and opportunities for consideration.

Internal information includes:

- reputation of the organisation in each product/service area;
- market share;
- qualities of human resources;
- premises;
- suppliers;
- synergies between products and potential products.

Each of these areas is capable of producing strengths and weaknesses for consideration.

An audit may be carried out simply, by:

1 a brainstorm of key individuals in the organisation;
2 by including customers and other stakeholders in a brainstorming exercise; or
3 by having a formal audit conducted by internal or external consultants (this latter option would take the form of a research exercise and deliver very objective data).

Commonly, in the NHS and Social Services, data are collected by methods 1 or 2. This is inexpensive and has the advantage of easily achieving ownership among essential managers. However, it can result in a major strategic planning exercise being based upon unproven information. It might be the case that, as appears in HM Armed Forces Regulations, 'Time spent on reconnaissance is seldom if ever wasted.'

Market analysis

A number of analytical devices exist that help to order the data collected in an audit. The simplest and most commonly seen in public sector industries is the 'strength, weakness, opportunity and threat' (SWOT) analysis, which sets out to order what is known for participant consideration. At worst, this is published in business plans with no obvious consequences, but at best it becomes a focus for a divergent-thinking exercise and changes the whole direction of the organisation. More complex analytical devices are available for use in devising a market plan and these can reward the planner with strategic direction improvements based upon sound scientific analysis.

Strategy generation

Examination of the audit analysis will show up areas for development of strategic directions. These strategic directions are intentionally broad-brush exercises stating the broad changes to activity that are to be achieved over a long period of time. For example, an NHS Trust may plan to reduce its investment in services to people with accidental injury and increase its investment in services to older people in response to its analysis of local industry decline and demographic trends. This strategic direction would be reflected in operational decisions in business and marketing plans. This route would incrementally implement the strategy. The reduction in accidents is an assumption, not a known event, and would need to be closely monitored.

Assumptions

In any plan, there will be areas where a factor is not known. Here the plan will be based upon assumptions. These assumptions are the best predictions that can be made, but must be distinguished from known fact. Above, an assumption was made about accident reduction. This assumption must be made explicit and a contingency plan created for implementation if the assumption proves false, i.e. if accidents continue to happen at the previous rate or above, how will the service move to ensure that services can be made available?

CASE STUDY 7.1   ASSUMPTION AND CONTINGENCY PLAN

It was assumed in a marketing plan that legislation for individual extra-contractual referrals (ECRs) would continue, and marketing effort was focused on making relationships with general practitioners (GPs) accordingly. This appeared as an assumption on the marketing plan. When the assumption was disproved and the White Paper *The New NHS* (DoH, 1998) abolished ECRs, the NHS Trust was immediately able to spot the change and implement the contingency plans associated with that assumption.

Implementation plan

Strategy is not directly implemented. One cannot simply drive to Scotland. Someone based in the southwest of England first drives to the nearest motorway, then journeys along a link motorway to access the M5, then travels north on to the M6, then joins the ... etc. Implementation is incremental through operational marketing and business planning practice, i.e. the service identifies short-term actions that will advance the drive towards the strategic objective. It is important that a strategy has milestones and timescales and that progress is closely monitored. Therefore the plan will show an overall aim and a number of specific, measurable, achievable, relevant and time-bound (SMART) objectives.

Operational marketing: the marketing mix

Developing a service or product in line with stated strategy might be addressed by application of the marketing mix. This involves attention to four main areas:

1 the product, along with any package building considerations
2 the placing of the service, in space and time
3 the price, seen in financial and other terms
4 the promotion of the service

Product

The product/service must be designed to best satisfy the demands of the customer and the consumer. This service design is done through market research in which need is discussed, a new product is proposed and its acceptability is thoroughly evaluated. This same approach is used to continually improve existing products. This should result in a constantly improving product/service base. If the organisation is to remain in operation in a dynamic environment its product/service offer must be constantly under review and constantly improved in line with customer and consumer aspirations.

Views about existing services, and services that customers and consumers yearn for, can be collected by a range of devices. These include: suggestion boxes, end-of-intervention questionnaires, focus group discussions, interviews, outcome evaluations, etc. The information collected should be through a variety of media: verbal and paper, formally and informally collected (e.g. questionnaires and over coffee when visiting a GP surgery), group or individual. Time must be set aside to make the best use of this information rather than, as is too common, collecting masses of data and making reports but never really acting upon what is learned.

Price

The price to be paid by the customer and the consumer needs to be kept to a minimum in health and social care services. In strict marketing parlance, price is 'whatever the market will bear', and this cannot be ignored. If the price of a service exceeds that of another provider because of inefficiency or even excessive quality, then customers and consumers will prefer the other service, and the other provider will take over the market. Customer loyalty and quality differentiation may in part mitigate this, but the problem of excessive price cannot be ignored for long. Marketing theory also says that the provider may price the service as high as the market will allow. This is the incentive that the marketplace offers to induce suppliers to enter sparsely served markets. However, in health and social care there is an ethical imperative not to charge more than necessary for a service, since to do so would take unnecessary resources out of the service, thus diminishing the service as a whole. This is reinforced by DoH instruction that price = cost (DoH, 1990). The financial price to customers must be as low as possible and certainly no higher than that of the competition.

The price to the consumer should also be considered. The claim that health care is free at the point of delivery is misleading, and an excessive price charged to the patient/client is unethical. If the consumer is forced to pay a price that he or she considers unacceptable, then he or she will cease to use the service and the contract will decline. This imperative to minimise the price to the consumer in a paternalistic system has only recently been a matter for serious consideration.

The patient may not pay full fees for health services but there are many other costs to him or her. Among many, these include:

- Financial costs in the form of lost earnings, paying for commercial child care, travelling/parking costs, co-payments, etc.
- Pain and discomfort as a result of assessment and treatment of illness. Who would not be willing to travel to access pain-free dental care? Does this not also apply to physiotherapy and osteopathy?
- Intrusion into private areas.
- Inconvenience and distress in the form of the stigma associated with some illnesses, long waits, difficult journeys, poor circumstances, poor courtesy, etc.
- Difficulties in accessing services, e.g. a mother of twins pays a high price for care if it requires her to push a double buggy for two miles to access treatment.

The service that minimises these costs to the patient maximises service uptake and shows greatest ethical respect for the individual.

Place
Where a service is placed will have a significant impact on demand from customers and consumers. This has already been reflected in part in 'Price', above. The mother of two babies cannot easily get to a hospital that is three bus connections away, or to a clinic where there is no public transport service. Where clinics are placed will therefore effect uptake.

The place a service is located can convey prestige. A service placed in a District General Hospital can assume an air of technical sophistication that is not possible when placed in a Health Centre. This may affect both the patient and his or her referring GP. There is always a queue of complementary practitioners keen to rent a room in a Health Centre, because of the implied approval conferred. Conversely, a service placed in a village hall can achieve an air of informality and approachability, and this might increase referral and uptake of service.

It is also important to consider when a service is placed in terms of time. An evening clinic will more easily attract employed and self-employed patients, and their dependants. A clinic timed to coincide with the referrer's clinic will be likely to attract more referrals.

CASE STUDY 7.2   PLACING IN TIME

Occupational therapists and physiotherapists were vying for orthopaedic referrals following a Tuesday afternoon hand trauma clinic. The physiotherapists offered an excellent service on Monday afternoons, and the occupational therapists offered an equally good service on Tuesday afternoons. The consultant was faced with a choice of two good services. 'I can get you seen by a physio next Monday, if you will come back then, or I could send you to the OT, who will see you later this afternoon and get your programme started'. Which service won the lion's share of the referrals?

Promotion

Once a service has been correctly defined, priced and placed in time and space, then it is necessary to let potential customers and consumers know that it is available and make sure that they realise how good it is. Thus, relevant individuals must be notified about the service. This notification must be adequately assertive to ensure that the audience comes to recognise the qualities offered. The promotion process is often also a good medium for collecting information about desired further improvements to the service. It should, therefore, be a two-way process. There is only a very limited place in health and social care for formal advertisement through leaflets and brochures, etc. The bulk of the work needs to be done through more fortuitous routes. This involves widespread involvement of clinical staff.

Clinicians meet referring consultants and GPs at case conferences etc., and this is a good opportunity to ensure that they understand what is being offered, and to comment on what they would like to see. Clinicians spend extended time with patients and clients, during which time they can ensure that patients understand the service provided and express any needs for changes.

In promoting a service, the marketer is seeking to move the consumer and/or customer through five stages leading from ignorance to demand. It is important to know where the customer is in this process because it is unlikely that desire will be achieved if the customer does not yet even know of the existence of a service. In good marketing the customer moves from ignorance, to awareness and interest, to desire, to demand and ultimately to satisfaction.

Awareness

It is frequently necessary to begin by making the potential consumer or customer aware that a service exists. For nursing or social work, this is not necessary because everybody knows about them, but for occupational therapy it may be essential.

Interest

Alongside awareness, it is necessary to induce interest. Until these have been achieved, there is no benefit in striving to achieve service demand.

Desire

When a potential customer is aware of a service and interested, it becomes necessary to move them to a position of desiring the service. This is necessary for all health care professions, and is achieved by giving them information about the benefits available to them if they use the service.

Demand

A desiring customer will only demand a service when he or she is willing to pay the price. This is addressed by discussing and minimising the price, in all of its aspects, and demonstrating value in relation to the benefits.

Purchase

A customer making a demand needs to be facilitated to a 'purchase'. Many 'sales' are lost because the necessary assistance is not forthcoming to make the purchase at the appropriate moment. Just as in a shop we may walk out because there is no assistant available, so a referring clinician may give up if the referral process is made too difficult, or the patient may not ask for a service if it is too difficult to access.

Satisfaction

After purchase, the customer and consumer should be aided through good after-care to achieve satisfaction in order for repeat and recommendation business to follow. This involves the way in which clinicians make reports to referrers and follow up patients, etc.

It is easy to see clinicians and service managers operating in all of these areas. However, this is often random in nature. Marketers need to assess exactly where the potential customer is on this progression and focus efforts to move them along.

Market research

Defining the most appropriate service to offer in health and social care, as with all industries, involves asking consumers and customers what they want. In the past, paternalistic professional practice has preferred not to ask patients and clients. Rather they have relied upon their professional expertise to tell them what is needed. However, since the 1990 reforms (the NHS and Community Care Act) there has been a growing willingness to consult, and many service improvements have been achieved as a consequence. Clearly, health care services are not available from a shopping list, and there will be a need to temper demand with professional knowledge. However, good market research will be needed to define the service that funders, referrers and patients/clients want. The closer the provision can be to that ideal, the easier it will be to achieve high satisfaction rates and increasing demands for service provision.

Segmentation and niches

Markets should not be seen as homogeneous. Each customer and consumer group can be segmented, e.g. to see GPs as one group might be inappropriate. A GP in an inner city practice with high social deprivation factors will have a different opinion and be responsive to different messages from a GP in an affluent rural practice. Thus, the opinions collected from one catchment will not be the same as those from another. This must be reflected in the market research approach adopted. It must also be reflected in the package of services offered. If there is one particular segment for whom the organisation has an ideal service, then it may be appropriate to focus energy on that area and aim for a very high share of that market, possibly at the expense of other segments of the market. This is known as niche marketing. Alternatively, a service provider may wish to address all segments of a market, but it must be recognised that different segments of a market may want different types of service and the offer must reflect local conditions.

The theory of household behaviour

It is the case that in some settings parts of a community are disenfranchised with respect to consumer choice. This is evident in a normal household. Consumers such as children are rarely able to exert their preferences over the choice of most household products. In this case marketing effort is aimed at the housewife, assuming that she makes such decisions. This is evident from a short study of TV advertising. The parallels in terms of health care are clear. Many patients abdicate their right to make decisions to their GP, parents, adult children, carers, etc., so marketing in this setting must take account of the this phenomenon. However, to assume abdication can be dangerous as well. Children may be indifferent to choice of soap and towels, but many have a strong view about breakfast cereals. Marketers talk in terms of benefits for the consumer, but these should be as perceived by the decision maker, e.g. parents.

A taxonomy of need

Need and demand are central to health care delivery.

- A need is a deficit affecting the individual requiring a service or product.
- A perceived need is a need that the individual recognises. It may also be that an individual perceives a need that does not objectively exist.
- A demand is a perceived need for which the individual is willing to pay all aspects of the price to receive goods or services.

Health care is generally delivered in response to demand, i.e. the patient/client must perceive that he or she has a need and be willing to pay the price in cash, time, discomfort, etc. Only when these conditions are fulfilled does a demand for service emerge in the form of presentation at a health centre.

The NHS and Community Care Act (1990) confirmed that the services provided should be based upon a priority of need, and the subsequent growth of evidence-based medicine has been a reflection of this requirement. Therefore for a service to be provided there must be a need, it must be perceived by the patient/client, he or she must be willing to pay the price of treatment and the referrer must be able to confirm that the proposed service will meet a genuine need. Marketing activity can be aimed at alerting needy patients/clients to their needs and giving them enough information to enable them to make a decision about their willingness to pay the price of treatment. This exercise is not simply about drumming up business. If providers do not make every effort to achieve this end, then the result is that the well-informed segments of the population benefit from services and the disadvantaged groups miss out because they do not have enough information to demand services. This results in care going to the segments of the population that least need them.

Value-added chains

The value of a service to a customer or consumer is an aggregate of all that has been done from the beginning to the end of the process. The maximum perceived benefit can be obtained by considering every stage of the process and ensuring that maximum perceived benefit is added at each one. To consider that benefit is perceived only at the treatment phase is misleading. The satisfaction a patient/client or referrer feels is affected by each stage. Careful consideration is needed at each stage. The marketer considers perceived as well as actual benefit. To perform as well as possible is an ethical imperative, but this excellence must also be perceived by influential players if the service is to be appreciated and to continue to be funded. In how people see a service, 'Perception is all there is' (Peters, 1989).

Referrer	Quality of interaction with referrer	Knowledge that the matter is being professionally addressed	Primary problems alleviated	Maximise referrer appreciation	Efficiency and support
	Referral ⟩	**Assessment** ⟩	**Treatment** ⟩	**Report** ⟩	**Discharge**
Client/P't	Quality of client/patient interaction	Instil confidence, show consideration, assure professionalism	Maximise benefit	Maximise appreciation of benefit	Information and support

Figure 7.2 The value added chain

Figure 7.2 shows the potential to add value to the service through every stage of the encounter, not just the treatment. This parallels the shopping experience in which customers choose supermarkets not just for product and price, but also for aisle space, checkout efficiency, layout, etc.

Queuing and queuing theory

A standing waiting list implies that the number of treatments is the same as the number of new referrals. Therefore the queue is a result of some past event, and is diminishing the quality and therefore the appeal of the service unnecessarily. A single initiative to clear waiting lists will increase the quality of all services thereafter. If the referral rate remains the same, then the same productivity will provide a service without delay. However, this will affect demand. If the queue is long, then referrers and patients/clients will not choose to use the service. When the list shortens, referrals will increase. On a hot day, we may wish to buy ice cream from a van. If, however, the queue is very long we may not bother, whereas when it is short we may join it. Thus, the queue is in some part self-regulating. The size of a waiting list may therefore be a useful tool for demand control, if used consciously, but it is far too influential to be allowed to float out of control. Occasionally, as with Morgan and Rolls Royce motor cars, there is a paradoxical effect that the waiting time adds to the value customers perceive for a product. However, to attempt to use such a mechanism in health and social care provision would be a dangerous strategy.

Requirements of a market economy

Under ideal conditions, the marketplace will ensure that all goods and services are available at a price and quality that is fair to supplier and customer. Competition prevents a supplier from charging too much for a product, because a competitor will charge a fairer price and take all of the customers. The price will not fall below an economic price, because there is no incentive for any supplier to operate at an economic loss. Were this to work in ideal conditions, then the consequences for health care would be excellent. However, for a perfect market, a number of requirements exist:

1 There must be perfect information, i.e. all suppliers and customers must have information about each other's products and prices. For this reason honest promotional activity will benefit health care generally.
2 There must be no externalities (desired benefits to parties other than supplier and customer/consumer). The health of one person affects that of another. For this reason, GPs are encouraged to make strenuous efforts to persuade parents to immunise children without waiting for demand from the parent. In addition, the service has the right to detain people with infectious diseases or dangerous mental health disorders regardless of their consent or any belief that detention will directly benefit the detainee. Otherwise, however, there are few externalities associated with health and social care provision.
3 There must be no predatory pricing, i.e. a willingness to sell at a loss for a period and thereby eliminate opposition. Legislation forbids cross-subsidisation, which is the only method by which a NHS Trust may sell a service at less than cost (the NHS and Community Care Act, 1990). However, the apportionment of overhead costs will effect the price of some prized services, and therefore providers may seek to subtly cross-subsidise services. Cross-subsidisation in the private sector is more common and more difficult to regulate.
4 There must be no cartels or monopolies, i.e service commissioners and providers may not collude and agree not to compete, thereby sustaining an unfair price. This is also outlawed by the NHS and Community Care Act (1990).

THE PRACTICE

Marketing of health and social care services is not carried out by extensive sales departments. The marketing of your services for the benefit of your patients/clients and of your NHS Trust, Social Services Department, etc. is the responsibility of clinicians in your service, with some planning contributed by managers.

Market audit

Market audit involves systematically identifying pluses and minuses in the internal organisation (strengths and weakness) and the external environment (opportunities and threats). These are most easily organised into a SWOT analysis (Figure 7.3). This exercise is best carried out by those near the point of service delivery, i.e. clinicians. The audit is often conducted as a brainstorming exercise. A large flip chart with a SWOT grid is posted and individuals place comments in boxes. Other participants build upon the comments made by colleagues and thus a comprehensive list is created.

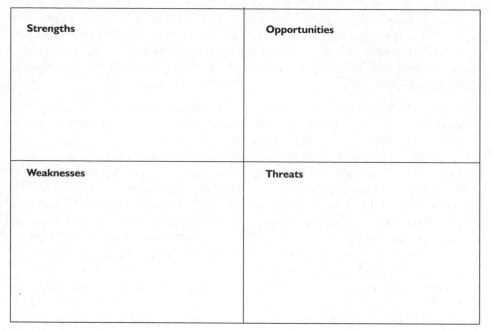

Strengths	Opportunities
Weaknesses	Threats

Figure 7.3 A SWOT analysis

This list will be more comprehensive if the participant list includes patients/clients, carers, family, colleagues and managers. When this happens, a comprehensive list is obtained. Although, by definition, nothing is found that was not already known by somebody, the interaction between involved people and the detailed attention always deliver far more than the group was aware of knowing and could therefore have been used in marketing planning.

This information can be supplemented with data collected from a variety of sources including the following.

Suggestion boxes

These do collect humorous content, but such items are easy to discard and much of value can be gained. Frequently, when consuming other services, you must have wished you could tell them just where they were going wrong, or occasionally right. A suggestion box, with pen and paper, will capture these thoughts in patients/clients, etc.; they often have all too much time to make such contributions when in waiting rooms. The content might inform or supplement the SWOT analysis.

End-of-intervention interviews

Sitting down with a patient, perhaps while he or she waits for transport home, is an ideal time to discuss how good the service is and how it could improve. This unpressured time delivers good information, and gives an air of consideration to patients who might otherwise think that staff no longer value them, because they are finished with.

Focus groups

If individual patients/clients are too nice to say where improvement is needed, a small group together may be far more forthcoming, through building on the comments of one another:

'Nurse was lovely.'

'Oh yes, she was. Mind you, I do wish that they wouldn't wake you so early.'

'Oh yes! And the way they serve tea in the morning. I can't manage it when I have just woken up ...'

This build-up of comment from one informant to another can deliver excellent information for improving a service.

Questionnaires

Simple questionnaires for completion at discharge will answer questions on any predicted subject. However, they will not give you information you had not thought to ask. That is why they work well in conjunction with focus groups. Questionnaires should be filled in and handed back there and then. Any promise to do it later and post it, even with a prepaid envelope, will deliver very few results, and these cannot be deemed representative. Anonymity may be important, so allow respondents to put the form in an envelope and place it among a number of others. This will allow them to be more honest. Although some criticism may be uncomfortable to receive, it is essential to know, or you cannot improve.

Informal opportunities

Many suggestions for changes or new services arise in conversation. You need to put yourself into situations where this can happen, and show colleagues that you are willing to hear these suggestions. This may be described as management by wandering about. If you can engineer to drop into a Health Centre around coffee time, you may hear many useful things from the staff there that you can use in marketing. It is important to capture these throwaway remarks, and to be seen to note them. This delivers much useful intelligence and is likely to result in repeat coffee invitations.

Market analysis

The information collected can be very great, and many NHS Trusts and Local Authority Social Services Departments (LASSDs) do not organise and use it. In some areas, it is collated into a report that is applauded and then used only to attract dust. Too rarely is this information integrated into hard plans.

The TOWS analysis (Figure 7.4) is a good tool for organising what is known and generating long-term plans to exploit that knowledge. Above, the data were sorted into strengths, weaknesses, opportunities and threats. Applying strengths to opportunities shows where possibilities can be immediately exploited. The interaction of strengths and threats shows you how to move to prevent losses and mishaps. Where there is interaction of weaknesses and opportunities, there is an urgent need to develop in order to take advantage of possibilities. Where there is interaction between weaknesses and threats, there is a need for development or disengagement. You may recognise that a service loss will occur and your plan must show the replacement of this business.

A TOWS analysis will generate a short list of strategic changes to the organisation and a further number of more immediate changes to make. This forms the basis of a strategic marketing plan.

	Strengths	Weaknesses
Opportunities	Strategies relating Strengths to Opportunities	Strategies relating Weaknesses to Opportunities
Threats	Strategies relating Strengths to Threats	Strategies relating Weaknesses to Threats

Figure 7.4 A TOWS analysis

Operational marketing: the marketing mix

The marketing mix may be organised by service managers, but if it is to be achieved, its enactment must be primarily achieved by clinicians. There are four points to consider: product, place, price and promotion, as described below.

Product

Defining and continually improving your service is a result of market intelligence collected by clinicians as described above. This must be in line with the organisation's strategy and must closely meet the demand of customers and consumers. It is your job to be constantly in touch with the demands of patients/clients/carers and referring agencies. You are responsible for noticing where the match could be improved and working with your organisation to bring about continuous improvement. Where there is conflict between the demands of (a) the referring customer, (b) the referred consumer and (c) your own clinical expertise, it is your responsibility to bring about reconciliation. You must find a way forward that satisfies the patient/client/carer, referrer/funder and your clinical conscience. In the ultimate case, however, if conflict really is not soluble, your accountability requires that your clinical knowledge of what is right must take priority. You cannot behave in a way that you know is wrong, either on doctor's orders or the client's wishes. If you did so, then you could be brought to account. (See Chapter 3.)

Price

There is a price paid for care by the consumer and the customer. You have the responsibility for minimising this price in all areas. You must identify and reduce the price paid by your patient/client, carer, etc. This may involve attention to a number of areas including:

Financial price

Consumers consume where they consider that the price is satisfactory. You must ensure that costs incurred by travel, loss of earnings, child care, etc. are minimised as far as is reasonable, by choosing a location and timing of clinics that best accommodate most service users. Ensure that they have free access to hospital car parks and can reclaim bus fares, wherever possible. This will reduce the number of clients who are put off by the financial cost of treatment. The old belief was that patients should be grateful for what they receive and not mind paying a bus fare. This paternal approach to medicine has only changed in very recent years.

Inconvenience and distress

If a service is inconvenient or distressing to access, then some patients/clients will not feel able to receive treatment. You must ensure that your clinic is sited where there is as little inconvenience as possible, e.g. where public transport access is good. Ensure that attendance attracts as little stigma as possible, e.g. for clients attending mental health services, and that there is suitable childcare assistance where needed.

Pain and discomfort

Discomfort will make a client less likely to attend regularly for treatment. You must ensure that any discomfort associated with treatment is minimised. This may involve a number of actions, such as selecting the least painful treatment media, careful pacing the treatment, suggesting that the patient takes any PRN analgesia prior to a session, removing anxiety by ensuring that the patient understands the treatment, maximising privacy, etc.

Place

The location of a treatment in space and time is crucial to ensuring high referrals and attendance. This was referred to under 'Price'. Discover, in conversation, whether referrers favour a clinic in the surgery or the hospital. Examine records to see whether patients/clients prefer one to the other. This may be indicated by data such as the 'did not attend' (DNA) rate for each setting. The clinician is in the best place to know which location will best attract referrals, attendance and funding. Management action may be needed to move a clinic's location, but the initiative and drive should come from the clinician.

Inconvenient placing may be erroneously used as a discreet form of rationing for an oversubscribed service. 'If it is made difficult, then only those who really need it will come.' In reality, a service difficult to access will favour the middle-class, middle-aged patient, who has access to private transport and communication skills sufficient to overcome poor information. The section of the community described in health care as 'socially deprived' will be disadvantaged by an inaccessible service, although it is known that this population needs health and social care most (Townsend and Davidson, 1982).

Promotion

The promotion of a service involves making sure that all audiences know what is available and know just how good it is or could be.

This promotion is often carried out by managers visiting important audiences and telling them about service possibilities. However, audiences such as GPs are very experienced at dealing with representatives, through their contacts with pharmaceutical companies, and are very sceptical about what they hear. A high percentage of leaflets and brochures are binned unopened. The best advertisement for a service is the clinician who is in contact with the referrer talking about live clients/patients.

There is no message or medium that will meet the need for all parts of the audience. Therefore, you should adopt a strategy for each target area. Much of the work can be a by-product of work happening already, such as case conference reports, if you alter the way in which you perceive these opportunities. Where extra effort is needed for promotional activities, then if the audience is seen in segments energy can be focused on the most influential area at any given time.

Promoting your service to the consultant
Consultants and junior doctors are key to nurses and Professions Allied to Medicine (PAMs) gaining referrals and contracts. If medical colleagues are not helped to understand the support offered by the professions they cannot make appropriate referrals or help them attract resources. Your immediate response might be to go and tell them. However, although being on an induction programme is helpful, there is little that medical colleagues will learn from a lecture, in terms of either new knowledge or change of attitude. Leaflets and brochures are also very unlikely to gain much attention, although they have value for reference once attention has been gained.

The best route for promoting a service to a medical colleague is through a case conference or ward round. You could use this as a time to state the minimum about a patient/client, and therefore do your job, or you could use it as a forum to show just what you can do with a patient/client and thereby promote your service as well as conveying the facts.

CASE STUDY 7.3 PROMOTING OCCUPATIONAL THERAPY

One occupational therapist in a department routinely says at case conference the like of, 'The patient can go home on Friday.' Another routinely says, 'When I examined the patient I found that he or she could not manage transfers, could not wash and dress and the bedroom facilities at home were no longer safe. I have conducted a home assessment, worked on the transfers, arranged for handrails to be fitted, and arranged for a home carer to call daily. He can now go home on Friday.' Which of the above OTs works on a ward where OT is understood and appreciated?

You may feel that a succinct answer is appreciated by any meeting, and rightly so. However, you have a number of reasons to be at the meeting, and you can pursue your professional agenda, to the good of patients generally, as well as satisfying the meeting's agenda. The caveat is, however, that you should not overdo this so that it is obvious what you are up to and so that your long-winded contributions become an annoyance.

Promoting your service to the GP
As with the consultant, the best approach to this sector will be through live patients. There is some opportunity for case conferences, and these should be maximised, but far more frequently you can reach a GP through letters about individual patients. Letters are normally written at the beginning and the end of an intervention. However, if your client group stays with you for a longer time, then you might consider regular reports at three or six month intervals. The important thing is that the report tells the reader about the service, rather than a minimalist comment that you are or are not involved.

CASE STUDY 7.4   PROMOTING PHYSIOTHERAPY

One physiotherapist courteously writes,

> I have been working with the above patient for three weeks and I have achieved as much as I can with his or her back problem. She reports some improvement.

> Please refer again if the problem recurs, or if there are similar cases.

Another writes,

> Thank you for referring the above patient. On examination, I found that he/she has a disorder of ..., which meant that he/she could not ..., therefore he/she was not able to attend work . I have treated him/her with ... and the pain is reduced by 80% as measured by the Chicago Pain Scale. He/she can now perform all normal activities and feels able to return to work.

> Please refer the patient back in the case of relapse, and I would be pleased to see any other patients in pain whose functional impairment is troublesome.

The second physiotherapist was more successful in attracting referrals than the first.

Promoting your service to the patient/client
The least understood profession is occupational therapy (OT). Or so say OTs. OTs solve problems for GPs they never knew they had. It is little surprise, then, that they gain little credit. Patients may report benefit to the doctor, saying, 'The lady from the welfare was a great help.' This advantages OT very little and in this situation, patients cannot ask for more OT because they do not understand that it was an OT who worked so well before or helped their neighbour. Therefore, when working with patients/clients, it is essential that each professional ensure that patients/clients know what profession they are and what is the point of what they are doing. Patients/clients, carers, etc. can watch a clinician going through the motions of treatment, but if it is not explained they will not have the opportunity to recognise the scientific method behind the activities they see. Without this explanation, many carefully prescribed treatments can seem trivial. Leaving the patient and carer ignorant of the point of what was done prevents them from asking for more treatment in the future or recommending the service to friends and their doctor.

Promoting your service to the purchasing DHA, PCG, etc.
District Health Authorities and Primary Care Groups / Trusts decide what health care services are provided in their catchment area. It is therefore essential that they know what your service is and how well it helps their patients/clients. Senior managers will, occasionally, be invited to address the Boards of each authority, and it is

essential that a succinct but thorough explanation is available, with audiovisual aids and comprehensive yet brief handout material. Multi-channel communication is known to convey more material to an audience than any single medium alone. Authorities have lay members (non-executive directors) who are keen to come to understand the services provided. When approached by lay members, you should recognise this as an excellent opportunity to become understood, rather that a threatening scrutiny. Many departments will be proactive and approach new DHA members to offer a visit and therefore give them the opportunity to understand better the business of health care from the sharp end. This also allows the service to promote themselves.

DHAs and PCGs are under pressure to focus resources on treatments that are proven through research to have therapeutic benefit (evidence-based practice). You therefore have a duty to know the evidence in support of your treatment and to explain how it informs the work that you carry out. It is frequently bemoaned that there is insufficient evidence, and that all clinicians should be supporting research in order to continue to be supported. This is correct, but there is also a wealth of evidence available that clinicians do not access and do not therefore bring to the attention of service commissioners. Your duty, therefore, is to ensure that every opportunity for contact with commissioners is exploited, that you know the evidence for your efficacy and efficiency, and that you present yourself in a focused, succinct and comprehensive way.

Promoting your service to the general public
Public opinion influences commissioning and referring practice. All clinicians have a part to play in helping the public to understand their profession and what it can offer. Newspaper advertising and poster campaigns are the domain of the professional bodies, and are of limited value if attempted by departments. However, offering to collaborate on an article describing your profession is of considerable value. These often take the form of 'A day in the life of ...' You could also contribute by speaking to the Women's Institute, church groups, men's/women's fellowships, etc. who are always hungry for different topics, and find health and social care of enduring interest.

Schools are important means for influencing children and parents. They welcome occasional lectures from professionals for career education reasons, but you might add a little education for the benefit of the profession. It may be possible to attach one member of your profession to each of the local schools, and over time build a string of valuable relationships.

Open days in departments are useful for fostering public understanding of a service, and if timed carefully can be used to accommodate those children who ask for a careers visit, rather than allowing each child to disrupt services by asking for an individual visit.

Promoting your service to colleague professions
Other professions may by contacted through case conferences etc. Additionally,

you can influence other professionals through being transparent in your working when collaborating over a client/patient. Journal clubs and similar meetings where research may be shared across professions offer a good opportunity for promotion of a service. Taking part in the training or induction of other professions allows you to be present when individuals are at their most receptive.

When promoting a service to a colleague profession you are seeking to gain referrals and, ultimately, business contracts. If this is seen as competition, then a colleague profession cannot be expected to help you. However, if you are operating a win–win approach to your collaboration you can talk in terms of developments that will allow your professions to benefit together. If occupational therapists seek to outperform physiotherapists, and vice versa, then both will fail over time. If, however, they work together to advance the case of occupational therapy and physiotherapy collectively, than both will steadily gain. Therefore, emphasise the ways in which you can both benefit through collaborative action.

Marketing yourself

All of the devices and practices described above for marketing an organisation or service can equally be applied to marketing yourself. You can market yourself in order to be seen to perform well in your present job, or to gain promotion, or a new job. You could also market yourself in your community and gain places on committees, etc., or even market a good diet to your children.

Self market audit

Conduct an audit of your strengths and weaknesses, and analyse your environment to identify opportunities and threats. This audit should be led by yourself, but you might collect information from colleagues etc., either individually or collectively in a brainstorm. You might consider a 360° audit in which you consult your manager, one or more peers and a number of subordinate staff. You might also include the views of patients/clients and those who know you in other settings such as at home or in any society you have joined.

When this information is collated, verified and sorted into a SWOT format, use a TOWS analysis to interact factors and devise strategies to advance yourself in any or all of the settings above. This should allow you to devise some long-term strategic directions so that your life goes where you want it to and at the same time some short-term tactics to move you in the right direction. This picture will change rapidly, so you may want to reaffirm your strategic direction and tactics at least annually.

Deciding on your strategic direction is the most difficult part of this exercise. Many people simply make incremental advances, each logical in the context of the last, but none calculated with a long-term intent to make your life meaningful as seen as a whole. You climb the ladder one step at a time. However, are you sure that it is leaning against the wall you really want to go up? One device is to consider what might be said in your obituary, or in marketing headlines on your headstone. If you continue as you are, what will be said, and is that okay? If it is not enough, then what would you like said? That points to your strategic plan. Alternatively, what will be your greatest regret on your deathbed? Few people will say, 'I wish I had spent longer in the office, or I wish I had made more money', so why do we seek so hard to do that now? Most of us will say, 'I wish I had made more time for family or church' or 'I wish I had bothered with people more', or 'I wish I had just stopped to smell the flowers'. So, why not add that to your strategic direction now? Check that the ladder you are on is going up a wall that you would like to be atop.

Avoid being seduced by the idea that more money or more importance is always positive. These are bought at the expense of something else, usually family, leisure, and art. The added income will certainly deliver increased quality of life (QoL). However, the loss of quality family time etc. reduces QoL. You might consider QoL as the base currency with which you make decisions. Will a promotion giving more 'money QoL' but costing 'family time QoL' deliver a net gain, or a net loss. Do not assume that all promotion delivers a net QoL gain for you or your family. It may, but it may not, so the sums should be examined carefully. Of course, you cannot devise a strict mathematical formula to carry out these calculations, but this does not invalidate the notion. Think in general terms about the gains and loss in any possible change, and decide whether they seem to you to aggregate to a gain or a loss. The answer will be different for different people. A promotion to Head Office involving daily commuting to London may result in a net loss to anyone who dislikes trains and the Underground railway system. However, it may be a net gain to anyone who can spend many hours per week travelling with equanimity and will not miss the extra time away from home.

Assumptions

Your life plan will be based on assumptions, such as 'The NHS will remain a growth area' or 'We expect to remain healthy into old age'. If an assumption proves wrong, it is essential to notice and review your plans accordingly. Be explicit with yourself about the assumptions that you make. Notice when one proves erroneous and take swift action to alter your plans accordingly. If your health, or that of somebody close to you, deteriorates, then your high-flying plans may no longer be in your best interest.

Implementation plan

Your TOWS analysis will have delivered tactics and pointed to plans. It will also show areas where you want to undergo development. Convert these into a long-term plan. If there is a MSc in there and counselling training as well as a long holiday to Australia, do not hold on to them in a vague way, because that way they will not happen. Draw up a long-term plan showing where each will fit. Then draw up a year plan showing where this year's components will fit. Know that you will realise these dreams and know when. This plan should be shared with your manager and other significant people in your life. Ensure that your partner has a plan, and that it is compatible with yours. The plan should show how it is to be funded, what consents are required, and how they will be obtained, what the assumptions are, etc.

The plan needs to be reviewed for success and modified to allow for failures or changes to circumstances.

Operationally marketing yourself: the marketing mix

Your product

So, what are the 'products' that you are offering? And to whom? The answers should be based upon your audit and analysis. These products must be the ones that best advance your strategy. Think in terms of services beyond your core function. You may have a main service based on your nursing skills, doing that aspect of nursing that you are especially good at and that your colleagues most value. However, you may also offer services such as mediating disputes, writing reports for the board, or giving public lectures. Your service list should be that calculated to get you the best reputation possible in the chosen and desired setting.

Price

Everybody pays a price for your cooperation and help. How difficult do you make this? If your contribution is at meetings, are you also a pleasant colleague to be at a meeting with. If the price of your eloquence at a meeting is that others have to listen to your views on every other agenda item, then you may not get invited again. If you can minimise the price paid by others for your services, then you will maximise the appreciation you gain.

Place

Where is the best place and time for your contribution? Careful timing and placing can make the value of what you do far greater. If you propose to make a virtue of your management report writing skills, what is the best venue to offer and deliver these? Choose venues where the value will be greatest for the minimum input.

Promotion

How you let others know what you could offer is crucial. Self-promotion is essential but can be counter-productive if it is too obvious. Too little, and you will go unrecognised, and too much and you will be blocked. Ideal promotion is by good word of mouth. This can be achieved by asking colleagues who recognised a good piece of work to bring it to the attention of influential others. If you promote a colleague in his or her presence, it is likely that he or she will reciprocate. If you promote everybody in his or her presence, you might get them all at it. There is no harm in joining mutual admiration societies.

If you produce a good piece of work, ensure that your name is discreetly but noticeably at the foot of each page. Wear a name badge and ensure that everybody knows whom he or she is talking to on the telephone. Always speak from the audience at meetings, and write papers on activities that go well. Do not claim all of the praise for yourself; be willing to share authorship with colleagues, and encourage them to reciprocate. Where you have a well-established colleague, work in tandem with them and benefit from their experience. A paper that you cannot get into print because you are a newcomer may well be printed if you collaborate with an established name and offer a joint publication. Later you can get on to the other end of this equation.

Value-added chains

Consider all aspects of each service that you offer and add value to each. Writing a paper is not the whole service. There are several stages to any process and you should seek to add value at each one.

In, for example, writing your paper, there are a number of stages: consultation, writing, proofreading, attribution, launch, follow-up.

Consider how you enhance your reputation when you are consulting on content. The more people you consult, the more people will have ownership of the product, even if you do not really need the help. Consult on drafts; again this will widen the ownership. In particular, ask influential names to look it over before the final print. Acknowledge influential individuals prominently in the paper, and they will ensure that it gets the best circulation. When the paper is released give advance copies as a favour. Get it a powerful launch, with good audiovisual support and, perhaps, a senior person to act as sponsor, introducing you to the meeting and getting you a good audience. Seek responses to your work and always thank respondents for their comments.

Conclusion

Marketing can appear aggressive and irrelevant in health and social care. However, ensuring that you are giving clients/patients what they really want, at the lowest price to them, where they want it and when, and then ensuring that they understand the opportunities, is entirely appropriate. Marketing is best conducted by clinicians and others with direct contact and coordinated by managers. Good marketing ensures good services and maximised benefit. It is therefore within the duty of every clinician and manager to market services.

To market yourself is to ensure that you are the best that the organisation and the patient/client could want. To ensure that everyone understands just how good you are is part of your duty to yourself. Active marketing can make you the driver of your career rather than the passenger.

REFERENCES

DoH (1990) *The NHS and Community Care Act*, HMSO, London.
DoH (1998) *The New NHS*, HMSO, London.
Peters, T. (1989) *Thriving on Chaos*, Harper and Row, New York.
Townsend, P. and Davidson, (1982) *The Health Divide*.
Townsend, P. and Davidson, N. (1988) *Inequalities in Health*, Penguin, London.
Wihrich, H. (1982) The TOWS matrix. *Long Range Planning*, 15(2), 54–66.

FURTHER READING

Frain, J. (1999) *An Introduction to Marketing*. International Thomson Business, London.

Lancaster, G.A. (1999) *Introduction to Marketing: A Step-by-Step Guide to All the Tools*. Kogan Page, London.

Proctor, R.A. (1982) Structured and creative approaches to strategy formulation. *Management Research News*, 15(1), 13–18.

Sheaff, R. (1991) *Marketing for Health Services: A Framework for Communications*. Open University Press, Milton Keynes.

Wheeler, N. and Proctor, T. (1993) Strategy analysis in the Health Service. *Journal of Marketing Management*, 9(3), 287–300.

8 The NHS

Introduction

The NHS was established in 1948, assuming responsibility for a diverse range of existing facilities. This constituted a major strand of the Labour government's post-war drive to create a welfare state in which individuals would receive essential needs irrespective of their ability to pay.

The NHS was founded on a number of principles, the most fundamental of which was that health care should be free of cost at the point of service delivery and accessible to all regardless of their resources. In addition to the treatment of illness, the new service was to make an active drive for health promotion through environmental improvement and disease prevention. It was believed that there was a backlog of need as a result of previous poor access to services and that, once that was overcome, there would be a decline in demand. Therefore, it was expected that the cost of the service would tail off.

A number of themes quickly emerged, which have been consistently present thereafter.

1 Funding has never been adequate to meet demand. The anticipated tail-off of demand did not occur, and in fact demand has increased to exceed supply throughout the life of the service. Although some illnesses have been eradicated as was expected and the associated costs saved, overall demand has increased. This is attributed to a number of factors:
   - Demographic change, with average life expectancy increasing, has changed the ratio of consumers to taxpayers.
   - Technological advances have resulted in many incurable diseases becoming treatable, with the resultant new treatment and aftercare costs
   - Increased resource reduces treatment barriers such as waiting times and increases demand.
2 Coordination of the disparate services has been difficult throughout the life of the NHS and has been addressed in every reform since its inception.
3 Equity of access, a driving factor in the creation of the service, remains unacceptable, with poor distribution and social fairness. Again, this has been addressed in every reform of the service.
4 The tension between central government control and local management has been a consistent issue, although there has been an evident trend towards decentralisation discernible in each NHS reform.
5 The interrelationship between the centrally funded NHS and local government funded Social Services has always been an area of discussion and the relationships have been altered repeatedly.
6 The relationship between clinical freedom and managerial control has been an area of contention throughout the life of the NHS, although a general trend

towards managerialism and the restriction of clinical freedom is discernible, culminating in the National Institute for Clinical Evidence, Evidence Based Practice and National Service Frameworks.

THE KNOWLEDGE BASE

Primary/secondary/tertiary

UK Health Services are divided into primary, secondary and tertiary provision.

Primary services are those provided by the general practitioner (GP) and the primary care team. Secondary services are those provided by the General Hospital
NHS Trusts and Community NHS Trusts. Tertiary services are those provided at
centres serving more than one DHA and are highly specialised. Private sector
health service providers are particularly active in the secondary and tertiary service
sectors.

The UK NHS is unusual in allowing patients direct access to primary care only.
Access to secondary care, e.g. hospital, is only on referral from a GP. (The exception to this rule is accident and emergency services.) Access to tertiary care is only
achievable through referral by a secondary care service clinician. Tertiary services
cannot generally be accessed directly by GPs. This rule even holds for most areas
of private practice. Access to a private practitioner in secondary care generally
involves referral from a GP.

The NHS Act (1947)

The NHS was set up in 1948 under the NHS Act of 1947. It assumed ownership
of pre-existing charitable and Local Authority facilities and evolved a plan for
development to achieve comprehensive coverage. Services were managed in three
strands: Community and Environmental Health services, General Practitioner Services and Hospital Services. This tripartite management system had difficulties of
horizontal coordination and regional variances of service quantity and quality that
were very difficult to resolve. These issues were well described in the 1950s and
continue to be cited as drivers for reform in the 1990 NHS and Community Care
Act.

The NHS Reorganisation Act (1973)

In 1974, the first NHS reorganisation saw the introduction of tiered management
with the government department, Regional Health Authorities (RHA), Area
Health Authorities (AHA) and District Health Authorities (DHA). (See Figure 8.1.)

Broad policy was set by the DoH and passed, with budgets, to Regional Health
Authorities (RHAs). Policies were interpreted by RHAs and passed, with budgets,
to Area Health Authorities (AHAs). Policies were interpreted by AHAs and passed,
with budgets, to Districts, who made local interpretation and passed instruction
and funds to Units (hospitals and community service managers). The amount of
funding passed from the DoH to each RHA was decided by the Resource Allocation Working Party (RAWP). The RAWP devised a capitation-based formula to

Figure 8.1 The NHS after NHS reorganisation Act (1970)

allocate resources. According to this formula, RHAs received funds relating to the size of the population, weighted for demographic profile, morbidity and, later, social deprivation.

Some services that were too specialised to be justified in a District (large town) were managed directly by the AHA (county) or RHA (about six counties). AHAs also had administrative and payroll responsibility for general practitioners, through Family Practitioner Committees (FPCs).

In 1982, AHAs were abolished (DoH, 1982), making the newly created DHAs directly accountable to RHAs, and removing an unnecessary tier of bureaucracy. In a few years, by amalgamation, many DHAs reverted to the boundaries formerly held by AHAs. They continued to manage Units and to administer FPCs

The NHS and Community Care Act (1990)

In the NHS and Community Care Act (1990) the managerial relationship between Districts and Units was severed and the Units were allowed to apply for NHS Trust status. The control of NHS Trusts by DHAs was to be through contracts in which DHAs passed funds to NHS Trusts in exchange for their agreement to treat patients for the diseases that historical knowledge and epidemiological study suggested would be encountered. The primary function of the DHA therefore became to assess the population's need for health care and contract with the health care providers of their choice for services. Contracts were one of three possible types:

- 'Block Contracts' in which the NHS Trust or other provider agrees to treat all comers for a fixed total price, rationing by waiting list if necessary;
- 'Cost and Volume Contracts' in which the NHS Trust or other provider agrees to treat a fixed number of patients for a fixed total price;
- 'Cost per Case Contracts' in which the NHS Trust or other provider agrees to treat as many patients as are referred at an agreed price per patient.

Where a patient attended an NHS Trust with whom his or her DHA of residence has no contract, then a fee for service was payable and he or she was known as an extra-contractual referral (ECR).

GPs were expected to refer patients to those NHS Trusts with whom the DHA had arranged contracts. However, some larger GP practices were allowed to hold the budget for their patients' secondary service needs and contract directly with NHS Trusts. These practices were known as General Practice Fund Holders (GPFHs). Although there was a limit to the range of services for which a GPFH could hold a budget, there were some experimental sites where large groups of practices held funds for all of their patient needs, known as Total Fund-Holding Schemes. These experiments were to provide information for the reforms of 1998: 'The New NHS – Modern and Dependable'.

FPCs were redesignated Family Health Service Authorities (FHSA) and became independent Authorities administering GP contracts.

As a result of the 1990 reforms, the DHA had a choice of NHS Trusts and other hospitals with whom to contract and the NHS Trusts had a choice of DHAs and

Figure 8.2 The NHS after the NHS and Community Care Act (1990)

other health purchasers with whom to contract (Figure 8.2). It was intended that this competition would constitute a marketplace that would be able to regulate service cost and quality through competition. This exercise was in part successful, but the costs of the marketplace infrastructure were considerable and some of the savings were lost.

The RHAs were abolished as Authorities and converted into DoH Outposts, effectively reducing the structure to a greatly enlarged DoH, operating centrally and regionally, and DHAs who contracted with NHS Trusts and other providers of services.

The NHS Trusts were allowed considerable business autonomy, particularly regarding financial management, but they remained owned by the DoH and a regulatory system was established by which NHS Trusts were directly accountable to a section of the DoH.

The 1990 reforms removed local government and other representation on Health Authorities, and established Boards of Directors for Authorities and NHS Trusts. A Board consists of five Executive Directors, who are the managers of the Trust/Authority, and five non-executive directors, who are local business managers etc. who contribute to the strategic management of the services. One of the non-executive directors is appointed Chair and it is the function of the Chair to appoint the Chief Executive Officer and other Executive Directors. In this, the Authorities and Trusts were to mirror the normal picture in industry. However, the DoH retained a strong influence over Board membership, and the Secretary of State has to approve the appointment of all non-executive directors.

The New NHS – Modern and Dependable (1998)

In 'The New NHS – Modern and Dependable' (1998), the purchasing functions of DHAs are progressively transferred to locality-based Primary Care Groups (PCG), constituted from members of the Primary Care Team, Unitary Local Authorities and officers of the DHA. Boards were created which included the above and non-executive directors from the community served. These groups assume responsibility for purchasing from NHS Trusts and other health and care providers on a schedule chosen by their Board. If the PCG chooses, it can become a Primary Care Trust (PCT) and provide direct services of the type formerly provided by Community NHS Trusts and take full responsibility for contracts and commissions with secondary NHS Trusts. This transfer of commissioning responsibilities to primary care teams is an important focus of these reforms, continuing the trend initiated in 1990, but the legislation also brought about a number of other important changes.

Contracts for services were to become longer. Three, four or five year contracts were to replace the one-year contracts common after the 1990 reforms. Coordination between purchasers was to be made easier by the agreement of local Health Improvement Programmes that would guide purchasing practice. Variations in practice were to be reduced by the issuing of National Service Frameworks that would set out the norms to be expected by patients. The National Institute for Clinical Excellence would collect, appraise and promulgate evidence about the var-

Figure 8.3 The NHS after The New NHS (1998)

ious approaches to health promotion and treatment available with a view to standardising around the proven best. Quality of services would be subject to more rigorous tests and poor practice would be more easily uncovered. The business mentality that had increased efficiency in NHS Trusts had also institutionalised secrecy and poor cooperation. A spirit of transparency and cooperation was to be established.

Primary Care Groups

A number of pilot exercises, such as locality commissioning groups and total GP purchasing groups, had tested the possibility of groups based around the primary care team taking responsibility for delivering or commissioning all secondary and tertiary services for the patients in their catchment. The establishment of PCGs brought clear responsibilities to larger groups of primary care staff for service commissioning. PCGs were expected to cover patches of in the region of 100,000 patients, but considerable variances were permitted in the first wave of PCG creation. In order to remove concerns about differentials between fund-holding and non-fund-holding practices, PCGs cover the entire population.

PCGs were given four levels at which they may operate:

1 As the minimum, PCGs may advise the DHA in its commissioning for their population.
2 PCGs may take a devolved budget and purchase, acting as a part of the DHA.
3 PCGs may become independent bodies, accountable to the DHA for their commissioning practice.
4 PCGs may become Primary Care Trusts (PCTs), remaining accountable to the DHA for their purchasing, but acting as a service provider for a range of community services.

The movement of responsibility for purchasing from DHAs to PCGs advanced a trend to empower the primary care clinician which had been evident in a number of NHS reforms:

1 The further involvement of clinicians in management was achieved. This development amalgamated the manager and the clinician and partially removed an insoluble tension between the two by giving budgetary control to the GP, who has always been the biggest spender in the NHS. No longer would GPs be at odds with DHA purchasing decisions because GPs would directly experience the constraints of budgetary limitations, make decisions according to their appreciation of priorities and then be expected to accept the consequent opportunity costs.
2 A continued devolution of service was achieved. Major decisions were to be made ever nearer to the patient and his or her clinician.
3 The shift of power from acute services towards primary care was furthered. This was initiated in the 1990 reforms and considerably furthered by the 1998 development.

As PCGs become PCTs and take direct responsibility for service delivery, the range of services formerly delivered by Community NHS Trusts is diminishing to include only services to people with learning disabilities and mental illness. It is anticipated that these NHS Trusts will amalgamate to form super-county providers.

Quality and efficiency management

The various reforms have sought progressively to improve together the quality and efficiency of the service, thereby eliminating difficulties where a tension is perceived between these two imperatives.

The 1998 reforms have created the National Institute for Clinical Excellence (NICE). This has the remit to promote excellence through audit and guidance. The Institute will critically examine the available evidence for effectiveness and efficiency, and encourage research in areas where insufficient evidence exists. This will allow it to advise on best practice, where a number of possibilities exist. This is not intended to remove clinical freedom, because it is recognised that every case is different. However, it is intended that practice will narrow down on to a small range unless there is a good reason for divergence.

The Institute will also publish National Service Frameworks (NSFs) that, based upon a detailed analysis of the evidence, can set out what a patient within a major care area can expect.

Clinical governance is introduced to set tangible controls on service quality. CEOs will report to the Board about the targets and achievement of quality standards and these reports are intended to attract the same attention and rigour as financial reports, i.e. NHS Trusts are to make the same efforts to ensure that quality is up to the mark as they currently do to ensure financial balance. Professions are expected to enhance their self-regulatory machinery to ensure that recognised standards are addressed. Additionally, they are to increase lifelong learning initiatives for continuing professional development (CPD). These requirements were reinforced by the Health Bill (1999), altering state registration requirements for the professions to make CPD an essential requirement for continued registration.

Adherence to the quality requirements will be monitored by the Commission for Health Improvement. This body is removed from government and can report on the extent to which quality machinery is being established, its effectiveness and the general impact on care. The Commission will carry out local reviews and work to assure as well as monitor quality service provision.

Health Improvement Programmes (HIMPs)

The DHA is responsible for leading and coordinating HIMPs for the residents in their catchment. The programme involves input from PCGs, service providers (NHS Trusts), the Local Authority and other agencies with an interest in public health. The HIMP will describe the major health needs of the population and the consequent service needs and set out the three-year strategic commissioning plan that will bring service provision into line with this agreed requirement. The programme will take account of national targets for improvements in services, morbidity and mortality.

The HIMP will be a resource that can be used to validate commissioning plans made by PCGs, thereby fulfilling the DHA's responsibility to supervise PCG purchasing practice. It will also assist with HR planning to identify future workforce needs in order to commission training of health professionals. (See Chapter 3.)

Conclusion

The UK NHS, although imperfect, has earned a good international reputation. It has consistently sought to provide high quality care with equity of access. A number of issues have been present throughout the half century of the NHS, including an inevitable resource shortfall against demand, equity, a constructive dynamic tension between clinical autonomy and managerialism, and ambiguity between central and devolved control. Debate around these issues is continually resulting in re-examination of provision, and the high public interest will ensure that the UK NHS is a volatile and dynamic public service.

REFERENCES

DoH (1947) *The NHS Act*. HMSO, London.
DoH (1973) *The NHS Reorganisation Act*. HMSO, London.
DoH (1982) *NHS Reorganisation*. HMSO, London.
DoH (1990) *The NHS and Community Care Act*. HMSO, London.
DoH (1998) *The New NHS – Modern and Dependable*. HMSO, London.

FURTHER READING

DoH (1949) *The NHS (Amendments) Act*. HMSO, London.
DoH (1951) *The NHS Act*. HMSO, London.
DoH (1952) *The NHS Act*. HMSO, London.
DoH (1979) *Patients First*. HMSO, London.
DoH (1989a) *Working for Patients*. HMSO, London.
DoH (1989b) *Caring for People: Community Care in the Next Decade and Beyond*. HMSO, London.
Donne, J. (1986) *Better Management, Better Health*. National Health Service Training Authority, Bristol.
Enthoven, A. (1985) *Reflections on the Management of the NHS*. Nuffield Provincial Hospital Trust, London.
Grice, D. (1994) The genetic therapist – a vision or a nightmare. In: *Wither the Professions Now?*: Conference Proceeding. Oxford Brookes University, Oxford.
Ham, C. (1991) *The New National Health Service: Organisation and Management*. Radcliffe Medical Press, Oxford.
Ham, C. (1994) *Health Care Reforms*. Macmillan, London.
Ham, C. (1997) *Health Care Reform: Learning from International Experience*. Open University Press, Buckingham.
Ham, C. (1998) *Boards of Directors: Are There Any Lessons for Health Authorities?* National Health Service Training Authority, Birmingham.

Maxwell, R. (1989) *Reshaping the NHS*. Policy Journals, Oxford.

Paton, C. (1996) *Health Policy and Management*. Chapman & Hall, London.

Pettigrew, A.M., Ferlie, E. and McKee, L. (1992) The leadership role of the new health authorities. *Public Money and Management*, April, 39–43.

Stewart, R. (1996) *Leading in the NHS*. Pan Business Books, London.

Wheeler, N. (1990) 'Working for patients' and 'caring for people': the philosophy. *British Journal of Occupational Therapy*, 53(10), 409–414.

INDEX